This is a revised and updated edition of a cross-cultural study of rituals surrounding death that has become a standard text in anthropology, sociology, and religion. Part of its fascination and success, also among a general readership, is that in understanding other people's death rituals we are also able to gain a better understanding of our own. Peter Metcalf and Richard Huntington refer to a wide variety of examples, from different continents and epochs. They compare the great tombs of the Berawan of Borneo and the pyramids of Egypt, the dramas of medieval French royal funerals and the burial alive of the Dinka "masters of the spear" in the Sudan, and other rituals that at first sight seem to have little in common. Many of the cases are anthropological classics, but Metcalf and Huntington bring them together into a new theoretical synthesis. A new introduction reviews developments in the anthropological study of death since the book first appeared in 1979.

CELEBRATIONS OF DEATH

CELEBRATIONS

OF DEATH

THE ANTHROPOLOGY
OF MORTUARY RITUAL

This book is due for return on or before the last date shown below.

18 NOV 09

PUBLISHED BY THE PRESS SYNDICATE OF THE UNIVERSITY OF CAMBRIDGE
The Pitt Building, Trumpington Street, Cambridge, United Kingdom

CAMBRIDGE UNIVERSITY PRESS
The Edinburgh Building, Cambridge CB2 2RU, UK   http: //www.cup.cam.ac.uk
40 West 20th Street, New York, NY 10011-4211, USA   http: //www.cup.org
10 Stamford Road, Oakleigh, Melbourne 3166, Australia

First published 1991
Reprinted 1992, 1993, 1995 (twice), 1997, 1999

Printed in the United States of America

Typeset in Goudy

A catalogue record for this book is available from the British Library

Library of Congress Cataloguing-in-Publication Data is available

ISBN 0-521-42375-9 paperback

CONTENTS

v

Contents

PART I.   UNIVERSALS AND CULTURE

PART II.   DEATH AS TRANSITION

Contents

ILLUSTRATIONS

PREFACE

In recent years, death has received new attention in the West. After three generations of silence, our mortality is again a topic of discussion. Seminars, courses, and television talk shows on death and dying are commonplace, where not so long ago they would have been considered in bad taste. Psychologists, sociologists, theologians, physicians, and social critics have all contributed to this new awareness. There is even a professional specialism of thanatology.

Our research was not initially directed to matters relating to death; instead we were interested in aspects of social life. But we found ourselves working in places (Huntington in Madagascar, Metcalf in Borneo) where funerals are important events and where people are remarkably open in their dealings with death. Back in Cambridge, we benefited from discussions of the similarities and differences in our two cases. In the process, we were led repeatedly to the same theorists, Arnold van Gennep and Robert Hertz, who also drew on material from Madagascar and Borneo, respectively. When they wrote their best-known essays in the first decade of this century, the comparative study of ritual forms was of crucial concern to the majority of scholars in the young discipline of anthropology. Hertz and van Gennep brought an impressive sophistication to the understanding of death rites, so that their work has hardly been improved on to this day. By midcentury, however, religion had retreated into the background, replaced by an obsession with kinship and social structure. The insights of Hertz and van Gennep were expropriated for different, and narrower, ends than they had intended.

We return here to the specific focus of their works to retrieve the full range of their insights on social reactions to death. We apply them to a wide variety of material, some of it exotic, some from closer to home. Many of our examples are taken intentionally from classics of ethnography, and we ask the indulgence of the authors for placing their work in analytic contexts quite different from those that they originally intended. By drawing together in this way many unconnected threads, we set out to construct a new anthropological synthesis on death.

This book is designed to be accessible not only to anthropologists, but also to others with an interest in culturally prescribed reactions to death. Chapter 1, "Preliminaries," is particularly addressed to those not already familiar with such figures as Edward Burnett Tylor and Emile Durkheim. Those who are may prefer to skip it. In the remaining chapters, the discussion, even where it concerns anthropological classics, is not simple recapitulation; the purpose is to put them to new uses in building a general argument.

This study has been a joint effort in the fullest sense. There is no part that has not benefited from the exchange of ideas and criticisms. There has been a division of labor, however, according to our respective areas of interest and research. Huntington is responsible for Chapters 1, 2, 5, and 7, Metcalf for Chapters 3, 4, 6, and 8.

Each of us owes many debts of thanks to teachers and to those who helped us during our research. Due to the double authorship, it would be unwieldy to list all these debts here; we have thanked these people elsewhere and will do so again. Relating to the original edition of this book, we thank our editor, Walter H. Lippincott, for his help and encouragement, and James A. Boon for his critical reading of earlier drafts. For help with the second edition, we thank Jessica Kuper and Richard Hollick at Cambridge University Press. Metcalf acknowledges support from the Wilson Gee Fellowship Program, University of Virginia, and Huntington the Teschemacher Fund, Harvard University.

Joint authorship is relatively rare in anthropology. This is largely a result of our highly personal and localized style of fieldwork in other cultures, which also encourages a tendency on the part of anthropologists to leap from minute and particular social fields toward global conclusions.

Preface

Moreover, field research can lead the anthropologist to put aside the cultural blinkers of his or her own society only to adopt in large measure those of another. Working together has expanded the empirical and experiential base for our study. Whether this has reduced some of the above-mentioned shortcomings while maintaining the sense of immediacy that derives from personal encounters, the reader must be the judge. For our part, we have found this collaboration tremendously stimulating, challenging, and enjoyable.

INTRODUCTION TO THE
SECOND EDITION

In the twelve years since this book was first published in 1979, the trend toward public discussion of deathways has continued. Inevitably, it has stimulated an interest in the comparative study of death rites, in which anthropology has the principal part to play. Our study was the first in a long time directly to pursue this project, following an epoch in which religion had been relegated to a merely supporting role in anthropological theory. It remains the only general and integrated (though not, of course, comprehensive) treatment that we know of, and it has evidently been found useful by scholars and teachers in several disciplines, including theology, history, and archaeology. For that very reason, perhaps, we have come in for our share of criticism from fellow social anthropologists, some of it generous, some snide, in the manner of academe. Interestingly, the criticism has revolved around just those issues that we used to provide the three-part structure of the book, indicating their continuing theoretical importance. In general terms, these issues are: the relation between ritual and emotion, the political significance of ritual, and the universal in symbolism. We feel that some recent approaches have been misleading, even retrograde. We take the opportunity of this new edition to review these developments, and to respond to critics.

Introduction

RITUAL AND EMOTION

In several respects, mortuary rites challenge our theoretical paradigms by making inescapable issues that are routinely avoided in other contexts. One of these is the relationship between ritual and emotion. The potentiality of death to release the most powerful emotions in the survivors is so obvious that it is often assumed to explain the rites that follow. In connection with other kinds of ritual, however, the issue of emotion is nowadays seldom raised. At the time when we were writing the book, a concern with emotion was very much out of vogue, especially in Britain, where it was associated with the discredited functionalist school. With the ardor of the reformed, British anthropologists excoriated A. R. Radcliffe-Brown for the psychological reductionism of his arguments. The best-known example concerns the extension of sentiment from near to more distant kin, which invokes a supposedly universal emotional process to account for a host of small rites of kinship.

We agreed with the criticisms of functionalism, but did not find it necessary to repeat them, with one exception. In Part I, we rejected the possibility of explaining complex and highly diverse death rites by resort to psychic universals. We did this at the outset for the sake of readers not familiar with the intellectual history of anthropology, for whom the appeal to emotions may seem "only natural." At the same time, however, we wanted to revive an interest in the examination of the emotional dimensions of ritual, the point being to substitute the sort of culturally nuanced account of emotion that becomes possible only after the weight of providing a catch-all explanation has been lifted. For a case study, we went back to a forgotten byway of functionalism, Godfrey Wilson's (1939) account of Nyakyusa rituals. Even within the confines of a mechanistic social model, Wilson succeeded in revealing something of the subtlety of the cultural dimension of Nyakyusa emotion. During the last few years, more sophisticated studies of emotion have appeared, and we would not use the same illustration now. In drawing attention to it, however, we anticipated the renewed interest, if we did not precipitate it.

Interestingly, our position on the connections between ritual and emotion has been attacked from opposite directions. Maurice Bloch and Jonathan Parry (1982) see the connection in directly causative terms, and privilege the role of ritual. By contrast, Renato Rosaldo (1984, republished in abbreviated form 1989), lays heavy emphasis on the power of emotion and is contemptuous of mere ritual forms.

The remarks of Bloch and Parry are provided as part of a long introduction to a collection of essays bearing on the theme of death. Theirs is the fullest treatment of mortuary rites in general to have appeared since our book and is consequently of special interest. Bloch and Parry begin by contesting our reading of Robert Hertz, whose essay is an important source both for them and us. Our discussion, they say, "almost totally ignores his central preoccupation with the social construction of emotion and with the relationship between the biological individual and the social collectivity" (1982: 5). At first, we were mystified by the charges, because we specifically deal with these issues, the first in Part I, the second in Part III. But all becomes plain when one realizes that Bloch and Parry hold a particular view of ritual, seeing it basically as a form of social control. One aspect of this is that society actively shapes the emotions of its members through ritual. As they consider this essential to the position of Hertz and his teacher, Emile Durkheim, they claim the mantle of the *Année sociologique* school. As we do not, and take a different view, we are portrayed as ignoring something vital to Hertz's essay.

It is certainly true that Durkheim makes much of emotion and emotional displays in his early essay on the individual and society (1895) and in his major work on religion (1912). In Chapter 2, we argue that he has a definite strategy in so doing. At first, he appears to be arguing that various celebratory rites are the result of a spontaneous upwelling of collective emotion, so that the latter calls the former into being. Some commentators have been content to read no further, and this view constitutes a kind of vulgar Durkheimianism. But Durkheim's calculated use of material on funerals, particularly descriptions of the reactions of Australian aborigines to a death in the band, from which we quote, shows that his view is really not so simple. First, he shows us the crowd working itself into a frenzy of grief, but then he confronts us with the observation that things are not as chaotic as they seem. Expressions of mourning, even those involving dire self-mutilation, are precisely assigned according to kinship roles. For all the violent displays of emotion, preexisting social arrangements govern them.

Thus far, Bloch and Parry agree with us, but they wish to go a step further, and positively set vulgar Durkheimianism on its head. They argue that the prescribed occasions of ritual function to call forth the

3

appropriate emotions in the participants. This is a strongly sociological reading of Durkheim: Society and its collective representations govern the individual's responses, and not the reverse. Consequently, Bloch and Parry call for an analysis of how rituals shape emotion and fault us for not providing it.

We carefully refrained, however, from taking that extra step. Nothing in Durkheim's examples requires a deterministic relationship between ritual and emotion. His point is that actions are prescribed, not emotions. How could we know what emotions are genuinely being experienced? The general conclusion is that the relationship between ritual and emotion is not causally determinative in either direction, but rather, cybernetic.

This conclusion fits our everyday experience. Take a mundane example: a shopping mall in the days before Christmas. The faces of the shoppers belie the notion that the greatest festival of our calendar is the result of a sudden general bonhommie. At the same time, many are later swept up in the festivities with friends and family, so that the rites may well succeed in calling forth the emotions appropriate to the season. Nothing is guaranteed, however. Any number of small crises or ancient quarrels could destroy the mood and leave the gathering disconsolately plodding through ritual forms that mock true feelings. This indeterminacy allows Durkheim to set aside issues of individual psychology and get on with his program of explaining culture in its own terms. By denying it, Bloch and Parry perpetuate Radcliffe-Brown's position, as set out in Chapter 2.

Meanwhile, Rosaldo (1984) attacks our position when he means to attack theirs. Rosaldo sets out to understand the frame of mind that, for the Ilongot of the Philippines, makes taking a head seem a natural reaction to the death of a loved one. He recounts his unsatisfactory attempts to explain Ilongot headhunting in terms of symbol systems, and so on, until he himself suffered the loss of his wife in an accident. Then, he tells us, distracted by grief, he finally understood the rage that Ilongot expressed in violence. Following this account, Rosaldo attacks the tendency of anthropologists to discount emotion, which he sees as the great shaper of human actions. As his prime example of this tendency, he quotes from the first paragraph of our Chapter 3, construing it to say that individuals rely entirely on rituals to accomplish their grieving. Had he included the preceding or subsequent lines, he would have found it harder to so willfully and completely misrepresent our position. It was and is our opinion that the psychic process of grieving only partially intersects with the performance of death rites. As we plainly say, it may be that ritual sometimes aids the process, but it could as easily be no help at all, or even an extra burden to bear.

Pursuing the same complaint, Rosaldo accuses us of conflating in our title the study of death and the study of death ritual (1984: 194). He has overlooked one sense of the word "celebration," which Webster's dictionary gives as a "religious ceremony." Consequently, both our main title and subtitle refer to the same topic. As it happens, the Ilongot are not much inclined to ritual elaboration, but, simple or complex, their rites are worth understanding. Rosaldo never offers any explanation, for instance, for why the outlet for Ilongot rage is chopping off heads. Why not hack the victim to pieces? Why not turn the violence in on themselves, like the aborigines, or channel it into ascetic practices? By his dismissal of ritual, Rosaldo discounts the force of religion in peoples' lives and effectively returns to a position of vulgar Durkheimianism.

In denying Rosaldo's charge, we do not doubt the interest of a genuinely comparative study of emotion. It has become abundantly clear that cultures vary widely in the ways that they perceive and evaluate emotional states. This goes deeper than classifying and naming. A decade ago, the pioneering essays collected by Paul Heelas and Andrew Lock under the title *Indigenous psychologies* (1981) showed that the individual may be culturally constituted *vis-à-vis* his or her emotions or temperament in various ways, and that all kinds of moral significance are attached to the expression or suppression of inner states. Michelle Rosaldo provides a remarkable study in this mode, describing the tension that Ilongot see between states of "knowledge" and "passion." Another example is Catherine Lutz's (1988) compelling account of *Unnatural Emotions* on a Micronesian atoll, demonstrating the social construction of emotion in specific circumstances. We have now passed the stage where vague generalizations about emotion are useful in the discussion of ritual, and by the same token, it has become pointless to argue which of two cultural phenomena is primary.

RITUAL AND THE POLITY

The feedback between ritual and emotion is but one aspect of the key issue in the Durkheimian tradition, namely, the relationship between the individual and society. We raised it early in Chapter 1, where we spoke of the tension between "the physical separateness of human organisms" and the "individual's identification with society." In their criticism of us quoted above, Bloch and Parry speak of the "relationship between the biological individual and the social collectivity." Note the similarity of the language. Where we differ from them is not, as they claim, in ignoring the issue, but rather in the emphasis that we place on the dynamism of the relationship. By contrast, they see ritual as simply a device of social regulation. This position owes something to Marxist theory but is for the most part a rigid version of functionalism.

The view of society promoted by Bloch and Parry is a brittle one, which leaves little room for surprises and reverses. Although we do not doubt that rituals are invariably caught up in relations of power, what is overlooked in their view is the uncertainty of the outcomes. Rituals may make a show of power, but they run the same risk as other shows: They may fail. In Part III, we discuss Berawan death rites as arenas in which leadership was asserted, or contradicted, and at each occasion, renegotiated. Ordinary villagers, by their enthusiasm or lack of it, held the success and failure of leaders in their hands. Communities rose and fell with their leaders. In Bali, the competition was even more theatrical, the politics equally fluid. In Thailand and France, where centralized states were stable for long periods, the elaborate death rites of kings were moments in ongoing political processes. We avoided flat assertions about the political functions of funerals precisely so as not to suppress their historical creativity. Similarly, Bernhard Helander (1988) shows that Somali death rites, far from enshrining the values of the social order, are actually subversive to them.

"LIFE" AS A POLITICAL RESOURCE

In support of their conception of ritual, Bloch and Parry elaborate a particular interpretation of the symbolism of rebirth in death rites. Following W. H. R. Rivers (1926: 40), we emphasized the finding that, paradoxically, death, the one true universal, is not "everywhere regarded in essentially the same light." Rather it is life that has a certain universal currency, and death appears only as its absence. Bloch and Parry take this notion further, and it is the most intriguing part of their discussion. Basically, their argument is that rites of passage, serving the ends of society and its masters, seek to drive a conceptual wedge between biological and social reproduction, in order to privilege the latter. The former, meanwhile, is progressively denigrated, so that the merely biological business of pregnancy and childbirth is overshadowed by the assertion of society's monopoly on the giving and withholding of life. In this view, "life" takes on an abstract existence, rather like the Gross National Product.

This argument resembles that made by A. M. Hocart in *Kings and Councillors* (1970), although Bloch and Parry do not mention him. Hocart's proposition, briefly, is that ritual originates as a technique for the acquisition and control of life. In the course of history it takes on a political aspect because the state, wherever it emerges, is obliged to press into service whatever institutions are available to perform the functions of government. Those preexisting institutions are ritual ones, and their primary mission is consequently modified by a new administrative role. The offices of state, for their part, long retain a sacral character.

Hocart's purpose in making this argument is to escape the dilemma in Western political philosophy between two, equally unsatisfactory, intellectualist theories of the origin of the state:

One was that government had been established by main force, and that its offices and forms were instruments of control and exploitation found convenient by autocrats. The other was that men had perceived the necessity and the advantages of government, and had come together to institute a social contract. (Needham 1970: xxv)

Since Bloch and Parry embrace the former theory, they have no need of Hocart's novel alternative. Instead, they take his concept of life and put it to other uses, making it just another "instrument of control." This requires the bifurcation noted above, so as to distance reproduction from biological processes.

To illustrate their theories, Bloch and Parry reanalyze our account of Bara death rites, given in Chapter 5. They fault us for taking a simplistic view of the Bara conception of femininity. They argue that women are not associated with the life-giving role that we too easily assigned them. On the contrary, they are identified with its very opposite, a threatening sexual pollution, which is in turn equated with putrescence and decay, and hence with death. Only men can keep these negative influences at bay through the techniques of ritual, which promote the reproduction of the lineage. As it is the elders who perform this task, their authority within the lineage is vindicated. This is how Bloch and Parry understand Bara ideology.

We respond that we did not make a simple equation between women and life. We did not associate either sex with life; on the contrary, we say plainly that, in the Bara view, life depends on a balance between male and female aspects. It is Bloch and Parry themselves that posit an equation, because they identify men with life, and women with death: This piece of sophistry requires us to see childbirth as unrelated to "life," a position that Hocart would not have found reasonable. Moreover, it projects onto the Bara some suspiciously Western ideas. Let us consider these issues in turn.

Recently, Louis Dumont (1978, 1986: 223–33) has criticized the tendency of English symbolic analyses of the sixties and seventies to be phrased in terms of a double column of paired oppositions. Rodney Needham (1987: 102–86) has defended these techniques, in part, by suggesting that Dumont reads more into them than was intended. What is clear is that dyads listed one on top of another may have incommensurable characteristics, and it will certainly do violence to the data to force all conceivable symbolic contrasts, of whatever type, into the same framework. In Chapter 5, we pointed out these pitfalls, drawing on the earlier critique of G. E. Lloyd (1966) and anticipating the current debate. Consequently, we refrained from simply associating one sex with life, which is not in our view appropriate to the Bara case. The crucial opposition that we saw in Bara ideology was between notions of order, on the one hand, and vitality, on the other. Life requires the two to be brought into rapport. At conception, female blood is ordered by male semen. At death, bone and flesh are radically estranged. By contrast with vitality and order, gender is less a matter of opposition than complementarity. There can be no question of whether a male or a female principle controls "life;" both are indispensable.

Moreover, we question whether Bara notions of the pollution peculiar to women means that all female bodily functions are polluting. It is one thing to consider menstruation polluting, and quite another to see childbirth in the same light. As Victor Turner pointed out (1967: 42–3) in connection with Ndembu color symbolism, menstrual blood is negatively evaluated precisely because it implies a failure to conceive, to fulfill the life-giving role. Again, Bloch and Parry (1982: 24–5) discuss cases, for instance in China, where women are seen to have the power to remove pollution, to somehow absorb it. If women are the source of pollution, how is it that they are simultaneously its antidote?

Recent feminist critiques have attacked the style of analysis that associates gender differences with, in the words of Carol MacCormack, "stark categories or metaphorical clusters of contrasts standing in wooden opposition to each other" (1980: 1). She warns that the contrasts made by our terms are as vulnerable to problems of translation as any other terms; they may not be significant in another culture, or they may be experienced differently. For example, both men and women may be seen as having "natural" aspects and "cultural" aspects. Instead of being identified with either nature or culture, women and/or men, separately or together, may play a mediating role between them. In this way a dynamic is introduced, a tension between the natural and the cultural that provides alternatives to Western understandings. Joanna Overing (1986) provides a nice example from the Piaroa of Venezuela.

Our analysis stressed a contrast between order and vitality that figures prominently in Bara expression. It is very much a dynamic, rather than a static, opposition. Although we did not explore the issue per se, it is plain that the nature/culture contrast does not neatly correlate with it, and that the concept of culture must be rather differently felt by the Bara. We would not want to identify culture with order, for this would make the dead the most cultured, although incapable of cultural expression.

Bloch and Parry's list of contrasts, by comparison, emphasizes a progressive domination of culture over nature, and men over women:

women	men
sexuality	fertility
death	rebirth
nature	culture
individual reproduction	lineage reproduction
negative aspects of death	positive aspects of death
biology dominant	biology mastered

This notion of the domination of nature is the hallmark of modern technological society. Michael Adas (1989) argues that it was elaborated in the nineteenth century as the ideology of Western dominance. To project it onto the Bara, along with its corollary notions of gender, is not convincing.

Western ideology is also echoed in a notion of "life" that is abstract but bankable, and largely under the control of an establishment, like the economists' concept of capital. Bloch uses it in his own chapter, later in the same book (Bloch and Parry 1982: 211–30), where he explains headhunting as a process whereby a more powerful group captures the vitality of a weaker. The idea is not original. At the turn of the century, the Dutch missionary ethnographer A. C. Kruyt (1906) attributed to the Toraja of Sulawesi the notion of *levensfluide*, "life-fluid," as an explanation for their headhunting practices. Later, he preferred the term *zielestof*, "soul-substance," but he made no claim that either term glossed any expression in the Toraja language. Moreover, his own fieldwork contradicts the interpretation, and he later abandoned it. In neighboring Borneo, the concept is likewise absent (Needham 1976). It may be that there are societies that have some concept of this type. But in the best-known cases, it appears as a mechanistic projection of Western physical concepts, only obscuring indigenous ideologies. It certainly will not stand as a universal explanation of headhunting. Bloch is not so much reinventing the wheel, as the flat tire.

THE UNIVERSAL AND THE PARTICULAR IN SYMBOLISM

In studies of symbolism, there is a delicate balance between the universal, or quasi universal, and the particular. We have been aware at least since the last century that there are certainly associations, valences, or metaphors that recur widely in diverse cultures, evidently because of, in Tylor's memorable phrase, "the like working of men's minds under like conditions" [1964 (1878): 3]. A large part of the program of contemporary anthropology has been to identify these like workings, and to account for their necessary conditions, either internal or external. Our study is within this tradition. But it must be emphasized that such research does not lead invariably to human universals. Far from it. There are pieces of symbolism that have purely local appeal; others seem to be restricted to particular regions, though not found everywhere within it; and others again are rare everywhere, but reported from all over the globe. All are equally part of the process that Tylor pointed out, and equally important to comprehend.

In the discussion on death rituals, there has been a tendency to ignore these subtleties of distribution and to proceed directly to unqualified universals. This is perhaps because of the universality of death itself, or because of the supposedly uniform emotional impact. Whatever the reason, the result is to mask the specialness of particular cultural configurations.

In this context, it is interesting to contrast the essays of van Gennep and Hertz. Van Gennep appears to set up a subclass of rituals, *rites de passage*. But in the hands of Victor Turner (1967, 1969), the category is fantastically expanded, to the point where it is hard to describe a ritual (or much else) that is not in some sense a rite of passage. Influenced by his writings, historians, literary critics, and dramatists press the concept into service. Its appeal is the universal symbolism of the liminal. For instance, the paradoxical prevalence of symbolism of rebirth at death rites appears simply as characteristic of postliminal phases.

Hertz's insights have proved less popularly accessible because they require more careful discrimination. His title "A Contribution to the Study of the Collective Representation of Death" shows that he did not conceive of his subject in narrow terms. Nevertheless, his focus really is on one special kind of ritual, rather than all kinds of ritual. In fact, the rites of secondary treatment of the dead that he discusses have a distribution that is somewhere between the second and third types noted above; they are relatively rare, but found worldwide, and at the same time they are particularly characteristic of certain regions, such as Southeast Asia. As an example of the application of the special-case method, Hertz's analysis sheds light on ritual reactions to death everywhere by revealing the dynamics of a particularly striking or extreme form of them. In this way, it invites us to look for similar dynamics in simpler or more familiar rites.

At the same time, considered as an ethnographic contribution, the essay inevitably sets us exploring particular cultural and regional transformations and variants. The model is remarkably exportable – that was Hertz's achievement – but it is not a simple, prepackaged "universal." Many studies in the last few years have extended Hertz's model in interesting ways. For instance, Nigel Barley (1981) describes the elaboration of a crucial wet/dry distinction among the Dowayo of Cameroon that incorporates corruption within a wider concept. New corpses are seen as similar to uncircumcised penises in that both are wet, and hence in need of ritual processing to become dry. In this view secondary treatment appears as a type of initiation. Again, Daniel de Coppet (1981) shows how such death rites are inherent in a complex pattern of murder and revenge killing. As neither of these extensions is remotely suggested in Hertz's original essay, the utility of the special-case method is confirmed.

In Part II, we explored some variations on Hertz's model. We drew on Elizabeth Traube's analysis of the funerals of the Mambai of Timor, now available as a full ethnography (Traube 1986), which reveals many echoes of secondary burial without its actual occurrence. Our principal example, however, was the Bara of Madagascar, who emphasize a different dynamic in their rites from that which Hertz found in Borneo. A full account of Bara notions of gender and society is now available (Huntington 1987). As regards the Berawan of Borneo, an ethnography expanding on the sketch provided in Chapter 4 finds, not surprisingly, that Hertz provides the key for understanding much about their death rites (Metcalf 1982a). Even so, there are aspects that lie outside his model. For instance, in the headhunting rites intimately associated with Berawan funerals, expressions of vitality and sexuality are conspicuous. Consequently, a theme central to the funerals of the Bara (who did not practice head-hunting) reappears in a different but related context among the Berawan – a nice example of the recurrence and transformation of symbolic elements.

In Chapter 3, we tried to approach the issue of less-than-universal symbolism. We noted that Turner's interpretation of the black-white-red color triad had many exceptions and deconstructed the simple correlation of percussion and transition, trying to give it a wider range of possible nuances. Then we explored some peculiarly Southeast Asian connotations of rotting, which may well cast the whole process of secondary treatment of the dead in a different light in that region. Perhaps we were too tentative, as our attempts to identify localized significations drew no response.

DEATH RITUALS AND EXCHANGE

Given the importance that mortuary rites often have, it is to be expected that they will be touched on in many ethnographies. For the same reason, they provide a convenient topic for collections of essays, of which there have been several recently (Humphreys and King 1981; Bloch and Parry

Introduction

1982; Cederroth, Corlin, and Lindström 1988; Watson and Rawski 1988; Damon and Wagner 1989). But the frequency with which the topic is discussed is matched by the diversity of aspects that authors pursue. As the editors of the collections discover, it is not easy to make out common themes in this literature. Nor is it possible to review all these contributions individually here. There are, however, a couple of important issues that have emerged.

One such issue is exchange. In Africa, inheritance tends still to be the main concern, as in Sally Falk Moore's (1981) study of changing rules of property among the Chagga of Tanzania. But recent ethnography from Asia and Melanesia has described mortuary exchanges as elements in a much wider system of prestations. For example, in a reanalysis of the funeral rites of the Khasi of Assam, Kaj Århem (1988) shows how they relate to the marriage nexus. As the Khasi practice both secondary burial and generalized exchange, two classic complexes intersect here. In eastern Indonesia, mortuary exchanges are important in the relations between wife-givers and wife-takers, as several of the essays in the volume edited by James J. Fox (1980) show. Shepard Forman describes them in detail and shows how they are an integral part of the structure of alliance among the Makassae of east Timor. As if to emphasize parallels between marriages and funerals, there is a payment that is called "the bridewealth of the dead" (Forman 1980: 165). Moreover, as Signe Howell (1990: 427) notes for the Lio of Flores, reciprocal relations may extend beyond the living to include ancestral spirits. The exchanges take on cosmological significance, as more is involved than things; it is life itself that flows through them (Fox 1980: 12).

Melanesia has long been known for complex patterns of exchange, in which death rites play an important, if underestimated, part. Andrew Strathern (1981) provides examples from the highlands of New Guinea. In her studies of the Trobriands, Annette Weiner (1976, 1980) emphasizes the neglected role of women's wealth objects in mortuary exchanges. For the whole Massim area, the volume edited by Frederick Damon and Roy Wagner (1989) is a valuable recent contribution that relates the death rites of each of several islands to the Kula cycle connecting them all. In her essay, Martha Macintyre (1989: 151) goes so far as to suggest that mortuary exchanges were the pattern and focus of all exchanges, both within the island that she studied and beyond. This perspective puts the venerable institution of the Kula, subject of so much controversy, in a new light, because it raises the possibility that the prominence that Bronislaw Malinowski saw in it may have been an artifact of the post-contact situation. Throughout Melanesia, colonial officers suppressed death rites, often involving secondary burial and exposure of corpses, because they found them repulsive, and condemned them as unhygienic. In the Trobriands, this suppression had already occurred by the time Malinowski arrived. Busy pioneering new techniques of direct observation, and perhaps already disposed to spurn "projective history," Malinowski was in no mood to attempt reconstructions of what he could no longer see for himself. No doubt this is why, in the opening paragraphs of his early essay "Baloma: The Spirits of the Dead" (1916), he casually dismisses the rituals of death as irrelevant to the study of Trobriand eschatology. Damon and Wagner do not take the same position, but they worry that it is now too late to assess the full significance of the rites (1989: 15). Nevertheless, several contributors to their volume find it useful to piece together what evidence is available to reconstruct precolonial ritual sequences.

RECONSTRUCTING DEATH RITES

The goal of reconstruction, although important to some social anthropologists interested in traditional cultures, is of much greater significance to archaeologists. With the advent of the "New Archaeology" in the 1960s, the possibility of reconstructing any and all aspects of defunct societies was confidently asserted, and a remarkable range of ingenious techniques have been mobilized to that end. At the same time, the results have been subjected to close scrutiny, and there has been vigorous controversy over both particular cases and theoretical premises. This debate is interesting because mortuary remains are among the most frequently used sources of data in making reconstructions, and because the account that we offered of the anthropology of death has been drawn on widely for support, sometimes by opposing sides in the same argument.

For the social anthropologist, a measure of reorientation is necessary to follow what is at issue in these arguments. Some years ago, Mark Leone observed that there is a "paradigm lag" in archaeology, such that it has been "consistently one stage behind" general anthropology

Introduction

(Leone 1972: 16). To the extent that this is true, there has certainly been a rush to catch up recently; now there are exponents of structuralism, symbolism, hermeneutics, reflexive and critical theory, to complement the more traditional approaches (Hodder 1982; Miller and Tilley 1984). But our reading is that there is less a lag in theory, than a shift in its import, as it is translated from one academic subculture and subject matter to another.

A useful summary of theoretical developments in archaeology up to 1981 is provided in the introduction to the collection of essays *The Archaeology of Death*, edited by Robert Chapman, Ian Kinnes, and Klavs Randsborg, and it is interesting to compare these with fashions in social anthropology. When the New Archaeology was announced, it stood opposed to the evolutionism of Edward Burnett Tylor and James Frazer, whose "rationalist intellectualism" was seen as mystification, and useless to the archaeologist, who cannot excavate belief. But at the same time, the materialist evolutionism of Elman Service and Julian Steward was enthusiastically embraced, so that the paradigm shift is not the same as that which occurred in British social anthropology in the period between the world wars, which involved a total rejection of evolutionism.

The brand of functionalism espoused was also different; where the British predominantly drew on the institutional cybernetics of A. R. Radcliffe-Brown, the New Archaeologists were closer to Malinowski's theory of needs. The source of their functionalism was, however, the same American materialism that inspired the cultural ecologists. Consequently, the occasional respectful references to Durkheim and Hertz are misleading, and there is no real sociological basis. Collective representations are, after all, as difficult to excavate as beliefs. This approach is often called "processual," though the connotations are somewhat different to those implied by Victor Turner's use of the term in social anthropology (1957, 1969).

These differences, in what appear at first sight to be similar theoretical shifts, help to explain divergent attitudes to generalization. The first programmatic statements of structural functionalism announced the framing of comparative laws as an ultimate goal, which was, however, postponed. As the years went by, it became less and less credible, or even desirable. By contrast, the New Archaeologists began nomothetically, because only through generalizations of some kind could they build a bridge between

Introduction

the physical evidence and their objective, a full reconstruction of a functioning society. Their mode of operation required that certain features be posited as indicative of, or correlated with, certain others.

In this phase, the role of social anthropology became that of spoiler: For every generalization advanced, there was an ethnographic case to contradict or invert it. Chapman (1987: 203) calls these "cautionary tales." In the mortuary context, the most frequently mobilized generalization was framed by Lewis Binford: "Other things being equal, the heterogeneity in mortuary practices which is characteristic of a single sociocultural unit would vary directly with the complexity of the status hierarchy, as well as the overall organization of society with regard to membership units and other forms of sodality" (1971: 14–15). The concern – one might almost say obsession – with assessing a society's scale of complexity derives from an evolutionary paradigm. It is to be met by assuming a direct correlation between elaboration of grave goods and architecture, on the one hand, and social hierarchy, on the other. The opening caveat seems designed to deflect the impact of "cautionary tales," but it did not succeed. It is easy to find ethnographic cases where an application of the hypothesis gives misleading results. In caste-organized Bali, for example, an archaeologist might look in vain for the grand mausoleums of kings and priests. Their ashes are scattered on the sea. In America, tomb architecture has become distinctly more egalitarian since the nineteenth century, with simple ground-level plaques replacing crypts and headstones, but it is hard to posit an equivalent narrowing of inequalities of wealth or power. As counterexamples multiply, exceptions overwhelm the rule.

The latter part of Binford's hypothesis, dealing with social groups, is more murky. Its elaboration has been associated particularly with the work of Arthur Saxe (1968, 1971). He and his colleagues have, for instance, detected evidence of descent groups in the clustering or variations in style of graves, but this involves a series of slippery subsidiary assumptions.

The Binford–Saxe hypotheses have provided the basis for many reconstructions in the last twenty years. There have also been studies that questioned them, however. For example, Randsborg (1980) argues that in some periods of Danish prehistory grave remains mirror social ranking, and in others they do not. Jane Okely (1979: 86) suggests that mortuary practices may in fact disguise social rank.

Introduction

In America, burial complexes in the South and East have attracted attention. For instance, Wright Mound in Kentucky has been analyzed by Andrew Shyrock as the necropolis of a chiefdom. He posits that those of lesser status were cremated elsewhere, and he rank orders the burials in the mound by applying the principle that "relative status can be operationalized as time expended in grave preparation" (Shyrock 1987: 249). From the comparative point of view, however, none of the graves are very elaborate, being at most shafts lined with logs. Their cost may have been marginal as compared to expenditure on the death rituals as a whole, so that they are an unconvincing indicator of status. Moreover, some tombs could be opened for reuse, and some disarticulated skeletal remains are present, suggesting secondary treatment. Perhaps the most high-prestige sequence involved primary interment in the mound, followed by cremation. In any event, there is little inherent reason to see some modes of disposal as belonging to "chiefs." In his critique of Shyrock, Robert Mainfort uses the Berawan case to show that tomb-building may be an element in competition between leaders who are less than chiefs, and that tombs may say more about the status of the builder than the interred. So far so good; but he goes on to say that multi-use tombs imply the "communal nature of the facilities," and hence competition between corporate groups rather than "big men" (Mainfort 1989: 171–2). He has stretched the Berawan comparison too far; contrary to his claim, grand Berawan mausoleums may well be "reused over a period of time," but, in a cognatic society, there are no competing descent groups. In rejecting Shyrock's chiefdom, Mainfort is set on substituting another standardized type, the lineage-based society.

In our reading of it, the basic issue in all of this is the use of ethnographic analogy. Some archaeologists have abandoned the possibility of reconstruction and see reality only in how the past is reconstructed and used in our museums and popular culture. This properly postmodern stance, illustrated in the work of Michael Shanks and Christopher Tilley (1987), presumably has little use for analogy. But, for the present at least, the majority even of postprocessual archaeologists are still concerned to probe into a substantive, if obscure, past. For them, working hypotheses, even if only guesswork, are still necessary to bridge the gap between the traces of a culture and the culture itself. In Ian Hodder's (1984) study of European megaliths, for instance, he castigates previous processual accounts for applying blanket explanations, and unconvincing ones at that, without regard for regional variations. In place of these, he explores some symbolic parallels between houses and tombs, with more stimulating results. But Hodder does not eschew generalizations; he only uses them more opportunistically.

There appear to be different ways of employing ethnographic analogy, however, and this causes confusion. At one end of the spectrum, some processualists advocate testing a generalization statistically, often by means of the Human Relations Area File. A correlation that holds in a significantly high percentage of ethnographically known cases then provides a valid "ethnographic analogy," that is, it is assumed to hold for some prehistoric culture or cultures. This technique is very different from analogy in the sense simply of apt comparison. For the latter, all that is required is a particular ethnographic case that bears interesting or suggestive parallels with the one being investigated. There are intermediary positions; one might, for instance, apply the statistical technique to a restricted culture area. The difficulty comes when the basis of inference is not made clear. The statistical method asserts a positivist and predictive power, whereas apt comparison can do no more than suggest interpretations. These must be substantiated, if possible, from the site data. The analogy proves nothing in itself, and that is the premise of our comparison in Chapter 6 between Berawan mausoleums and Egyptian pyramids, which disclaims any evolutionary suggestion.

In a discussion of techniques of reconstruction, Chapman begins "Here we make the assumption that not all societies are unique" (1987: 202). A social anthropologist is startled by such a beginning; surely we study particular cultures precisely because they *are* unique. Chapman is presumably referring to the possibility of statistical generalization: For any given feature there will be some norm; in which case his statement is a truism, and he has no need of assumptions. Only a few paragraphs later, however, he compares the "archaeological signatures" of particular New Guinea societies with those of prehistoric cultures on other continents, to see if the institutions of "big manship" that ethnographers have found in New Guinea could be attributed to societies elsewhere. This technique resembles "apt comparison," and it is not a positive method.

Even so, for postprocessual archaeologists, the matching of their data to suitable comparative cases in the ethnographic record is surely an important tool, and it at last gives social anthropology a constructive role, in place of the subversive one that it played in the previous phase, depending on a shared notion of interpretation.

It is worth distinguishing between analogies that are relatively more close or more distant. When Chapman looks to New Guinea for insights on American mounds, that is a distant analogy. It may still provide insights, but a host of major differences must be taken into account, because any one might invalidate the comparison. By contrast, if a comparison is made with an ethnic group known to be closely related to the one represented at the site, linguistically, ethnologically, or historically, then the analogy is close. As features characteristic of a culture area or tradition may be shared between the two, similarities and contrasts stand out more clearly. Early contact accounts are particularly valuable, because they often describe behavior. In a coherent culture area, they may provide clues at some distance. In his study of the Indians of the Virginia piedmont, about whom little is recorded directly in the historical record, Jeffrey Hantman (1990) is careful to assess the value of information from a close reading of English accounts of the Indians of the Chesapeake shore, so adding a new level of interpretation to data from excavation. This style of detective work, which does not rely on shotgun generalizations, is representative of the most convincing examples of current reconstructive studies.

We should remind ourselves, however, that reconstruction is not the only, or even the principal, goal of archaeologists. Many retain a primary interest in tracing long-term sequences of cultural change, and here again the contrast between archaeology and social anthropology is obvious.

DEATH AND THE LONGUE DURÉE

Social anthropologists sometimes question the utility of archaeological reconstruction, when ethnographic research into living traditions can provide directly the sort of data so painstakingly won from excavation. The reciprocal complaint is that ethnographers base their accounts on only brief encounters with another culture. Chapman (1987: 205) points out that Metcalf's (1982a) analysis of Berawan eschatology is based on just nine major funerals. He leaves out of account the funerals of children (alas, numerous) and the very old, which are not ritually elaborate. But his point is well taken. Even prior to the recent vogue for demystifying

Introduction

fieldwork, most thinking ethnographers were painfully aware of the limits of their experience of the cultures they studied. It is often possible to make some assessment of trends over a period longer than the year or two of fieldwork. Berawan death rites, for instance, evidently became more grand in this century than they were in the previous one, because of the availability of credit from traders (Metcalf 1981). Increasingly, anthropologists trying to escape the confines of functionalism are concerned to recover what they can from historical records or accounts of first contact by Europeans. But often the message seems to be *plus ça change, plus c'est la même chose*. A nice example is provided by Olivia Harris (1982), showing how among the Laymi of Bolivia indigenous concepts of the dead, and even deathways, have stubbornly resisted suppression by the Catholic church. It is an important theme, but it does not address the changes that characterize what Fernand Braudel calls *la longue durée* (1980: 27–34). For those, we look to archaeologists and historians.

Historians have recently directed new attention to the context of mortality. In England, Clare Gittings (1984) provides an interesting survey of the deathways of both rich and poor in the sixteenth and seventeenth centuries, drawing on such documents as wills, probate accounts, and parish registers. John Morley (1971) demonstrates the remarkable elaboration of mourning and funereal art in Victorian Britain. The essays edited by Joachim Whaley (1981) are interesting but range over topics too diverse to summarize common themes, a tendency even more pronounced than in collections by social anthropologists.

It is in France, however, that historians have displayed most interest in death, and John McManners (1981) explains why. Ever since the revolution, French republicanism has taken an anticlerical stance, but public figures of progressive views, novelists, philosophers, and the like, have had a disconcerting habit of reconciling with the church at the end. Consequently, deathbed scenes have taken on a compelling drama, a tug-of-war between enlightenment and religious ideologies. Such scenes figure in Philippe Ariès's ambitious study (1978), which attempts to describe European reactions to death over several centuries in terms of what he calls *mentalités*, or attitudes characteristic of each of the epochs that he identifies. In some respects, his approach resembles the "culture and personality" school in American anthropology, and it is vulnerable to the same charges that were leveled against the latter, namely excessive subjectivity. Ariès switches criteria for identifying different epochs and *men-*

talités idiosyncratically and often stresses elite culture at the expense of general trends. The same charge cannot be made concerning Pierre Chaunu's equally well known study (1978). He bases his account firmly on, among other things, a mass of statistics documenting the varying death rate in Paris over three centuries. In this emphasis on quantification he follows a well-developed pattern of the *Annales* school. As Stuart Clark (1985: 181–85) argues, this pattern reflects a basically materialist program in contrast to Ariès's idealism. Nevertheless, it does not follow that Chaunu's conclusions lack interpretive leaps. Whaley (1981: 10) makes the point that Chaunu's final goal also is to reveal attitudes, but not impressionistically. However, he takes for granted that he can translate objective circumstances into inner states. He assumes, for instance, that in periods of high infant mortality parents became hardened to the loss of children. Such presumed psychic universals are risky. Chaunu came under fire for discounting the force of ideas in shaping peoples' responses, but critics had different ideas about which ideas mattered. Some thought that the teachings of the church may have had as much influence as the death rate, whereas other intellectuals objected to the intrusion of the church into the discussion, so that death remains as politicized as ever in France (Favre 1978; Lebrun 1971; LeGoff 1984; McManners 1985; Vovelle 1976).

In much of this literature, analytic goals and premises go unstated. At the same time there is no common understanding of them, so that studies do not much relate to one another. Historians generally do not share basic theoretical tenets, beyond the professionalism involved in scholarly use of written sources. Instead, they make a virtue out of devising interpretive frameworks ad hoc, by common sense criteria. In the last couple of decades, the retreat from positivism has moved anthropology away from sociology and closer to history. But anthropologists have a century of experience in the pitfalls of "common sense" explanations of cultural differences, and the suspicion with which we regard unselfconscious narrative still divides us from historians. This complicates an integration of historical and ethnographic materials, but it is a complication with which we must deal if we are to fulfill the promise for a dynamic, postfunctionalist approach. In Chapter 7, we had this goal in view of juxtaposing histories of French and English monarchs with some classic ethnographies of sacred kingship. A fascinating recent essay in this mode is Gary Ebersole's (1989) study of the intrigues and political maneuvers surrounding the secondary burial rites of emperors in early Japan, making use of ritual poetry as a source. China offers a rich field for research of this kind, and the collection edited by James Watson and Evelyn Rawski (1988) is a valuable exploration into a complex topic.

DEATH AND REFLEXIVITY

American historians have shown less interest in responses to death than their French colleagues. David Stannard's *The Puritan Way of Death* (1977) is well known, but until recently there has been no account of that peculiarly American configuration of embalming, viewing, and storage in a concrete vault, other than a mostly technical account commissioned by the Funeral Directors Association (Habenstein and Lamers 1955). This gap has now been filled by James Farrell (1980), who shows how the American funeral took shape in the crucial period between 1830 and 1920. Since then, it has proved remarkably stable. We thought that our discussion of it in Chapter 8 might soon be rendered obsolete, as values shifted and the death awareness movement directed scrutiny toward the power of the death industry, but it was not so.

Another surprise is that our account has not been outdated by new research. Richard Kalish and David Reynolds (1976) provide a caveat to the impression of uniformity in American attitudes to death, by describing differences that have persisted in some ethnic minorities. But many recent trends remain to be investigated, and made sense of in cultural terms. It is twenty years since David Sudnow (1967) showed the subtleties of class involved in deciding who was classified as "dead on arrival" at a California hospital, so that it was possible to speak of the "social construction of death." With the medical resources now available, the issue of who is dead and who is not has become infinitely more tangled (Gervais 1986; Lamb 1985). The phenomenon of near-death experience, made more common by improved emergency treatment for victims of heart attacks, has redirected attention to eschatology (Cherry 1986; Ring 1984). AIDS has replaced cancer in the American imagination as the most appalling affront to technical values, the uncurable disease (Shilts 1987). We know nothing about the clientele of the temperature-controlled mausoleums, touted for their views of the sea or closeness to shopping malls. Most importantly, we have learned little

Introduction

about the wellsprings of American culture that have kept deathways stable through years when much else seemed to be changing.

Meanwhile, American death rites are probably the most elaborate in the industrialized West, and certainly the ones most likely to be regarded as exotic by people from other countries. Consequently, they are an obvious focus for studies in the reflexive or critical mode. Anthropology has for decades made the claim that it allows us a new view of ourselves by escaping for the moment, at least, and partially, the confines of our own cultural horizons. To try to make good on that claim, we turned to American death rites in Chapter 8, even though we risked undermining what went before if our interpretations proved unconvincing or superficial. Evidently for some they did. In a survey of current work in cultural critique, George Marcus and Michael Fischer remark only that our discussion is "developed through secondary sources and appended as a provocation" (1986: 157). They are correct; neither of us has conducted fieldwork in America, then or since. Nevertheless, we set out to probe an unexplored area, using the same theoretical guides that we had employed throughout the book: We tried to show the limitations of psychological and materialist arguments. We noted the symbolism of the corpse as it related to a constellation of ideas about life and death and looked at the ways in which death rites intersected with institutions of the political center. In the process, we put into practice the strategy of "defamiliarization by cross-cultural juxtaposition" (Marcus and Fischer 1986: 157). It is a strategy that comes readily to hand after experiencing the horrified reactions of the "cultural other" to our practices (Metcalf 1978). One cannot help wondering whether Robert Hertz, reading in the library of the British Museum at the turn of the century, might have made embalming his special case, rather than secondary burial, if he had found as much material about America as he did about Borneo, and what twist that might have put on the anthropology of mortuary ritual.

23

1

PRELIMINARIES

DEATH IN LIFE

What could be more universal than death? Yet what an incredible variety of responses it evokes. Corpses are burned or buried, with or without animal or human sacrifice; they are preserved by smoking, embalming, or pickling; they are eaten – raw, cooked, or rotten; they are ritually exposed as carrion or simply abandoned; or they are dismembered and treated in a variety of these ways. Funerals are the occasion for avoiding people or holding parties, for fighting or having sexual orgies, for weeping or laughing, in a thousand different combinations. The diversity of cultural reaction is a measure of the universal impact of death.

It is not a random reaction, however; always it is meaningful and expressive. This study is about the rituals by which people confront death, and in so doing, celebrate life. Anthropologists have, of course, no special understanding of the mystery of death. We can at best only recount the wisdoms of other cultures, wisdoms that have found expression in song and dance, as well as solemn rite, for funerals elsewhere are often rowdy affairs in comparison with those of mainstream America. This is true in the islands that provide our most extended case material, Borneo and Madagascar, as it is in much of Southeast Asia and Africa. Closer to home, one thinks of Irish wakes or the jazz bands that traditionally accompany funeral processions in New Orleans. Even where cus-

24

tom calls for restraint, it often happens that the pleasure of a reunion of family and friends bubbles up amid the prescribed hush. It is a very frequent aspect of funerals that evidences of life and community eclipse representations of death and separation.

The study of death rituals is a positive endeavor because, regardless of whether custom calls for festive or restrained behavior, the issue of death throws into relief the most important cultural values by which people live their lives and evaluate their experiences. Life becomes transparent against the background of death, and fundamental social and cultural issues are revealed. For example, in Madagascar, the pervasive opposition of maleness and femaleness that underlies the structure of that society achieves its most powerful and focused expression in funeral ritual. In Africa, the politically fragmented Nyakyusa and Dinka peoples reveal in their funerals basic survival values of warriorhood and cooperation. In centralized kingdoms everywhere – Africa, Europe, Asia – events surrounding the death of the king reveal most strikingly the nature of each polity and the structure of its political competition. In the United States, the individualism, materialism, and commercialism that characterize our national ethic seem to stand in particularly sharp relief in the context of our funeral industry. Peoples' customary responses to death provide an important opportunity for sensitive probing into the nature of human life.

THE "DEATH AWARENESS" MOVEMENT

Currently, there is a growing interest in all facets of death. It is now fashionable to deal frankly with this formerly taboo subject. The legal, medical, and moral issues surrounding death and our new abilities to delay it are discussed frequently in the general press and in professional journals. The introduction of "death education" in the public schools is almost as controversial as the introduction of sex education. This is no accident: Some association of sex with death occurs in nearly every culture in the world. In another vein, a popular book (now made into a feature film) presents the reports of people who have "died" and then been revived to describe the nature of *Life After Life* (Moody 1975).

In many respects, this "death awareness" movement began with the popular success of Jessica Mitford's exposé of *The American Way of Death*

(1963). Mitford attacked the American funeral industry for profiteering by selling unnecessarily expensive services and goods to a captive clientele under great temporary stress. She questioned the appropriateness of the funeral ritual itself, especially the elaborate treatment and display of the corpse. With this public reassessment of the ritual, there began a broader reconsideration of all aspects of the experience of dying and the significance of death in modern society. Mitford saw the normal American funeral as irrational, and by the standards of most of the peoples of the world, it is indeed strange. So thoroughly have Americans sealed themselves off from death that many have never seen a corpse. Others have seen one only in the carefully stage-managed context of the funeral parlor, the body elaborately packaged and beautified. After delivery to the undertaker, the corpse

. . . is in short order sprayed, sliced, pierced, pickled, trussed, trimmed, creamed, waxed, painted, rouged and neatly dressed . . . transformed from a common corpse into a Beautiful Memory Picture. This process is known in the trade as embalming and restorative art, and is so universally employed in the United States and Canada that the funeral director does it routinely without consulting corpse or kin. He regards as eccentric those few who are hardy enough to suggest that it might be dispensed with. Yet no law requires it, no religious doctrine commends it, nor is it dictated by considerations of health, sanitation, or even personal daintiness. In no part of the world but in North America is it widely used. The purpose of embalming is to make the corpse presentable for viewing in a suitably costly container; and here too the funeral director routinely, without first consulting the family, prepares the body for public display. [Mitford 1963: 54]

Remembering the oddities of our own funeral practices, we can avoid any tendency to feel superior toward the other cultures we are about to examine. Conversely, the exploration of the death rituals of other cultures will allow us to observe American funerals with a new and more balanced perspective.

Several serious studies of Western attitudes toward death and dying preceded Mitford's book. Most notably, sociologist Geoffrey Gorer (1965) compiled a detailed study of mourning practices in England, and historian Philippe Ariès (1967) documented the changing Western attitudes toward death over eight centuries. Collections appeared containing numerous empirical studies of the social-psychological reactions of people to death, both their own impending deaths and those of others (Feifel 1959; Fulton 1965). Even as these academic studies multiply, our death customs are themselves undergoing changes. On the one hand, consumer groups have organized to procure simpler, less expensive, more "rational" funerals. Although this movement has attracted wide interest, few people actually choose these streamlined funerals for themselves or for their loved ones. On the other hand, many funeral businesses are shedding their traditional cloak of restrained respectability and are mounting more explicit promotional campaigns for a greater variety of funeral arrangements. Innovations such as drive-in wakes and motorcycle funerals would not startle Mitford, however. In spite of such variations, or perhaps because of them, there is today a widespread desire to examine the nature of our institutions.

DEATH RITUAL AND NINETEENTH-CENTURY ANTHROPOLOGY

If a frank concern with the way that we die is a relative novelty, an interest in the death rites of exotic cultures is not. Given the extraordinary variety of rites found worldwide, which we noted at the outset, it is easy to see the potential in them for sensationalism. For some theorists in a young discipline busy trying to establish its scholarly credentials, this very feature counseled avoidance and in part explains why the study of ritual in general, and death ritual in particular, has gone in and out of fashion. But even in its most sober phases, anthropology has had to deal, implicitly at least, with the essential facts of our mortality, because of their relentless subversion of merely human arrangements.

In archaeology, a concern with disposal of the dead is well-nigh inescapable, since it provides an important context for the deposition of artifacts. Data from burials have furnished some of the earliest evidence of cultural activity. For the oldest civilizations, mortuary structures have yielded impressive and revealing evidence about ancient ways of life.

Meanwhile in social anthropology, interest in death rites has vacillated. Curiously, in both this century and the last, there has been a similar oscillation. Beginning with a preoccupation with types of social organization, the focus has gradually shifted to broader issues of ideology. In the midnineteenth century, writers such as Lewis Henry Morgan and John McLennan were engrossed in the evolution of marriage, the family, and the clan. Metaphysical ideas seemed to these writers less amenable to their comparative method, which alone could provide scientifically valid reconstructions of the progress of humanity. This opinion had reversed itself, however, by the end of the century. For Edward Burnett Tylor and James Frazer it seemed obvious that the most interesting aspect of primitive life was the conception of the universe that it engendered. Tylor posited an entire religious system that arose from the contemplation of the phenomena of death, and of dreaming. From dreaming came a notion of the bifurcation of the individual into a material and an immaterial component, which then provided an explanation of death in terms of the separation of body and soul. This in turn gave rise to ideas of the afterlife, and in due course, to a cult of the dead. This mode of argumentation, involving the empathetic reconstruction of the ratiocination of early humans has been dubbed "intellectualist." Note, however, that Tylor's interest in religion did not translate into an enthusiasm for religion; like most of his anthropological contemporaries, he viewed it as simply an erroneous precursor to science. Tylor's primitives may have been intellectuals, but their thinking was wrong.

DURKHEIM AND THE SOCIOLOGY OF RELIGION

The work of the French sociologist Emile Durkheim directly opposed this intellectualist emphasis of the English tradition of anthropology. Durkheim argued that religion expressed the moral cohesion of society rather than the fears and imaginings of individuals. As we shall see in Chapter 2, funeral rituals and the expression of anguish in the confrontation with death were also important data for Durkheim's theories, but they are utilized in a very different way.

Whereas for Frazer and Tylor primitive beliefs relating to death provided easy solutions to questions about the origins and nature of religion, for Durkheim conceptions about death were part of the problem, not a solution. This is because, from his point of view, the very nature of the individual as an entity differentiated from the group is the central problem to be investigated. Durkheim's theory focuses on the integration of individuals into communal life. In this process, beliefs and ideas play a role that is much more complicated than that envisioned by Tylor and Frazer. Durkheim devoted much of his career to investigating the complexity of collectively held beliefs and concepts, and exploring how such "collective representations" unite individuals even while simultaneously specifying their separate identities. Throughout Durkheim's work, there is a dynamic tension between the autonomy of the individual and the individual's identification with society; between the physical separateness of human organisms and the necessity to transcend it through the use of language and symbols. Within this theoretical framework, the event of death is an important but difficult topic that brings to the fore the ambiguities and contradictions of human social existence and definition.

During the first decade of this century, Durkheim and his students produced a remarkable series of essays on the sociology of religion, many of which were published in their journal, the *Année sociologique*. One by one these essays took up the topics of sacrifice, symbolic classification, magic, sin and expiation, and body symbolism. They reformulated these classical theological issues within the sociological framework established by Durkheim's work. This was truly a cooperative effort, and most of these essays are collaborations of two authors. English-speaking anthropologists have only recently begun to accord these works the attention they deserve. It was the belated translation and republication of these essays that was largely responsible for the great florescence of studies of symbolic forms that has been one of the chief developments in social anthropology during the last twenty years.

One of these essays, Robert Hertz's 1907 study of secondary burial, provides the primary point of reference for our analysis of death ritual. In 1909, another Parisian scholar, Arnold van Gennep (who was conversant with but not associated with Durkheim's group) published *The Rites of Passage*, which dealt with funerals as one of a large class of rituals. Both appeared in English translation in 1960; together they provide an original perspective on the nature of death ritual.

VAN GENNEP'S RITES OF PASSAGE

Van Gennep identified a class of rituals concerned with transitions from one state to another, such as those of initiation, or marriage, or the annual round. His thesis is that they all share a common tripartite

Preliminaries

death	ONE DISTINCTION	marriage
alive / dead	TWO CATEGORIES	single / married
alive → dying → dead	THREE STAGES	single → engaged → married

Figure 1. Schema of van Gennep's rites of passage.

structure, involving, first, separation from one status, then a liminal period, followed by reincorporation into a new status. At first sight, the proposition seems innocuous enough, merely the assertion that rites have a beginning, a middle, and an end. The force of his analysis is that he shows how similar are the beginnings, middles, and ends of a vast array of diverse rituals. As he himself remarked, others before him had noticed recurring symbolic themes, but he demonstrates a logic behind this recurrence: In the course of a lifetime, a person undergoes several changes of status. At each change, an old self perishes, as it were, and a new one is born. For people everywhere, death and birth provide the obvious metaphors with which to imagine lesser transitions, and that is why each is routinely expressed in the symbolism of a rite of passage, predominantly in the opening and closing phases respectively. This occurs regardless of the occasion; skulls and skeletons intrude incongruously at a harvest festival, whereas death rites are filled with the symbolism of rebirth.

It is principally van Gennep's analysis of symbolism that concerns us here, but the structuralist aspect of his work also deserves mention, especially as it is often overlooked. The tripartite structure is generated by a binary opposition (see Figure 1). Moreover, it may not be consciously employed; pervasive as it is, the structure must be made out "beneath a multiplicity of forms" (van Gennep 1960: 191).

Van Gennep's essay, like much that was written in Paris during the first decades of this century, is strikingly modern in style. It allows us to make sense of rituals in particular social and religious contexts, and equally in our own or in remote cultures. By contrast, evolutionary anthropologists such as Tylor and Frazer were interested in bizarre beliefs and practices only as evidence of supposed previous stages of human social and intellectual development. Their sheer irrationality made it obvious that they could only be survivals of more primitive epochs. But this appearance of irrationality was itself a product of the assumptions that the evolutionists brought to their study. Franz Steiner provides an insight into this odd Victorian view of ritual:

The Victorian era was a rationalist age which differed from the previous Age of Reason in that it attributed importance not only to the various attempts at rational explanation, but also to the residual context which did not yield to the solvent of reason. This was particularly true of religion, which was then being adapted to the needs of an industrial society. Now the ground held by religion could be covered by various ethical theories, but there remained, unaccounted for, some very important attitudes which were not susceptible to the same kind of treatment and which, indeed, seemed irrational under such examination. These attitudes and contexts, which had thus been divorced from their background and from institutional functions, became isolated to a degree which was new in human history. The more the links, props and joints of the socio-religious thought structure were absorbed into theories of rational ethics, the more isolated became the little islands of prescribed ceremonial behavior. [Steiner 1967: 50–1]

These attitudes colored the perception of ritual in the nineteenth century. The interest of ritual lay in what it could say about the past, not the present. It was noticed, for instance, that peasants in some parts of Europe had an odd preliminary to marriage. The male kin of the groom arrived at the bride's house fully armed and made a show of abducting her. The bride's kin were careful to stay away while this little charade was played out. Here was prime evidence, so the evolutionists thought, for a previous epoch when genuine marriage-by-capture had been the rule, and on this frail basis whole sequences in the prehistoric evolution of the family were postulated. Van Gennep subverts this logic simply by showing that the rite has a meaning as it stands, regardless of whatever antiquity it may or may not have. It expresses, directly and poignantly, the separation that a woman undergoes in these societies when she leaves her natal family and joins that of her husband.

Van Gennep helped to reduce the acute ethnocentrism of nineteenth-century anthropology by making ritual everywhere accessible to a similar logic. The concept of the rite of passage stands close to three major contemporary issues: the integration of the individual into society, the nature of symbolism, and the moral relativity of cultures.

Preliminaries

LIMINALITY

The aspect of van Gennep's work that has received the most attention recently is his notion of liminality. Victor Turner's brilliant elaboration of this concept (1967, 1969) is largely responsible for the wide currency of van Gennep's terminology. Building on van Gennep's insight that the transitional phase sometimes acquires a certain autonomy from the rest of the ritual, Turner develops a view of "a state of transition" (1967: 94), the inhabitants of which are "betwixt and between" normal social roles, and close to some transcendent and sacred core of social and moral value. Turner follows van Gennep's lead in exploring the characteristic ways humans represent change with symbols drawn from biological processes such as menstruation and decomposition. Turner's focus on the autonomy of liminality eventually leads him far afield from specific rituals of transition. As he notes, with self-deprecating humor, it is:

a hypothesis that seeks to account for the attributes of such seemingly diverse phenomena as neophytes in the liminal phase of ritual, subjugated autochthones, small nations, court jesters, holy mendicants, good Samaritans, millenarian movements, "dharma bums," matrilaterality in patrilineal systems, patrilaterality in matrilineal systems, and monastic orders. Surely an ill assorted bunch of social phenomena! [1969: 125]

Turner's development of the theme of liminality extends far beyond its initial application to Ndembu initiation rituals. But van Gennep's original emphasis on the autonomy of the liminal derives most strongly from his consideration of death rituals. The chapter titled "Funerals" opens as follows:

On first considering funeral ceremonies, one expects rites of separation to be their most prominent component, in contrast to rites of transition and rites of incorporation, which should be only slightly elaborated. A study of the data, however, reveals that the rites of separation are few in number and very simple, while the transition rites have a duration and complexity sometimes so great that they must be granted a sort of autonomy. [1960: 146]

Van Gennep's survey of death rituals throughout the world emphasizes the ways in which this theme of transition seems to dominate funeral symbolism. Water journeys and islandlike afterworlds appear over and over again. Additionally, van Gennep noted that, surprisingly, the theme of regeneration and growth expressed in symbols of agricultural and human fertility is equally common. Where Turner has emphasized that the symbolisms of growth and fertility, on the one hand, and degeneration and putrescence, on the other, are functions of liminality per se, van Gennep was cautious. He noted that this liminal phase of funerals is not entirely autonomous, not entirely interchangeable with liminal phases of other rituals. He carefully left room for a special relevance of these highly charged and sensuous symbols to death itself.

In van Gennep's formulation, liminality is never divorced entirely from its ritual context. Where it most nearly approaches autonomy is in the context of funerals, perhaps because death is so much more profound a mystery than other transitions. Moreover, van Gennep's concept of liminality is never separated from the notion of change, process, and passage. It is not extended as a fixed complementary category, as in some of Turner's developments. Although such an extension enables one to explain a staggering array of phenomena, it makes the concept of liminality static, in contrast to the dramatic changes of death.

HERTZ'S STUDY OF SECONDARY BURIAL

As van Gennep himself noted (1960: 190n), the only other writer to appreciate the importance and character of the liminal phase of ritual was Robert Hertz. This is not surprising given that Hertz's special concern was with death rituals. Funerals provide only a part of the data of van Gennep's wide-ranging survey. They are, by contrast, the sole concern of Hertz's essay "A Contribution to the Study of the Collective Representation of Death" (1907), one of the most original analyses pertaining to death written in this century.

Hertz discussed those societies that do not see death as instantaneous. Although such a view of death is not uncommon in the world, Hertz drew much of his material from Indonesia, particularly the island of Borneo. In this region, many peoples conceive of a period when the mortal is neither alive nor finally dead; this Hertz called the "intermediary period." The end of this period is marked by the "great feast," during which the remains of the deceased are recovered, ritually processed, and moved to a new location. Hertz noted that the length of the intermediary period may be prolonged by several factors, such as the need to accumulate a surplus for the feast. But the irreducible minimal duration is the time required for the bones to become dry and free of decaying flesh.

The fate of the corpse is to suffer putrescence and formlessness, until only dry bones remain, hard and imperishable. It was Hertz's insight that, in Borneo, the fate of the body is a model for the fare of the soul. As the corpse is formless and repulsive during the intermediary period, so the soul of the dead person is homeless and the object of dread. Unable to enter the society of the dead, it must lead a pitiful existence on the fringes of human habitation. In its discomfort, the soul is liable spitefully to inflict illness upon the living. Elaborate observances are required to divert its hostility. The "great feast" terminates this miserable period by honoring the now dry bones of the deceased, confirming the soul's arrival in the land of ancestors, and marking the reestablishment of normal relations among the survivors.

Such an explanation is hardly a general postulate comparable to van Gennep's schema of the rite of passage. Hertz used a different but equally powerful lens through which to focus on death, viewing the issue through one type of burial custom. Yet Hertz's concerns were no less general than those of van Gennep; the difference is largely one of sociological style. Hertz followed Durkheim's method of the special case. Rather than survey all forms of a phenomenon, one example is chosen, the analysis of which will illuminate a wide range of related forms. The classic example of this is Durkheim's choice of the topic of suicide as the special case on which to test his theories of the integration of the individual into the larger social group. In studying the representation of death, Hertz chose the custom of secondary burial as an elaborated form of the general tendency toward representing death through manipulation of the corpse.

Hertz's treatment of general issues wholly within a single ethnographic context was, in this way, a forerunner of the modern tradition of social anthropology. Whereas the value of van Gennep's approach can be appreciated in comparison with the style of anthropology that preceded it, Hertz's work makes most sense in the context of what followed. As a student of Durkheim, he shared in the development of comparative sociology:

Hertz's essays exemplify this descriptive integration, the meaning of the facts being shown to lie not in themselves, considered as separate facts, but in their interrelation; the art of the anthropologist being to reveal this and hence their meaning. We do not understand what the double disposal of the dead in Indonesia means till we know also about the beliefs held about the ghosts of the dead and also about the rules of mourning, but once we have grasped the pattern of these three sides of death – corpse, soul and mourners – we see that each expresses the same idea of transition; and we further understand why a ruler's death cannot be announced, why widows may not be immediately inherited or remarried, why corpses of the very old and of small children are treated differently, etc. [Evans-Pritchard in Hertz 1960: 15]

Central to this approach was a new form of comparative analysis. Hertz was careful to concentrate on a limited range of facts from one area of the world, and not to lift facts out of context from widely divergent societies. The representation of death is a problem of universal scope and even the seemingly bizarre practice of secondary disposal of the corpse is more widespread than is generally realized. Examples could be cited from Central Asia (Lopatin 1960: 90–114), North America (Driver 1961: 450), South America (Crocker 1977), Melanesia (Haddon 1908: 149; Tuzin 1975; Wagner 1972: 147–50), and elsewhere. Reburial was a part of the Jewish tradition (Meyers 1971) and is still practiced in Greece (Alexiou 1974: 47–9). But Hertz stuck for the most part to the rich material from Borneo and Indonesia. It is on this empirical base that his analysis, whatever illumination it might cast on behavior elsewhere in the world, must stand or fall. In the context of Bornean ethnography, Hertz's analysis can be put to the test.

In his analysis of the symbolism of the decaying corpse, Hertz borrowed from his colleagues' account of the nature of sacrifice (Hubert and Mauss 1899). What connects secondary disposal with sacrifice is the conception that objects must be destroyed in this world in order that they may pass to the next. Hertz saw that what applied to the sudden destruction of sacrifice also applies to the slow one of decomposition. In this way, he placed himself in the tradition of W. Robertson Smith (1889) in exploring the subtle interaction between the nature of a concept and the "material husk" within which it must be wrapped in order to have form (Beidelman 1974: 56–7).

Preliminaries

MODERN DEVELOPMENTS
OF HERTZ'S THESIS

Although Hertz's essay is often cited, there are few places in the anthropological literature where it is discussed in much detail. The most prominent of these discussions (Goody 1962; Miles 1965; Bloch 1971) draw their inspiration from the sociological side of Hertz's analysis. For example, Jack Goody's study of *Death, Property and the Ancestors* discusses Hertz's analysis of the problem of restoring the social fabric after death has rent it. This approach provides an effective base for Goody's emphasis on the transformation of economic, social, and emotional relationships wrought by the funeral rituals of a West African people. But the symbolic aspects of Hertz's argument have been passed over.

Meanwhile, those anthropologists responsible for the revival of interest in Hertz's symbolic analyses have paid little attention to his essay on death. By translating and publishing it along with Hertz's "The Preeminence of the Right Hand: A Study in Religious Polarity," Rodney Needham highlights Hertz's concern with body symbolism (Hertz 1960). The introduction to that volume, by E. E. Evans-Pritchard, is a general discussion of the *Année sociologique* with but a few lines specifically referring to the death essay. Needham's development of Hertz's work has built mainly on the essay on the polarity of the human body rather than on the essay relating to its mortality. The former was again reprinted in a large collection of articles on left-right binary symbolism (Needham 1973). The older volume containing the death essay is now out of print. Other anthropologists, notably Mary Douglas (1970), have also expanded on Hertz's insights regarding the body as a "natural symbol" for moral phenomena. The complex issues raised by the death essay have yet to be discussed.

The elaborations of Hertz's insights wrought by scholars such as Goody, Needham, and Douglas have been fruitful and stimulating. However, the separate developments of the sociological and symbolic aspects of Hertz's work serve to point up how specialized anthropology has become in recent decades. In his short essay, Hertz tried to encompass a problem larger than those that exercise his successors. He tried to cover the whole range of human activity: the symbolic, the social, the pragmatic, and the emotional. Perhaps it was his situation as a young man working in a new discipline during its formative years that permitted him to be so ambitious.

No doubt Hertz's essay is flawed in several respects, largely due to its attempt to achieve grand aims based on limited and secondhand data. At times it seems as though he is attempting desperately to bridge this gap with every analytic device available to him. Explanations drawn from studies of Hindu pollution and Hebrew sacrifice are applied directly to the cultures of Borneo. Exceptions to his thesis are argued away with the same utilitarian reasoning that he elsewhere rules out as inadmissible. But no one claims that Hertz's death essay is a measured and mature piece of work. Indeed, it is his intellectual daring that makes Hertz so rewarding. His crucial proposition remains: Close attention to the combined symbolic and sociological contexts of the corpse yields profound insights regarding the meaning of death and life.

THE FORMAT OF THIS BOOK

It is not our intention in this book to provide either an encyclopedia of the world's funeral customs or a history of the anthropological study of death rituals. We limit ourselves to a few outstanding cases that provide striking illustrations of the major themes that concern us. Our interest in these cases lies in the details of cultural practices relating to death and the treatment of the corpse. In order to keep close to the poignant human drama of death, we supplement these descriptions with several vivid eyewitness accounts of specific funerals in these societies. Our study is divided into three main parts, each of which consists of two chapters that explore complementary sides of the issue at hand, and a concluding part comprising a single chapter.

In Part I, Universals and Culture, we look at some of the attempts anthropologists have made to establish universal theories about responses to death.

The undeniable universality of death suggests the attractive possibility of an uncomplicated panhuman explanation of funeral rites. Anthropologists have often stressed a certain "psychic unity of mankind," so postulating that whatever different beliefs people have, whatever different types of societies or environments they inhabit, they nonetheless share the same emotional and cognitive qualities. However, the question remains: Can these qualities, if they can be identified, serve to explain mortuary practices? The strong negative emotions of fear and sorrow that seem naturally to accompany death are candidates for a universal cause of funeral rites. Chapter 2 explores attempts to base a theory of society on the ritual expression of emotion. We conclude in this first chapter that the strong emotional aspects of funerals, although nearly universal, are too malleable and too various to provide a general explanation for the forms of funeral ritual.

Universal symbols have also been postulated by anthropologists. An important example is provided by Hertz in his essay on the association of the right hand with good and the left hand with evil. Given the natural binary form of moral evaluation (good/bad) and the fact of human two-handedness, it is logical that this means of moral representation should be utilized by most of the world's peoples. Throughout this book, we regard the corpse as a similar sort of natural symbol. In Chapter 3, we examine the symbolism of two widespread practices: the use of loud noises in association with the presence of the dead; and the application of certain techniques of processing to the corpse. As with emotional responses, these symbolic quasi universals prove too ambiguous to provide a general explanation for the forms of funerals.

In the chapters of Part II, Death as Transition, we look at the kinds of ethnographic case material that led Hertz and van Gennep to portray death as a gradual process. If death is to be seen as a transition from one state of being to another, then it must be placed in the context of the period that follows and the period that precedes it.

Hertz noted that in much of Borneo, Indonesia, and Melanesia, the extended rituals of burial, exhumation, and reburial relate directly to beliefs about the afterlife. In Chapter 4, we test Hertz's analysis against the data of modern field research among a particular ethnic group of Borneo. We also make some comparisons with other Indonesian groups outside Borneo.

In Chapter 5, we focus on death as a transition from life, rather than to death. Van Gennep noted that of all the rites of passage, funerals are most strongly associated with the core of life values. Turner has also demonstrated how the symbols of liminality tend to be drawn from the biology of sexuality and fertility. Because much of van Gennep's writings before the appearance of *The Rites of Passage* concerned the religions of the peoples of Madagascar, it is appropriate that we should return to these data to analyze how the links between death, birth, and life are revealed in one Malagasy society.

The chapters of Part III, The Royal Corpse and the Body Politic, examine two sides of the socio-political question of the deaths of kings, under which rubric we include all manner of leaders, chiefs, pharaohs, and headmen.

In Chapter 6, we examine the uses to which royal relics are put in dramatic political competitions and the ways construction of elaborate death edifices such as pyramids in Egypt and mausoleums in Borneo can be instrumental in the establishment of authority.

Chapter 7 explores various uses of the corpse as a symbol of the corporate continuity of the kingship and polity. How can a mortal represent a supposedly eternal polity? We look at the classical case of ritual regicide among the Shilluk people, who inhabit the Upper Nile region. The Shilluk postulate that their king must be killed before his body, the symbol of the nation, becomes weak with age. Elsewhere effigies are used to replace the imperfect king. We explore the different uses of royal effigies in Renaissance England and France and relate these differences to the political philosophies of each culture.

Finally, in Chapter 8 we turn back to contemporary American culture. We note that from our wider comparative perspective American deathways no longer seem as exotic and irrational as they appeared to Mitford. Although our death customs, like those of others, are characterized by certain unresolvable paradoxes and ambiguities, they make sense within their cultural context. The elaborate preparation of the corpse so that it appears natural, healthy, and comfortable for its last public appearance relates directly to important American cultural values concerning the nature of the individual and of life.

PART I

UNIVERSALS
AND CULTURE

2

EMOTIONAL
REACTIONS TO DEATH

Surely one of the most prominent aspects of death is its potential for intense emotional impact on the survivors. The reasons are as numerous as they are obvious. There is the simple but often searing fact of separation from a loved one; the realization that he or she will no longer enjoy the fruits of life; the suddenness with which death strikes. There can be fear for one's own life, and fear of the power of death in general. There may be anger, directed diffusely at the deceased, or at the persons or powers held responsible. Finally, there are various strong reactions to the corpse itself.

The interpretation of emotion presents, however, special problems for the anthropologist, because we are not well equipped to deal with inner states. Even within our own cultures, it is hard to be sure that outward appearances match true feelings. How much harder will it be where the meaning of no posture, or gesture, or tone of voice can be taken for granted? Observers who imagine that they can see plainly into the emotions of people of different cultures are bold indeed. Having learned how diverse and complicated the perceptions of such apparently simple matters as space, time, and color may be, how can we assume a constancy for such complex states as love and hate, sorrow and joy? For all the importance of the emotional aspect of human experience, it is fraught with difficulties for a discipline that attempts to escape systematically from the biases of our own worldview. Even a very brief exploration of the emotions expressed at funerals in different parts of the world will serve to show that we cannot assume that any are universal, nor even that similar reactions correspond to the same underlying sentiments in different cultures. Take, for example, weeping, which seems as transparent as any expression of emotion could be.

SENTIMENTS AND SOCIETY: RADCLIFFE-BROWN'S THEORY

In our own society, it is quite permissible to cry at funerals. It is common for some individuals, especially some of those close to the deceased, to be overtaken with emotion and shed tears, sob, or occasionally cry out loud. In many societies, crying at funerals is not merely tolerated, it is required by custom, and at predetermined moments the entire body of mourners will burst into loud and piercing cries. Just as suddenly, the weeping halts and the tears that had just been running so profusely cease. An early attempt at understanding this custom of ceremonial weeping is found in Radcliffe-Brown's *The Andaman Islanders*. We turn to this work not only for the interesting analysis of ritual weeping, but also because Radcliffe-Brown based his entire theory of society on the ritual expression of sentiments.

It seems simple enough to explain why people cry at a funeral. After all, it is a sad occasion. But this fails to explain a number of features of Andamanese weeping. Radcliffe-Brown insists that any explanation of ceremonial weeping must cover all its manifestations in Andamanese culture. There are, it appears, seven different occasions when an Andamanese "sits down and wails and howls and the tears stream down his or her face" (Radcliffe-Brown 1964: 117). This is not a spontaneous expression of feeling. It is mandatory, and the individual is in complete control. Radcliffe-Brown reports how he once asked some people how it was done, and they immediately sat down and provided a demonstration, effusive tears and all. The occasions for such a display are as follows:

1. When two friends or relatives meet after having been for some time parted, they embrace each other and weep together.
2. At a peacemaking ceremony.

3. At the end of a period of mourning, the friends of the mourners (who have not themselves been mourning) weep with the latter.
4. After a death, the relatives and friends embrace the corpse and weep over it.
5. When the bones of a dead man or woman are recovered from the grave, they are wept over.
6. On the occasion of a marriage, the relatives weep over the bride and bridegroom.
7. At various stages of the initiation ceremonies, the female relatives of a youth or girl weep over him or her.

In examining this list, Radcliffe-Brown notes that there are two varieties of weeping. In the first three instances, the weeping is reciprocal; two parties cry over each other and embrace each other. In the latter four examples, the wailing is one-sided; one person or party weeps over a passive person or object. Radcliffe-Brown insists, then, that in order to understand the weeping at Andamanese funerals, one must take into account all seven instances and also explain their division into reciprocal and one-sided varieties.

Radcliffe-Brown's explanation, in keeping with his theory of society, is that this ritual weeping is "an expression of that feeling of attachment between persons which is of such importance in the almost domestic life of the Andaman society. In other words the purpose of the rite is to affirm the existence of a social bond between two or more persons" (Radcliffe-Brown 1964: 240). In those cases of reciprocal weeping, then, it is obvious enough that a social relationship is being mutually stressed. Reunions between friends, former enemies, or between mourners and their nonmourning friends are all occasions for stressing and affirming social ties. Radcliffe-Brown insists that although participants may not actually feel the sentiments that bind them, participation in this mandatory rite will strengthen what positive feelings they do have and create such sentiments where they were previously absent. As a general theory of weeping, this is perhaps rather shallow, but he points out that the Andamanese also refer to such situations as ones of intense emotion, calling for some act to cover the "shame" of reaffirming ties.

For the reciprocal weeping that marks the end of mourning, Radcliffe-Brown shows that, according to Andamanese custom, the mourners are associated with the world of the dead, and hence separated from the rest of society. At the end of the period of mourning, they are reunited with the rest of the community. This mutual weeping stresses that in spite of the death, and in spite of the temporary seclusion of the mourners, they now renew their bonds with the community of the living.

The second variety of ceremonial weeping, in which one party cries over a passive person or remains, serves to express the continued sentiment of attachment in spite of the fact that social bonds are being altered and lessened. Radcliffe-Brown maintains that such weeping cannot be explained as due to the sadness felt at the weakening of a relationship. Such weeping, when looked at in the total context of Andamanese weeping, is also a positive affirmation of the continuity of social ties even though they may be modified by initiation, marriage, or final reburial.

Much of this explanation can be neither demonstrated nor disproven. But there are a number of positive aspects to Radcliffe-Brown's approach that take us beyond the obvious and uninformative observation that people cry because they are sad. For one thing, Radcliffe-Brown separates sadness and the expression of sadness. These are not spontaneous outbursts. Sadness and its expression are related, however, and this relationship is the reverse of what we might expect. For Radcliffe-Brown, the sentiment does not create the act, but wailing at the prescribed moment and in the prescribed manner creates within the wailer the proper sentiment.

What makes Radcliffe-Brown's analysis stimulating is that he takes a seemingly obvious item, weeping, and places a number of sensible methodical constraints upon his analysis, and hence arrives at conclusions that are illuminating of Andamanese culture. Andamanese wailing at funerals, we can see, has a very different meaning and takes a very different form from the expression of grief in, say, American funerals. Radcliffe-Brown's contextual analysis of all the situations calling for weeping, combined with his interest in the native explanation, leads away from a simple but plausible analysis based on the universality of sorrow and toward an investigation of the symbolism of wailing in Andamanese ritual.

This path is, however, cut short by Radcliffe-Brown's tendency to revert to universals. In his grand theory of persons and society, these ritual expressions of motion hold a central place. The wailer comes to feel the appropriate sentiment, and, as we have seen, this sentiment is not merely a negative sentiment of sorrow and loss, but a positive emotion of social bonding:

. . . ceremonial customs are the means by which the society acts upon its individual members and keeps alive in their minds a certain system of sentiments. Without the ceremonial those sentiments would not exist, and without them the social organization in its actual form could not exist. [Radcliffe-Brown 1964: 324]

This global claim for the function of ritual is based on the assumption that all participants of all rituals in all cultures come to feel positive sentiments of social bonding through joining in the prescribed behavior.

That Andamanese ceremonial weeping is a symbol not only of sorrow but of social ties seems valid given the range of occasions when weeping occurs, the two varieties of weeping behavior, and the statements of Andamanese informants. In other societies, ritual wailing follows very different patterns. For example, the Bara of Madagascar perform such on-cue crying only at funerals, and only at two times: while the body is lying in the women's hut before burial, and just before the secondary burial of the exhumed bones. Also, weeping is absolutely prohibited during the preparation of the body for burial and during the exhumation of the bones for reburial. Only the women are expected to cry, although it is tolerated where closely related boys and men join in briefly. Also, such wailing is done only by day. As another example, consider the ritual lamentation for the dead in Greek villages. For this event, female specialists are hired to sing heartrending laments as part of a highly theatrical performance (Alexiou 1974). In each case, if we follow Radcliffe-Brown's method of (1) noting carefully the range and variation of social contexts of ceremonial weeping, (2) remembering that this weeping is a symbol with meaning and not a spontaneous show of emotion, (3) relating the weeping to indigenous beliefs, and (4) collecting indigenous explanations of the weeping, then we will discover much about the meaning of this practice in each culture.

If, instead, we follow Radcliffe-Brown's more general notion that all ritual activity, including wailing, in whatever form and style serves to channel sentiments of social bonding, then the careful contextual analysis of the ethnographer is for naught. All roads lead to preserving the social system.

It was Radcliffe-Brown's insight that expressions of sentiment in ritual are not merely reflections of feeling, but symbols whose meanings can be discovered through careful analysis. It was Radcliffe-Brown's mistake immediately to forsake this sound view for the meretricious charms of an instant universal theory.

DURKHEIM AND THE ABORIGINES

The universalistic theory of Radcliffe-Brown was greatly influenced by the work of Durkheim. For this reason, and because of his influence on the anthropological study of religion generally, it is instructive to examine how Durkheim dealt with the emotional aspect of death rituals. Durkheim discussed the ritual expression of sentiments in terms similar to those later used by Radcliffe-Brown. However, there is a crucial difference in emphasis. Where Durkheim was seeking to understand the integration (or nonintegration) of the individual into society, Radcliffe-Brown took the problem to be the solution. He assumed, as a starting point, that society is based on a system of shared sentiments. Durkheim, on the other hand, was involved in a lifelong search to know to what extent society could be defined in relation to "collective representations," what might be the nature of such representations, and how we might discover and demonstrate their nature. Within the framework of this search, the material on the funeral rituals of the native Australians presented Durkheim with a unique rhetorical opportunity.

First, let us observe the rites, for they contain an intensity of emotion that, although not entirely beyond our abilities of empathy, seems far more bizarre and shocking to our sensibilities than does the custom of ritual wailing. Durkheim opens his discussion of funerals with this vivid description:

Here is a scene which Spencer and Gillen witnessed among the Warramunga. A totemic ceremony had just been celebrated and the company of actors and spectators was leaving the consecrated ground when a piercing cry suddenly came from the camp: a man was dying there. At once, the whole company commenced to run as fast as they could, while most of them commenced to howl. "Between us and the camp," say these observers, "lay a deep creek, and on the bank of this, some of the men, scattered about here and there, sat down, bending their heads forward between their knees, while they wept and moaned. Crossing the creek we found that, as usual, the men's camp had been pulled to pieces. Some of the women, who had come from every direction, were lying prostrate on the body, while others were standing or kneeling around, digging the sharp ends of yam-sticks into the crown of their heads, from which the blood streamed down over their faces, while all the time they kept up a loud, continuous wail. Many of the men, rushing up to the spot, threw themselves upon the body, from which the women arose when the men approached, until in a few minutes we could see nothing but a struggling mass of bodies all mixed up together. To one side, three men of the Thapungarti class, who still wore their ceremonial decorations, sat down wailing loudly, with their backs towards the dying man, and in a minute or two another man of the same class rushed on to the ground yelling and brandishing a stone knife. Reaching the camp, he suddenly gashed both thighs deeply, cutting right across the muscles, and unable to stand, fell down into the middle of the group, from which he was dragged out after a time by three or four female relatives, who immediately applied their mouths to the gaping wounds while he lay exhausted on the ground." The man did not actually die until late in the evening. As soon as he had given up his last breath, the same scene was re-enacted, only this time the wailing was still louder, and men and women, seized by a veritable frenzy, were rushing about cutting themselves with knives and sharp-pointed sticks, the women battering one another's heads with fighting clubs, no one attempting to ward off either cuts or blows. Finally, after about an hour, a torchlight procession started off across the plain, to a tree in whose branches the body was left. [Durkheim 1965 (1912): 435–6, with the permission of The Free Press, a Division of Macmillan Publishing Co., Inc., and Unwin Hyman, a division of HarperCollins Publishers Ltd.]

Reports from other parts of the continent tell the same story. People gouge their faces, slash their thighs, burn their breasts, and attack their friends. Much of this activity is so ferocious that it is not uncommon for mourning to add to the death toll. But the violence is not as random as it appears; on the contrary, it is meted out according to definite rules. Women, in particular, are enjoined to considerable displays of suffering. They are reported to be the most prominent victims of some of the physically aggressive melees; they lead in much of the howling and lamenting, and, to highlight this, they are prohibited normal speech during mourning. Sometimes whole villages of women are under sentence of speechlessness for long periods. The habit of communicating by signs develops and grows as mourning rites follow mourning rites, and it is not uncommon for some women to cease speaking altogether for the remainder of their lives. All in all, the rites are marked by extreme displays of anguish, anger, and aggression tinged with sexual implications, and destructive tendencies.

When Durkheim confronts the reader with this startling material, he had already outlined his basic theory emphasizing the positive cohesive effects of public celebrations. He has already suggested that a certain renewal of common values, a reaffirmation of communal conceptions, and a strengthening of social bonds is the unique function of ritual. This famous demonstration (Durkheim 1965: 385–92), however, pertains to calendrical rites in Australia, when groups gather together after the dispersal of the dry season. That such joyful rites, performed by people reuniting as a group even as they unite themselves to the rhythm of the earth's seasons, should promote a positive mood of solidarity is plausible. But Durkheim wishes to demonstrate that it is a feature of ritual in general. How can he make the same claim for the violent, destructive, unplanned-for, and negative behavior surrounding a death?

Durkheim faces the same difficulty that Radcliffe-Brown brushed aside. On the one hand, we cannot assume that people actually *feel* the sorrow that they express; and we certainly cannot claim that the ritual expression results from inner emotions. On the other hand, for the rites to fulfill their supposed sociological function, these acted sentiments must become real. Radcliffe-Brown claimed that people participating in the ceremonial weeping come to feel the emotion. But the emotion he said they feel is not sorrow but togetherness (Radcliffe-Brown 1964: 240). Durkheim is quite clear, however, that the emotions that develop and are amplified by participation in the funeral rite initially are feelings of sorrow and anger.

If he weeps and groans, it is not merely to express an individual chagrin; it is to fulfill a duty of which the surrounding society does not fail to remind him. . . . Sorrow, like joy, becomes exalted and amplified when leaping from mind to mind, and therefore expresses itself outwardly in the form of exuberant and violent movements. But these are no longer expressive of the joyful agitation which we observed before; they are shrieks and cries of pain. Each is carried along by the others; a veritable panic of sorrow results. When pain reaches this degree of intensity, it is mixed with a sort of anger and exasperation. One feels the need of breaking something, of destroying something. He takes this out either upon himself or others. He beats himself, burns himself, wounds himself or else he falls upon others to beat, burn and wound them. [Durkheim 1965: 446]

Obviously, the sentiments expressed and amplified in this ritual do not automatically transform themselves into social solidarity. Durkheim stresses, however, that although the mood of this rite is different from others, the fact of emotional arousal is common to rituals of joy and of sorrow. A death is a shock to the family group. Its members feel the family lessened and weakened, and so they draw together in reaction to the loss. What Durkheim finds important to his sociological theory, however, is the way that other members of society feel moral pressure to put their behavior in harmony with the feelings of the truly bereaved. Those who feel no direct sorrow themselves will nonetheless weep and inflict suffering and inconvenience upon themselves. Can this be other than a positive affirmation of their commitment, not only to their suffering neighbors, but also to an abstract value of neighborliness, of society?

One need not join Durkheim in answering in the affirmative. But let us be clear how important this funeral material is to his theory. The two most important criticisms of Durkheim's explanation of how the "external" society is inculcated into individuals through ritual are both weakened in the face of this material. First of all, it has been suggested that Durkheim bridged the gap between individual and society with a crude use of crowd psychology. But the funeral material, as Talcott Parsons (1968: 437) noted, provides a crucial demonstration that crowd psychology was not what Durkheim intended. The power of crowd behavior derives from the fact that the crowd is an unorganized, ad hoc assemblage. The rituals that Durkheim describes are, by contrast, minutely organized. Intense emotion and tight organization go hand in hand even in these funerals, where the obligations of slashing one's thighs or burning one's abdomen are precisely determined by kinship (mother's brother and mother, respectively). The funeral material makes it clear that emotional "effervescence" does not replace structure but, on the contrary, results from structure. Durkheim's approach stands in contrast to later debates in anthropology that saw explanations based on "structure" and those based on "sentiment" as mutually exclusive.

The other important criticism is summed up in Lévi-Strauss's aphorism that Durkheim's theory of religion "starts with an urge, and ends with a recourse to sentiment" (Lévi-Strauss 1963: 70–1). The circularity of Durkheim's theory is quite obvious regarding the calendrical rites, for there can be no source to explain the welling up of the urge to perform the ritual that produces the sentiment of solidarity. Durkheim's case regarding funerals is stronger, rhetorically and sociologically. One can readily accept that, at a time of death, some people genuinely feel the great emotions that are expressed. This provides a source for the senti-ment that is transformed in ritual. Durkheim's claim that a broad sense of social solidarity derives from ritual is stronger in this funeral case when those who personally feel no sorrow are nevertheless compelled to put themselves through such extreme discomfort. In his analysis of the calen-drical rites, Durkheim has the sentiment of solidarity bubble up naturally out of the expression of joy. But the dialectic between sorrow and com-fort, loss and gain, real emotion and obligatory display that emerges from the discussion of these terrifyingly intense funerals provides more solid grounding for his theory of the social function of ritual. One does not know Durkheim's intentions, but it is characteristic of his style of argu-ment that this strongest evidence is presented last, and cleverly intro-duced as a supposed negative case.

There is perhaps another advantage to presenting this funeral material toward the end of *The Elementary Forms of the Religious Life*. It allows Durkheim to dissociate his theory from those that viewed primitive man's contemplation of death as the source of all religion. In this way, Durkheim's sociological theory contrasts with Tylor's intellectualism, as described in Chapter 1. Where Tylor saw religion as the outcome of con-templating the fate of the soul in death, Durkheim placed priority firmly on ritual: "men do not weep for the dead because they fear them; they fear them because they weep for them" (Durkheim 1965: 447). In this, Durkheim followed W. Robertson Smith (Beidelman 1974). The relation between belief and practice remains an embattled issue, but we need not pursue it further here. It is, however, important to note that although death rites provide Durkheim's strongest evidence, he carefully avoided any implication that they might be the source of religion and ritual and hence, in his framework, of society. To this, we concur. Death rituals often provide the most interesting and challenging material for the under-standing of people and their cultures, but in spite of our devotion of this book to the topic, we see no reason to add unnecessarily to the claims death makes on the shape of human institutions.

There is in Durkheim's approach the possibility for illuminating analyses of particular ethnographic situations. This would demand, of course, the sort of intimate knowledge of the people and culture that Durkheim, writing from Paris, lacked. His theory suggests a subtle dynamic of social interaction that could be apprehended only through the type of sustained personal field research that became the hallmark of anthropology in the generation following Radcliffe-Brown. Unfortunately, that generation largely turned away from the study of religion. When anthropologists returned to the study of religion, the analytical emphasis had shifted so that studies were focused on systems of belief with little direct reference to the intimate social interaction that would provide the locus for a truly Durkheimian analysis.

"A PASSION OF GRIEF": NYAKYUSA FUNERALS

One of the few early anthropologists who attempted a systematic analysis of the emotional aspect of funerals based on firsthand experience was Godfrey Wilson (1939). In his essay "Nyakyusa Conventions of Burial," Wilson demonstrated how illuminating a cautiously Durkheimian approach can be for understanding the expression of sentiment in a ceremonial context. Emotions may be vague and irrational, but when the analyst knows the culture and the particular participants, has personally shared in the events, and furthermore, is scrupulous of the level of verifiability of each piece of evidence, then the study of the emotional aspect of life yields great dividends.

Wilson asks three general questions through his exploration of the Nyakyusa conventions of burial. First, noting that Nyakyusa burials are jolly affairs in comparison to English funerals, he asks why the emotional tenor differs from one culture to another. Second, he questions why it is that the normal emotional response of people at a funeral is never random, but falls within an obligatory pattern. One *must* dance and flirt at a Nyakyusa funeral just as one *must* wear black and be solemn at an English funeral. Third, he asks what are the social dynamics that preserve the conventions of funeral behavior or lead to their modification. One can begin to answer these general questions only by taking a detailed look at another society's customs in contrast to our own. Godfrey Wilson's essay refers only to the burial ceremony. For an analysis of the full funeral cycle, see Monica Wilson (1957).

Nyakyusa social relationships are determined by membership in three groups: family, village, and chiefdom. These social relations are largely established, expressed, and maintained in two ways: exchange of cattle and attendance at funerals. When a death occurs, messages must be sent to all kin, affines, villagers, and the chief. If anyone is overlooked, he or she will be extremely angry at the affront. On the other side, should anyone receive the message and then deliberately not attend, this act will be considered a serious breach of the social relationship. This obligation to attend the burial ceremony holds not only for representatives of each family. Men, wives, and children over the age of ten must attend, for otherwise they would be accused of having helped cause the death through witchcraft. Many other people come voluntarily, to enjoy the feasting and dancing, and they are welcomed. The size of the crowd depends on the amount of meat made available by the obligatory sacrifices.

The main activities of the burial ceremony are divided according to sex; the women wail and the men dance. The women begin their ceremonial wailing at the time of death and continue intermittently until the end of the burial activities, three or four days later. The female "owners of the death" spend most of their time inside the house that is the center of the wailing. The rest of the women sit and wail just outside the house, or else they enter and wail upon arrival and then move to the group outside. Men and boys may wail once, and then they join the male "owners of the death." Old women are the most persistent wailers, providing around-the-clock support for the grieving women in the house. The corpse is kept in the house until it is buried later on the day of death or the next morning. Until burial, the women hold the body in their arms and the wailing is intense. One Nyakyusa told Wilson that they like to delay burial long enough for the women "to weep and assuage their grief, for they always wail more before the body is buried, when they can see the dead man" (Wilson 1939: 8).

In addition to grief, Nyakyusa reactions to death express several elements of fear: fear of the afterworld, fear of the spirits, fear of not performing the ceremony properly, fear of contagious disease, and fear of witchcraft. It is within this particularly Nyakyusa framework of explicit fears that the purpose of the various funeral rituals is to be understood.

Emotional Reactions to Death

Their stated purpose is "to drive the spirit away." The Nyakyusa fear further contact with the spirits of the deceased, which are believed to have the power to send misfortune and insanity upon the surviving kin.

Many Nyakyusa had converted to Christianity by the time of Godfrey and Monica Wilson's field research, and the comparisons between Christian and non-Christian Nyakyusa are instructive. One of the chief attractions of Christianity in this area was its reassurance on the topic of death. Christian preaching about heaven is seen by old Nyakyusa as a strong threat to the traditional social order. The old men complain that fear of death no longer motivates the young people to attend properly to burial ceremonies. These changes and laments only serve to highlight the prominent role of fear in Nyakyusa concepts of death.

Women bind one another's bellies with strips of bark-cloth during the wailing ceremony. Relatives and friends provide a woman mourner with numerous cloths. One of them explained to the Wilsons: "I give them these to tie round their bellies because they are all atremble, they are full of fear." The men don't wear belts, say the women, because "They are not afraid like women, they do not tremble much" (Wilson 1939: 12).

Gradually the focus of activity shifts from the women to the men, from the decreasing wailing to the increasing dancing (see Figure 2). Dancing is led by young men dressed in special costumes of ankle bells and cloth skirts, often holding spears and leaping wildly about. Women do not dance, but some young women move about among the dancing youths, calling the war cry and swinging their hips in a rhythmic fashion. The number of dancers slowly increases, as does the number of drummers and the crowd of onlookers. The noise and excitement grow and there are no signs of grief. Yet when Wilson asked the onlookers to explain the scene, they always replied, "They are mourning the dead" (Wilson 1939: 12).

This burial dance is traditionally a dance of war. Conventionally, Nyakyusa men say that they dance to honor the deceased, who was also a great warrior, a powerful man of the spear. If the deceased is a woman, they claim to honor the fact that she gave birth to warriors. The dance, of course, also expresses the virility and courage of the dancers themselves. And there is a strong sexual component to the dance, which, as the era of interchiefdom raiding recedes, is rapidly becoming the dominant motif. In either case, male strength and courage is emphasized in contrast to female fear and trembling.

Figure 2. Nyakyusa men dancing at a funeral. Though stylized, the pos-
tures of the dance are extremely energetic (from Wilson 1951: 131,
with permission of the International African Institute).

Additionally, Nyakyusa men state that the dance helps them express
and overcome their grief and anger over the death of a kinsman:

This war dance is mourning, we are mourning the dead man. We dance because
there is a war in our hearts – a passion of grief and fear exasperates us. . . .
A kinsman when he dances he assuages his passionate grief; he goes into the
house to weep and then he comes out and dances the war dance; his passionate
grief is made tolerable in the dance [literally, "he is able to endure it there, in
the dance"], it binds his heart and the dance assuages it. [in Wilson 1939: 13]

Wilson's careful translation of these statements, especially his renderings
"passionate grief" and "exasperate," demonstrate that the Nyakyusa view
these acts as expressing and relieving certain unbearable emotions.

This dance is a vehicle for the expression of a considerable range of
emotions; grief and exasperation merge into an act of honoring the warlike qualities and virility of the dead man. This leads into feelings of pride
and exhilaration of the dancers' own courage and virility, often resulting

in fighting among the young men, or lovemaking between some of the youths and the girls. Traditionally, the outbreak of violence was common at burials because the endemic raiding among chiefdoms left many open disputes waiting for the sort of provocations that the war dance afforded. Now that the emphasis has shifted more to the sexual aspect of male prowess, violence is less common. But in a society in which almost every girl is betrothed at puberty, these romantic encounters can also produce social turbulence: "So far from ceremonies having the sole function of promoting social integration, as some would have us believe, the burial ceremonies of the Nyakyusa were occasions on which existing antipathies continually found overt expression in fighting and new antipathies arose" (Wilson 1939: 14).

The Nyakyusa, like many other peoples, seem to feel the need to confront death with an assertion of life. They express a desire to turn their attention away from the contemplation of death, which holds only fear, sorrow, and uncertainty for them, and gradually toward "a realization of present life in its most intense quality, to the war-dance, to sexual display, to lively talk and to the eating of great quantities of meat" (Wilson 1939: 24). This transfiguration of the sorrow of the chief mourners requires, in the Nyakyusa view, the active and sympathetic celebration of others. That transformation of mood, with its interaction between those whose grief runs deep and those whose sympathy for the mourners leads them to dance, is a subtle process, the action of which escapes a general description of the Nyakyusa conventions of burial. It is, however, poignantly evident in Wilson's description of a particular burial:

Here is a description of one of the pagan burials which I observed. It is the second day; the man, who was quite young, died yesterday afternoon and was buried early this morning. I arrive at 7:30 a.m. to find that the wailing is the dominant activity. The dead man's house is full of weeping men and women, shedding tears and wailing in the conventional high-pitched voice. His sister, his young wife, a step-mother, a classificatory brother and two half-brothers, with many other women, are inside the house. The noise is considerable. The rest of the women, fifty or more, are seated just outside, in and around an unfinished bamboo house which he died leaving half-built; they too are weeping and wailing. A few men are seated in a group on the opposite side of the swept place facing the women; they are either silent or talking soberly.

The emotion pitch is very high. The classificatory brother leaves the house and walks about round the new grave with his hands to his head, shedding tears and calling: "Alas! Alas! What kin are left? Alas! What kin are left?" He is a mature man about forty years old. Then he takes by the hand a half-sister of the dead man, a woman of thirty or more, smothered in mud and pot-black, her belly supported by many bark cloths, and with a baby on her back; together they walk over the grave weeping and wailing, addressing each other in words that I fail to distinguish, and stumbling about as though blind with grief. The baby sleeps quietly all the time. Then comes an old woman, step-mother of the dead man, leading a daughter in each hand (his half-sisters), all wailing, shedding tears and calling out indistinguishable words. They sit down on the newly-filled grave, first making towards it gestures of extreme grief; and there they sit with their arms on one another's shoulders rocking to and fro' and weeping. More people keep arriving and in the background now is the insistent wailing of seventy or a hundred women in and outside the house.

For the first hour after my arrival the drums are only occasionally beaten, and a few young men rush across the grave brandishing spears, but only spasmodically.

The two half-brothers, after wailing in the house, come outside and walk up and down together still weeping. Then they each take a spear and run back and forth several times wailing the dead man's name. One of the half-sisters, meanwhile, rolls over and over in the fresh earth of the grave in passionate contortions, with tears running down her cheeks. Gradually a group of women relatives collects on the grave, eight or nine of them; they sit huddled up together with their arms on one another's shoulders wailing. One woman, before she sits down, makes a series of trembling gestures towards the grave, crying out "Avaunt!" in fearful grief.

Then, at last, the drums begin in earnest and the young men start to dance. To me, as well as to the Nyakyusa, the insistent vital rhythm of the drums and the sight of the leaping dance fall on the senses gratefully, bringing relief from the almost unbearable tensions. [Such a subjective account of the observer's feelings is, of course, quite valueless in itself; but we have already proved that the Nyakyusa protagonists have feelings of which these are but a sympathetic image (Wilson's note).] The situation begins to change. Still in the house the wailing is loud and continuous, but the women on the grave give place to the dancers and return to the house, while the group of women outside gradually ceases wailing and turns all its attention to the dance. The conversation among the men changes also, none are silent now and the talk is more eager than before. Soon the dancers begin to cut the bananas; one stem falls full on a young man's head, causing loud laughter among the onlookers. But at first the dance, though lively, is by no means wholly gay. The male kinsmen dance with grief in the looks, calling out "alas!" as each shakes his spear.

No women are yet dancing at all; two or three kinswomen wander about distraught, and one of the half-sisters in particular seems quite blind to the dancers, who have to get out of her way. The situation is, however, a lively one, and it becomes livelier still as the young men from another village come to join in, bringing three more drums with them. Six drums are now being beaten and about thirty young men are dancing. Two hours have passed since I first arrived.

At four-thirty p.m. I am back again to find the scene changed once more. There is no sound of wailing, not even inside the house, and the dancers are having a glorious time. About a hundred men are either dancing or standing round looking on, with a number of girls walking rhythmically about among the dancers. These girls are non-relatives and adorned with great finish.

The young men leap and dance, some with more agility than others; they stamp, roll on the ground, leap in the air, turn somersaults, hurl their spears into the earth and fight invisible enemies. All the spectators, save the chief women mourners and one or two of the men, seem lively and excited. I see the young wife [She will die herself four days later. There has been a series of deaths in this family which gossip attributes to the sorcery of an enemy (Wilson's note).] of the dead man looking tired and sad, and she and the other women mourners spend most of the time in the house; but one of the half-brothers, on the other hand, who appeared to be so greatly affected seven or eight hours before, is laughing gaily as he dances.

Two cows have been killed and are now being cut up. As the sun sinks and the dancers go away home, taking their meat with them, the relatives and near neighbors gather round fires and begin to roast and eat the meat. Some is given separately to the groups of friends from other chiefdoms; and by the next morning the whole of the two cows is finished. "It was a grand burial," people say afterwards, "we have seen him on his way (to the place of the spirits) properly." [Wilson 1939: 24–7, with the permission of Witwatersrand University Press]

CULTURE AND SENTIMENT

The examples we have presented in this chapter are from societies whose customs seem violently emotional in comparison to the norm in our own society. Throughout the world, death is generally a time for the expression of strong emotional response. There are societies, however, that surprise us in just the opposite way by the seeming equanimity with which death is greeted. Clifford Geertz describes the funerals of the Javanese as "a calm, undemonstrative, almost languid letting go, a brief ritualized relinquishment of a relationship no longer possible" (Geertz 1960: 72). Geertz mentions the case of a young girl who was crying slightly after her father died suddenly. Her relatives hushed her gently into a show of composure by telling her that she could not continue participating in the ritual if she cried, that such crying made it hard for the deceased to find his path to the grave. The proper emotional state to be achieved is called *iklas*, a "willed affectlessness," an evenness of feelings from which the peaks of elation and the troughs of despair have been eliminated (Geertz 1960: 69–74). For the Javanese, mortality does not seem to hold any great terror and they discuss it with little show of anxiety. In part, this calmness is due to a pervasive fatalism about dying; it is all in the hands of God. In part, death is often asserted to be a good state, empty of desire and striving.

Although the emotions and beliefs of the Javanese and Nyakyusa are very different in content, both are enforced by subtle social pressures. How social pressures lead people to place their behavior in sympathetic harmony with their fellows in times of loss is amenable to the analysis of an experienced and sensitive field researcher. Such an analysis is difficult, however. It demands an intimate knowledge of the society and the language; it calls for many observations of burial rituals so as to become attuned to the elements of social interaction, to appreciate the importance of slight variations, and to be certain that some key aspects hold true in spite of the uniqueness of each event. Additionally, when dealing with sentiments, the temptation toward unwarranted universal conclusions is particularly great. The temptation is also great to attribute to participants feelings that they may not experience. Far from providing some kind of universal explanatory framework for analysis of death-related behavior, the emotional aspect demands from the researcher the most subtle awareness of cultural variations.

Cultural differences work on human emotional reactions, just as they do on supposedly universal modes of reasoning or requirements of institutional arrangement. Although we clearly recognize emotions that are familiar to us, the range of acceptable emotions and the precise constellation of sentiments appropriate to the situation of death are tied up with the unique institutions and concepts of each society. The Australian aborigines, the Andamanese, the Nyakyusa, the Javanese, and others that we shall examine, express different emotions at funerals and may experience somewhat different feelings in each case. Uniformity of human emotion does not explain the rituals of societies. The baffling combination of the familiar and the strange, the universal in the culturally particular, confronts the anthropologist even when examining emotional reactions to death.

3

SYMBOLIC
ASSOCIATIONS
OF DEATH

Though often intense, emotional reactions to death are too varied and shifting to provide the foundation for a theory of mortuary ritual. A recent cross-cultural study concluded that grief is shown at funerals in most societies, but not all. Even this weak result was achieved only by defining grief so widely as to include virtually any negative emotion, namely, "sorrow, mental distress, emotional agitation, sadness, suffering, and related feelings" (Rosenblatt, Walsh, and Jackson 1976: 2). These authors approach funeral practices assuming that they fulfill certain pan-human needs to perform "psychological work." But the need to release aggression, or break ties with the deceased, or complete any other putatively universal psychic process does not serve to explain funerals. The shoe is on the other foot. Whatever mental adjustments the individual needs to make in the face of death he or she must accomplish as best he or she can through or around such rituals as society provides. No doubt the rites frequently aid adjustment. But we have no reason to believe that they do not obstruct it with equal frequency.

Despite the perennial appeal of such theorizing, something more is needed to explain the remarkable richness and variety of funeral rituals. In succeeding chapters, we turn away from emotion in order to explore the meaning of these rites in social terms. But we are not yet ready to leave behind the nagging issue of universal, or at least general, features of behavior. Are there not regular features of funerals that crop up again and again?

Indeed there are. One obvious example is color symbolism. Although it would be an error to assume that our cultural association of black with death and mourning is universal, there is a wide distribution among the cultures of the world of the use of black to represent death. Turner (1967) suggests that there exists an almost universal color triad of red, white, and black. In many societies, white relates to such things as purity and fertility, red to both good and evil aspects of power and life, and black to decomposition and death. Turner suggests that the wide distribution of this symbolic color triad may relate to the association of these colors with bodily fluids, especially white with milk and semen, and red with blood. Black, he notes, is rarely associated with a bodily excretion, but tends to be associated with loss of consciousness, such as when one faints or "blacks out" (Turner 1967: 89).

Throughout the world, black often provides the funeral hue. But there are many exceptions. White is sometimes appropriate in Christian funerals to symbolize the joy of eternal life, which the Resurrection promises to each believer. Some of the peoples of Madagascar provide another exception: Their funeral color is red. An important item in their funeral rituals is a large number of expensive, brightly colored, striped shrouds. These come in many colors, but they are always called the "red cloths." Red is used in these funerals to represent "life" and vitality in opposition to death. In both these exceptions, the funeral use of white or red is in symbolic opposition to the blackness of death. But in parts of Borneo white is the color of mourning because it is directly associated with the pallor of death and the whiteness of bones. (Figure 4 below shows mourners wearing white cloths and headbands.)

A second example concerns the mourners' hair. As Edmund Leach (1958) notes, practices involving special cutting of the hair have a world-wide distribution, and they are particularly prominent in funeral ceremonies. Frequently survivors are enjoined to shave their heads as a sign of mourning. Elsewhere, the custom is reversed; the mourners, especially men, forgo their usual habits of shaving and trimming beards, mustaches, and hair and hence emphasize a hirsute dishevelment for the time of mourning. And it need not be one way or the other. Often in a single society, even within a family, some mourners shave entirely while others put away their razors. Hence there is a generality about the use of such practices, but not about their meaning.

In this chapter, we examine two additional symbolic items having a wide distribution and association with death rituals. The first is what we may call a purposeful noisiness, the second relates to symbols of rotting. At first sight, these two items appear dissimilar, and their selection consequently arbitrary. Whereas the former seems mysterious and unaccountable, the latter seems obvious (although we must remember that it is possible for decay to be cheated, for instance by cremation of the corpse). But however dissimilar, it is an empirical feature that din and corruption are constantly associated, as Lévi-Strauss has demonstrated in his monumental mythological studies (1973: 296–475, specifically 310, 396).

DRUMMING: SYMBOL OF DEATH, LIMINALITY, OR DIVINITY?

In many parts of the world, funerals are noisy affairs. This is already apparent from our examples in Chapter 2. It is also very much the case among the Berawan, a small ethnic group of central northern Borneo, to whom we shall turn for case material at several places in succeeding chapters. The Berawan comprise just four communities, each of several hundred people and occupying a single massive wooden longhouse. Great tracts of dense rain forest separate the villages from one another, and in precolonial times each was a sovereign political unit. The Berawan gain their livelihood by growing hill rice in clearings made anew each year, by foraging in the jungle, and by fishing in the great rivers that also provide the only means of transportation in the interior.

During funerals, the Berawan gather great crowds of people into their longhouses. Drinking and socializing are enjoined upon the guests, and all but the close kin are encouraged to enjoy themselves as gustily as possible. The general hubbub can be heard half a mile away through the quiet forest. But not satisfied with that, the Berawan have additional ways to make noise at funerals. There is the great brass gong that is used initially to announce that a death has occurred. A special tattoo is used, and the deep reverberations can often be heard several miles away, summoning people from their farms. Then there is the large drum that can only be played during funerals. Its boom can be heard day and night, producing rhythms that are proscribed at other times. The same rhythms are played on gongs large and small, which together make up an orchestra with several players. The larger gongs are hung vertically, and struck with a padded mallet to produce a deep, resonant sound. The smaller gongs are strung horizontally in descending order of size on two strands of rattan stretched across a frame. The player holds a piece of firewood in each hand and plays rapid tinkling figures, further augmented by the staccato clatter of children beating on bamboo slit gongs.

But even the music of the gongs and drums is lost in the din of games in which noise is supposedly only a by-product. Tops are played outside, in an arena overviewed by the veranda of the longhouse, which provides a grandstand. Men compete to see who can fling their own top in such a way as to knock a target top set spinning in the center of the arena out of the area of play. The men jostle for position to take a shot, holding their heavy hardwood tops in the upraised hands. When they throw them, a dull moaning whirr is heard. If the shot is well judged, the two tops make a loud clack on impact, and the target goes flying out of the ring. Then a great roar of approval goes up from the veranda. The men must remain alert to avoid being hit by a ricocheting top.

Meanwhile, another game played inside the house uses rice pestles. This is a game in which women excel, though men may play. The pestles are hardwood poles about five feet long and three inches wide at each end, tapering slightly to the middle. Normally they are used to pound rice free of its husk, in conjunction with a mortar that consists of a heavy slab of hardwood with a hemispherical indentation about six inches in diameter. In the game, two pestles are placed side by side across two bulks of timber such that they are about four inches above the floor. A woman sits on each side, grasping the adjacent ends of each pestle in either hand. The two women begin to beat the pestles, two strokes downward onto the bulks of timber, then two sideways, clashing the pestles one against the other. The player stands off to one side, flexing her knees and bobbing her head to get the rhythm. Then she dances nimbly across the clashing poles, trying to execute fancy steps without getting a blow on the ankle. This game is invariably played indoors on the raised plank floor of the longhouse, which provides a massive sounding board for the crashing of the pestles. This activity is in addition to the regular pounding of rice, which is a continuous chore during funerals due to the number of guests to be fed.

Finally, when the corpse is moved out of the longhouse to the barge that will carry it to the graveyard, a series of shotgun blasts punctuate the wailing of the womenfolk.

All this cacophony at Berawan funerals would come as no surprise to Rodney Needham, whose paper "Percussion and Transition" (1967) first pointed out how widespread this phenomenon is. He expands upon an idea originally stated in "The Origin of Bell and Drum" by Maria Dworakowska (1938), who argues that the use of bells and gongs at funerals derived from the use of drums, which in turn originated from "coffin-logs." Hence the association of these instruments with the dead. Needham accepts this association, shorn of its historical speculation, but criticizes it as too narrow. First, the list of instruments is too restricted: drums, gongs, bells, xylophones, metallophones, rattles, rasps, stamping tubes, sticks, resounding rocks, clashing anklets, and other objects are all used in these contexts. Berawan funerals could add a couple more items to the list, as we have seen. Needham shows that the only feature shared by these instruments, if such they may be called, is percussion. Not all of them are capable of producing a melody, or even a rhythm, so these attributes are not the relevant ones. Second, he shows that such percussive noise is not restricted to funerals. It is found at weddings and birth feasts, initiations and harvest festivals, and all manner of rites of passage.

Needham states his conclusion as follows: *There is a connection between percussion and transition.* As to why this connection exists, Needham is unable to offer an explanation, and he is pessimistic that anthropology is capable of finding one. So universal is the phenomenon, he believes, that its grounds must be sought in the "general psychic character of mankind" (1967: 394).

Concerning the association that Needham points out, we can make surmises similar to those concerning color and hair symbolism. A percussive noise seems to punctuate and divide time ("mark time") the way a line or a wall demarcates space. Hence it is a natural symbol for marking a temporal change in status, especially one as irreversible as death. Furthermore, the drumbeat has an obvious affinity with the heartbeat and rhythm of life. Or equally, it can resound

66

with the hollow finality of death. There is plenty of room for multiple symbolizations.

Another aspect of percussion, in addition to its rhythmic characteristics is its potential for making loud noise. Noise or silence, individually or in alternation, provide, like white and black, shaven and hairy, opportunities for symbolic representation and heightened drama. In another well known and intriguing paper, Needham (1964) traces the connections that hunting peoples of Malaya and Borneo make between "Blood, Thunder, and the Mockery of Animals." Thunder in Malaysia, he writes, is "an appalling natural phenomenon, seeming to crack and reverberate menacingly on the very surface of the forest canopy and shaking the guts of the human beings cowering underneath" (1964: 281). The great noise of thunder has, in many such places, associations with power and divinity. Noise is sometimes seen to facilitate communication between humans and the supernatural, as when the psalmist enjoins "Make a Joyful noise unto The Lord, all ye lands" (Psalm 100).

Cosmological and calendrical events such as solar eclipses and new years are characteristically greeted in many cultures with the loudest clatter the technological level permits (Lévi-Strauss 1969: 287). Over the centuries, fireworks, gunshots, horns, and sirens have been added to the initial stock of drums, bells, and gongs. In the din of the modern world, we may forget how extraordinary and rare truly loud noise was to most of the previous generations on the earth. It continues to connote power, as with electronically amplified music and roaring car engines, but it has lost its sacred character.

Our problem in dealing with the significance of noise is to cope with too many associations, not too few. Already we have three correlations of increasing generality: drums and death, percussion and transition, loud noise and supernatural power. There is little point in discussing which is the correct correlation. For instance, all are present in the Berawan events mentioned above. There is the great drum that resounds only for death. There are the gunshots that specifically punctuate the transition to the graveyard, and there is the continuous tumult of games and music associated with the presence of spirits of the dead. Many threads of significance are woven together in the Berawan use of noise. As van Gennep noted, the funeral is, of all rites of passage, the one with the greatest emphasis on liminality. It is not surprising that symbols used at the funeral are often vague and indeterminate, and yet connote mystery and power. Death and liminality must, of their very natures, retain a certain elusiveness.

RITUAL ACTIONS AND DAILY ACTIVITIES

Noise production is a cultural feature, yet its use in funerals achieves the same kind of universality as the emotion of grief. Percussive noise is frequently found in rituals of transition, and examples can be found in every region of the globe. But that does not imply that all societies use noise in this way or use it to a similar extent.

It follows that the observation of the quasi universality of grief and percussive noise at funerals does not exhaust those topics. Contrary to Needham's formulation, the variation that occurs from one society to another, and one culture area to another, is equally demanding of explanation, and implies a cultural dynamic rather than a psychic universal. As an example of this, we examine the special propensity for percussion that is found in Southeast Asia, and we draw on the work of Marie Jeanne Adams (1971, 1977).

Adams is concerned with repeated patterns of behavior occurring in ritual contexts that seem to parallel everyday work activities. The similarities are often striking, but Adams is careful to avoid the implication that either is derived from the other. On that score, we simply have no evidence. However derived, these recurring actions appear to lend a power and intensity to the rituals that is difficult for the outsider to grasp.

Adams pays particular attention to pounding: a very simple technical process to be sure, but especially pervasive in Southeast Asia. Pounding actions figure prominently in the production and preparation of many foods. Breaking up the ground prior to planting is often accomplished with a heavy digging stick that relies more on momentum than sharpness for its effect. Alternatively, in irrigation agriculture particularly, buffalo are used to pound the topsoil in the newly flooded plots with their hooves. Even in slash-and-burn systems, where no soil preparation occurs as such, the seeds are planted in shallow conical holes made with a heavy dibble.

Many foods are inedible without preparation involving pounding. Most obvious in this connection is rice, which must have its husk removed before cooking. For those accustomed to agriculture based on wheat, grinding is the process that immediately comes to mind. But in Southeast Asia the grinding of rice is associated with the Chinese. Indigenous peoples prefer some kind of pounding technique usually involving a pestle and mortar. The rhythmic thump of the women pounding rice is often the first noise that one hears on approaching a village. In some societies employing sago, the woody part of the palm is separated from the nutritious part by beating.

But even foods that can be cooked just as they come from the ground are often preferred in some processed form involving homogenization by pounding. The favored way of eating many kinds of beans is to beat them into a paste. Corn, peanuts, and edible seeds are reduced to crushed powder. Fruit such as bananas are preserved by drying and then pounded into a thick paste. Fish are dried and then pulverized.

In trades, crafts, and all manner of technical processes, pounding constitutes an important step. In the making of rope and yarn, vegetable fibers are obtained by prolonged beating of the raw material to remove pulpy parts of the plant. We need hardly point out the importance of this technology for everything from fishing to house building. Pottery techniques in general spurn the wheel or hand molding, and instead employ the paddle-and-anvil method. Surprisingly, weaving also involves a good deal of beating. Heavy flat wooden wands are used to close up the weft and make the fabric tight and hard wearing. Sharing some of the features of weaving and fiber making is the production of bark cloth. In this process, beating is employed only to soften woody fibers, not to order them in strands.

Metalworking involves much beating. Without modern furnaces, iron cannot be brought to its melting point, and so must be worked by hammering the red-hot ingot. Iron for blades is produced by layering ingot on top of ingot and then beating them wafer thin. But even with metals that could be cast, like brass and silver, hammering methods of working are preferred. Decorative patterns are punched onto the finished product.

One final example. Anyone who has watched women washing clothes in Southeast Asia will have noticed the way that the women roll them into a ball, soak them in water, and then beat them on a stone. Alternatively, they swing the wet cloth over their heads and bring it down smartly on a washboard or a convenient rock. Seldom do they employ the rubbing actions that come most naturally to Westerners.

Pounding actions appear with equal frequency in ritual contexts in Southeast Asia. The Berawan again provide an example. At funerals, drums, gongs large and small, slit gongs, and rice pestles are all unambiguously pounded. At other festivals, such as weddings, the gongs are played (using different rhythms), but the big drum and the funeral games are prohibited. This lesser level of percussion is consonant with the relative unimportance and ritual simplicity of all life-crisis markers other than death. The only rites that compete with funerals in terms of duration and complexity are head-hunting festivals, and they have their own peculiar percussive practices. When new heads are brought into the house, the men break into a stamping dance quite unlike the graceful, light-footed warrior's dance seen on other occasions. Also the felicitous opportunity is taken to expel evil influence from the house in the following manner. A crowd of people, mostly women, line up at one end of the longhouse veranda armed with rice pestles, canoe paddles, or heavy sticks. Together they march down the veranda, pounding these implements on the floor. Three times they go up and down the house, supposedly driving bad spirits before them.

We cannot conclude that these pounding actions in ritual derive in any simple way from similar ones in everyday life. That this cannot be the entire cause for their occurrence has already been shown by Needham, for the worldwide use of percussion cannot be explained by localized technologies of food production. However, it is still possible that the special frequency and importance of pounding technologies in Southeast Asia augments a universal resort to percussion for making noise. Though drums and gongs may be very widely employed at funerals, there is a particular intensity to the crashing, clanging, booming noisiness of Berawan rites.

Moreover, there may be cultural differences of emphasis in the significance of noise. The reason that is given by Berawan for the restriction on the playing of tops to funerals is that the whirring noise that they make is like the speech of ghosts. Normally it would be dangerous to attract ghosts with such noises, but at funerals the generations of the dead are invited anyway. Percussion is associated in the same way with the presence of the ancestors. Drumming and gong playing cease at the moment when this intercourse is broken off and the souls of the living are summoned back to the longhouse away from the departing dead.

LIMINALITY AND THE CORPSE

We cannot leave this consideration of the general and the particular in funeral practices without considering the corpse. It is our thesis throughout that attention to the symbolic attributes of the dead body provides insights into a culture's understanding of the nature of death. These attributes have the same kind of quasi universality and subtle variability in connotation as do color symbolism and the use of percussive noise.

Corpse symbolism is a special case of the use of the human body as a symbol. As we have mentioned, Hertz's essay on the representation of positive and negative moral qualities through the opposition of the right and left hands is one of the classic studies in body symbolism. The mourning usages involving shaving the head or letting the beard grow touch on another aspect. Throughout history and in most cultures, the human body has been used to represent moral and social verities. In connection with circumcision and scarification at initiation, van Gennep writes that "the human body has been treated like a simple piece of wood which each has cut and trimmed to suit him" (1960: 72). If the human body in life provides such a reservoir of moral representations, this same body after death carries its own possibilities for symbolic expression.

The surprising thing about corpse symbolism is how widely it is used in contexts divorced from death per se. Van Gennep saw that an immense variety of rites involve a rebirth in a new status, either for the individual or the whole society. But birth in the new condition presupposes death in the former, so that all liminal conditions involve deathly, terminal representations. Turner has paid great attention to the recurring symbols of liminality:

The symbolism attached to and surrounding the liminal persona is complex and bizarre. Much of it is modeled on human biological processes. . . . They give an outward and visible form to an inward and conceptual process. . . . The symbols . . . are drawn from the biology of death, decomposition, catabolism, and other physical processes that have a negative tinge. [Turner 1967: 98]

In Turner's view, it is the process of rotting, of dissolution of form, that provides the metaphor of a social and moral transition. Hence the prevalence of disagreeable remainders of dissolution at otherwise optimistic rites such as initiations and installations. Following Turner, one could argue that the corpse is associated with death because its decay is a metaphor of liminality. However, the direct connection between the two is so obvious as to hardly require such sophistry. Whether death or liminality is seen as primary depends upon whether one begins with funerals or other rites of passage. It is useful to explain liminality in initiation rites as deathlike, but it is tautologous in connection with funerals. However, Turner shows us a way to pursue the symbolism of the corpse by focusing upon the process of dissolution. Though, like percussive sound, corruption is a nearly universal symbol, it varies greatly in its metaphorical significance.

ROTTING, FERMENTING, DYEING, AND DISTILLING

Adams (1977) shows that in Southeast Asia there are strong parallels between certain manufacturing processes and the whole format of mortuary rites.

Blue-black dye is the most common color used for decorating cloth in Southeast Asia. Its preparation from indigo is widely practiced, and one of the simplest methods is that employed by the Meo of Thailand (Bühler 1972). Two pits are dug side by side, but at slightly different elevations. In the higher pit, the roots and stems of the indigo plant are soaked in water and left to rot. The liquid is then drained by a bamboo connecting pipe to the lower pit. Lime is added, and after a week or so of fermentation, a sediment forms. This is the dye, recovered by draining the pit. Elsewhere in Southeast Asia, clay pots are used to hold the liquids, but the process is the same.

In the preparation of hemp for cordage, the hemp stalks are left to rot in water for some weeks, after which the useful fibers can be separated from woody or pulpy material. Fermentation is widely employed as a means of rendering toxic food edible, or of preserving perishable foods. Fish and vegetables are stored for future consumption by means of partial anaerobic rotting in tightly sealed containers. These techniques were probably even more common 100 years ago, when rice was a less available staple and root crops made up a larger part of the diet of Southeast Asians (Pelzer 1945: 6–8). Even where not strictly necessary, fermented foods are often preferred because of their astringent flavor, such as shrimp paste and fermented tea leaves for chewing.

All these techniques involve decomposition – decomposition to produce useful things like dye and hemp or tasty things like shrimp paste and pickles. But there is a formal symmetry between these techniques and rotting in a less utilitarian context, the secondary treatment of the dead. Both involve the three stages of preparation, decomposition, and extraction.

The Berawan of Borneo do not prepare dyes and only occasionally ferment foods. The most familiar process of this kind for them is the making of rice wine, which is consumed in large quantities at social gatherings. Rice is first washed, cooked by boiling, and sprinkled with yeast. Then it is rolled into tight balls, which are stacked in large earthenware jars. The jars are sealed and left for some days, during which time a watery liquid runs off the balls of fermenting rice and collects in the bottom. When the crowd is assembled and the party about to start, the jars are opened. The remains of the rice balls are picked out and squeezed to remove the last drops of the liquor. The rice wine is now ready for consumption, after straining to remove the sediment. One characteristic Berawan method of treatment of corpses is wholly similar. After washing and dressing, the corpse is stored in a sealed jar. Decomposition proceeds similarly, except that it is the sediment that people wish to retain this time, not the liquids. The latter are drained off by means of a bamboo tube inserted in the bottom of the jar. The bones are removed from the jar finally, and placed in a smaller container for final storage. The jars used for rice wine are identical to those used for primary storage of corpses. Often several such jars are kept in the kitchen of a family apartment, and occasionally one is seen standing upside down. If one inquires why, the answer may be: Grandmother (or grandfather) has picked out this one for herself, and does not want it used for wine (Metcalf 1987).

All these processes of fermentation or rotting produce a strong smell, often a nauseating smell. Making indigo dye is infamously stinky, and many Westerners dislike the preserved foods that we mentioned because of their pungent scent. The familiarity that Southeast Asians have with such smells may indicate different attitudes to corpses. It was not our experience that the Berawan were indifferent to these smells of decomposition, but they did show fortitude in the presence of corpses. Rotting does not have the *wholly negative* connotations for them that it does for us. Consequently, there may be a radically different set of attitudes to the decomposition of corpses than those found in the West.

A second feature of Southeast Asian uses of techniques of decomposition is the notion of extraction. In the making of indigo, hemp, rice wine, and so on, raw materials are refined to produce valuable finished products that are of less bulk. From something perishable, inconveniently bulky, and useless in its present form, something long lasting, compact, and useful is obtained. The bones of the deceased partake of this nature, so that it is logical to take the time to recover them and store them with the other ancestors, from where they may exercise a benign influence upon their descendants. We cannot show that secondary burial rites like those found in Borneo evolved out of techniques for processing dyes. Nevertheless, the parallels are there, and they are striking. It may be that at some subconscious level, familiarity with practical techniques of distillation and fermentation makes the practice of secondary treatment of the dead more acceptable to Southeast Asians than it is to other peoples. If at some remote period, such practices were more widely distributed in the world, it may explain their persistence in some parts of Southeast Asia. These are the strongest statements that we can make.

Finally, it is worth noticing that this analogy is not inconsistent with Hertz's analysis of secondary treatment. Hertz pointed out that in these rites the fate of the corpse provides a model for the fate of the soul. Adams would only add that both are refined: the body to ossiferous relics, the soul to perfect spirit.

THE UNIVERSAL AND THE PARTICULAR

In the first part of the book, we have rejected the possibility of a simple panhuman explanation of the forms of funeral rites. Although we may posit a general psychic unity of mankind, the identification of vague quasi universals does not preclude variation at levels lower than that of the whole species. In trying to understand why Berawan funerals are so noisy, we were led to examine the worldwide use of percussion, the special propensity for pounding in Southeast Asia, and items of belief peculiar to the Berawan. Great care is needed to sort out the nature of variation

from one place to another. Hence the need for case studies. Placed in
the context of a particular ideological, social, and economic system, rituals of death begin to make sense in a way that they cannot if we pursue
elusive cultural universals.

Caution is doubly necessary in connection with death rites because
of an odd paradox. Contrary to what one might expect, conceptions of
death are not only elusive, but also highly variable. Rivers remarked many
years ago:

Death is so striking and unique an event that if one had to choose something
which must have been regarded in essentially the same light by mankind at all
times and in all places, I think one would be inclined to choose it in preference
to any other, and yet I hope to show that the primitive conception of death . . .
is different, one might say radically different, from our own. [Rivers 1926: 40]

Meanwhile, concepts of life, which seems so much more complex a
notion, have a certain universal familiarity about them. Ethnographers
the world over constantly report the same symbols occurring in rites
designed to promote fertility and the preservation of life, and the museums are full of life-promoting charms and ritual equipment. Death is
more intangible:

. . . on the whole there does commonly seem to be a contrast between a relatively patent and apprehensible conception of life and a more obscure and per-
plexing conception of death. One reason for this readily suggests itself. We have
our being in a life that we know; we are struck down into a death that we can
only surmise. [Needham 1970: xxxv]

PART II

DEATH AS TRANSITION

4

THE LIVING
AND THE DEAD:
A RE-EXAMINATION
OF HERTZ

In common with several of the influential essays originally published in
the *Année sociologique*, Hertz's "A Contribution to the Study of the Collective Representation of Death" is more complex than is immediately
apparent. At first sight, it appears to follow one topic in a direct fashion.
Scholars already wedded to a particular theoretical viewpoint find it easy
to pick out only familiar lines of argument. But a closer study reveals
several interwoven themes. This is what makes the essay useful. Each
argument is worth following out; each suggests a new interpretation of
one's field data. But in order to make full use of Hertz's insights, it is necessary to tease apart the distinct threads of argument.

THE THREE SIDES OF HERTZ'S ANALYSIS

The most direct way to begin is with Hertz's dramatis personae: the
corpse, the soul, and the mourners. Each part of the essay is devoted to
one of these, producing a tripartite structure made explicit in the section
headings. In his introduction to the English translation, Evans-Pritchard
pointed out the "three sides" of Hertz's argument. But contrary to what
Evans-Pritchard implies, the arguments differ not in which of the actors
takes center stage, but in which *pair* of actors is brought into dialogue.

Death as Transition

We may imagine the arguments as the sides of a triangle, the corners of which are the aspects of the corpse and its disposal, the soul and the dead, and the living and the mourners (see Figure 3).

A nice example of the three sides of Hertz's argumentation concerns the answers that he gives to the deceptively simple question: Why is the corpse feared? What is the origin of the horror that surrounds it? At first glance, the answer seems obvious enough. Surely disgust at the process of bodily decay, even before death, but especially after death, is natural. However, the strength and the character of this reaction vary widely from one culture to another. Some dispose of the corpse hurriedly, others slowly and with painstaking attention. Americans do not often witness a death, but will readily view the corpse once suitably treated. Even within one culture, reactions may vary according to the mode of dying. In many parts of Borneo, for instance, the cadaver of a woman who dies in childbirth is the subject of special revulsion. Nor are attitudes to the process of decomposition always the same, as we saw in the concluding section of Chapter 3. For Hertz, the expression of fear is important as evidence of cognitive and sociological motivations, not as an adequate explanation in itself. But he rejects at the outset any explanation of it that relies on natural disgust:

This is not a matter of hygiene (as we understand it), nor even, exclusively, a concern to ward off foul smells: we must not attribute to these people feelings and scruples about smell which are foreign to them.[1960: 32]

Near the end of the essay, Hertz offers this explanation:

The horror inspired by the corpse does not spring from the simple observation of the changes that occur in the body. Proof that such a simplistic explanation is inadequate lies in the fact that in one and the same society the emotion aroused by death varies extremely in intensity according to the social status of the deceased. . . . At the death of a chief, or a man of high rank, a true panic sweeps over the group. . . . On the contrary, the death of a stranger, a slave, or a child will go almost unnoticed. [Hertz 1960: 76]

This argument is explicitly sociological, because it turns upon the social status of the deceased. The passing of an influential person, on whom many people depend for leadership or livelihood, is a momentous event and perhaps a calamity. It leaves a large rent in the fabric of society. The same is not true of the socially insignificant.

The Living and the Dead

Earlier in the essay, Hertz offers a different explanation:

These tribes thus explicitly connect the dissolution of the corpse and their belief in a temporary stay of the soul on earth, together with the obligations and fears that derive from this belief. . . . This representation is linked to a well-known belief: to make an object or a living being pass from this world into the next, to free or to create the soul, it must be destroyed. . . . As the visible object vanishes it is reconstructed in the beyond, transformed to a greater or lesser degree. The same belief applies to the body of the deceased.[Hertz 1960: 46]

The corpse is feared because, until its reconstruction in the beyond is complete, part of its spiritual essence remains behind, where it menaces the living with the threat of further death.

These two explanations are not identical. The important point in the present context is that it is not necessary to choose which of the explanations is the correct one. Both have validity and utility, but they are of a different order; they simply *explain different things*. The second shows why the death of any person causes anxiety and fear. The first shows why this reaction varies in scale from one person to another. Moreover, each has a different utility in trying to understand death ritual. The first explains why some funerals are large and some small. The second provides the formula for a particular shape that the rituals may take – in this case secondary burial. It follows that the two explanations are different in the level of their generality also. The first might be applied to grand funerals anywhere, but the second applies only to one category of death rites. In this chapter and subsequent ones, we will pursue the implications of these two lines of argumentation.

Nor is the nature of the fear the same in each case. The horror of death is not the same as the shock of some particular death, and neither is identical with the fear of the dead. But Hertz has yet a third explanation to cover that reaction:

Death . . . by striking the individual, has given him a new character: his body, which . . . was in the realm of the ordinary, suddenly leaves it; it can no longer be touched without danger, it is an object of horror and dread. Now we know to what degree the religious or magical properties of things are regarded as contagious by "primitives": the "impure cloud" which, according to the Olo Ngaju, surrounds the deceased, pollutes everything it touches.[Hertz 1960: 37–8]

At first sight, this explanation appears the simplest, and not very different from the hygienic rationale that Hertz rejects at the outset. But *this* pollution is supernatural, not literal. It occurs even where no physical contact exists, as with the land, even the trees, owned by the deceased (1960: 38). Also there are practices that seem directly to contradict the avoidance of pollution. The widow may be obliged to rub the products of decomposition of the corpse on her own body, for instance (1960: 51). Typically, Hertz offers two explanations for this practice: that for the widow, pollution is inevitable anyway, and that by so doing she deflects the animosity of her husband's ghost.

In the Indonesian context, pollution is not fundamentally a matter of contact with, but of relationship to, the source of contagion. Nonkin may sit near the corpse, and even touch it, without incurring infection. But close kin, wherever they happen to be, are immediately struck by the "petrifying thunderbolt" when a death occurs. More distant kin and fellow residents of the longhouse are affected to a lesser extent (Hertz 1960: 39). Unlike the Hindu or Semitic case, already well described in Hertz's time, pollution is not a conspicuous feature of Indonesian religions. In fact, it is found almost exclusively in the context of death. Meanwhile, their evaluation of rotting differs from our own. Though they certainly do not find it an attractive process, it has positive connotations that it does not have for us, having to do with the release of the dead from the bonds of the flesh.

Kin are contaminated by death because they partake in the death. Each severed relationship leaves a living person that much reduced: a social and psychological amputee. Of all relatives, the widow is the most disfigured. Like the dead man, she must undergo a liminal phase during which her identity is readjusted. To a lesser extent, the entire community goes through a period of redefinition.

Hertz's third explanation for the fear that death engenders turns, then, upon the extinction of the social person. What appears at first sight to be a statement about the corpse is in reality an explanation that relates the soul (in the form of the memory of the dead) to the living. Meanwhile, the first explanation that we reviewed above relates the corpse and its disposal to the mourners, and the second explanation relates the fate of the soul to the body, giving us the three-sided argumentation diagrammed in Figure 3.

Moreover, each type of explanation can be utilized to account for different aspects of the funeral rites. Explanation 1 shows why the scale of

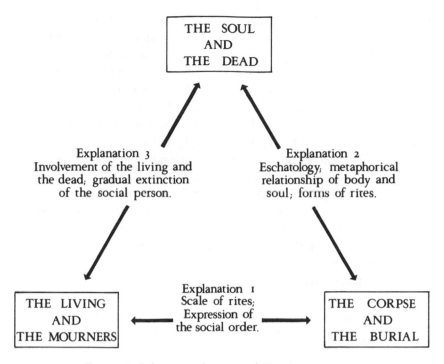

Figure 3. Schematic diagram of Hertz's arguments.

funerals varies, and consequently how the rites express the social order by differentiating between people of unequal status. This type of argument lends itself to extension in many directions. Hertz himself connects it with the practice of preserving relics of individuals of high esteem, and hence the origin of ancestor cults (1960: 57). In a detailed analysis of the Merina of Madagascar, Bloch (1971) shows the importance of funeral rites in organizing the society of the living. Because the tomb that an adult Merina plans to occupy plays an important part in defining the corporate group to which he or she belongs in life, it follows that the society of the dead structures the society of the living. As Bloch acknowledges, his study is primarily sociological (1971: 220). We utilize arguments of this type in Chapter 6, where we examine how the remains of important men are manipulated to serve broad societal functions or the narrow ambitions of their would-be successors.

The arguments that can be elaborated out of explanation 3 are different in character. They focus on the gradual disentanglement of the living and the deceased. This theme is very pronounced in the funerals of the LoDagaa of West Africa, described in an important study by Goody (1962). The funerals of the LoDagaa involve several large ceremonies spread over many months. Goody shows that the effect of the rites is to dismantle the legal and emotional roles of the deceased and redistribute them among the living. The weightiest issue is the inheritance of property, which is not accomplished at once, but in stages. However, the LoDagaa carry the process through with unusual thoroughness. Even such nonjural and seemingly uninheritable roles as friend and lover are reallocated. "The LoDagaa are loath to extinguish any of the dead man's relationships; hence the funeral ceremonies provide institutionalized methods for the taking over of these roles by other persons. During the course of the burial service certain relationships that have been marked by satisfactory personal feelings are provisionally re-organized, and among these are . . . friend and lover" (Goody 1962: 133). This formulation is similar to van Gennep's: The living pass through a liminal phase during which society is reintegrated without the lost member. The liminal phase has both a sociological dimension, concerned with rents in the social fabric, and a symbolic or psychological one, having to do with society's image of itself. Hertz did not fail to notice the latter: ". . . when a man dies, society loses in him much more than a unit; it is stricken in the very principle of life, in the faith it has in itself" (1960: 78). This societal crisis is most severe in the case of sacred kings, and it is the symbolic aspects of the death of kings that we take up in Chapter 7.

Different insights again are furnished by explanation 2 which has a unique power. It enables us to penetrate the meaning of mortuary rituals by paying attention to the details of the treatment of the corpse. In his essay, Hertz demonstrates "A kind of symmetry or parallelism between the condition of the body. . . . and the condition of the soul" (1960: 45). This relationship makes it possible to derive eschatology from the metaphorical relationship of body and soul. Consequently, such analyses have a symbolic character. Given the extraordinary variety of methods used throughout the world and at different epochs to dispose of the dead, we are provided with a rich vein of material for analysis. This approach enables us to deal with the *particular forms* of death rites, so that their specialness and individuality are not lost.

The Living and the Dead

This line of argument is the most original feature of Hertz's essay, yet it has so far received very little attention. We shall follow it in subsequent chapters by keeping the corpse clearly in view.

It is an approach that can be applied to any type of funeral. Hertz chose to apply it to one particular variety of mortuary rite, that of secondary disposal. He drew much of his data from Borneo, where there were instances of the practice that were already well documented in his day. However, Hertz was obliged to rely on the accounts of travelers, in which this bizarre custom figures prominently. The Berawan of central northern Borneo still practice secondary disposal, and they provide an appropriate test of Hertz's analysis in the light of detailed field data.

AN APPLICATION: BERAWAN DEATH RITES

Berawan rites of secondary treatment   Between Berawan communities there are many differences in the details of ritual of secondary treatment of the dead. Nevertheless, there is an overall similarity of format. Briefly, there are two major ceremonies, each lasting several days and involving many people, separated by a period of at least eight months, and sometimes as much as five years.

The first ceremony begins immediately after death occurs. The corpse is displayed on a specially built seat for a day or two. When all the close kin have seen it, it is inserted in a coffin or large jar. At the end of four to ten days, depending upon the status of the deceased, it is removed for temporary storage. This may be within the longhouse, or more frequently on a simple wooden platform in the graveyard. When the time has come to perform the second ceremony (*nulang*), guests are summoned from far and wide to attend. The coffin or jar is brought from its place of temporary storage to a small shed built onto the longhouse veranda. If the initial storage container is damaged, the relatives may decide to open it, clean the bones of the deceased, and store them in a new jar of smaller size. The ceremony lasts four to ten days, and every evening there is a boisterous party on the veranda adjacent to the jar or coffin. Then the bones are transferred to their final resting place. This may comprise a single massive post, often richly carved, with a niche near its head into which a small jar may be inserted. Alternatively, the remains may be stored in a large decorated wooden mausoleum raised on one or several supporting posts, and housing several coffins. The second ceremony comprises what Hertz called the "great feast."

What is the significance of these rituals, spread out over so long a period? The answer that the Berawan give is that the rites, and in particular the death songs sung at the "great feast," conduct the enduring spiritual component of the deceased to the land of the dead. But an inconsistency immediately appears in this account, because Berawan also claim that the entry into the land of the dead occurs immediately at death, indeed, this is the definition of death. In order to resolve this contradiction, it is necessary to understand how the spiritual component of human beings is perceived.

Berawan notions of the soul, sickness, and death   The Berawan conceive of the living human being as the conjunction of the body (*usaa*) and a spiritual component (*telanak*). The obvious gloss for *telanak* is "soul," but we must beware of the tendency to assume that the two concepts are identical. They differ in at least two ways. First, the Berawan soul changes its nature and manifestation in different contexts. At healing sessions it appears as minute and particulate, so that the shaman is able to catch it on a sword blade. But in the death songs we find it paddling a canoe and singing laments, in short, appearing as a homomorphic counterpart of the deceased. Second, the Berawan soul is not considered eternal. On the contrary, the soul of a dead person changes some time after death into something else, and the word *telanak* is no longer used in connection with him or her.

What the soul changes into is called *bíli' letd'*, a spirit of the dead. *Bíli'* (spirit) is a word often heard in Berawan prayers and in casual conversation. Supernatural agencies ranging from the Creator, to omen birds, to mischievous sprites that are assumed to be behind any unusual occurrence, however trivial, are all parts of a limitless spirit world (Metcalf 1989: 59–69). The spirits of the dead inhabit a region called *lía dé lo letd'*, simply, "the place of those who are dead." Berawan refuse to speculate on where it is, replying to enquiries with the pragmatic answer that they are only human and cannot know. They do, however, assert that the land of the dead is a beautiful place full of radiant spirits (Metcalf 1982a: 233–56).

The unaging perfection of spirits contrasts with the infirmity of humans. Some common ailments, such as skin diseases and upset stomachs, are attributed to environmental causes without supernatural implications. Others, including some serious conditions, are believed to result from violation of a taboo. But the most important category of illness stems from "soul loss." The soul wanders from the body in sleep, but should not be long absent. If it is tardy, or is ensnared by some malevolent spirit entity, then illness soon results. Curing practices center around recovery of the soul, and its restoration to the body of the patient. This is the province of the shamans, who control many techniques for the location and securing of errant souls (Metcalf 1982b).

If sickness is caused by the prolonged absence of the soul, what is death? The unanimous and immediate answer to this question was that if the soul continues to wander, and eventually strays so far that it enters the land of the dead, then at that moment the victim is dead. One informant told the following story to illustrate graphically his answer. Once, as a young man, he had been seriously ill and had lose consciousness. He had dreamt that he was paddling upriver, and had turned off into a stream that he later realized was the route to the land of the dead as described in Berawan death songs. He paddled up the stream and beached his canoe at the foot of a steep hill, which he climbed. On top of the hill were beautiful people dressed in fine clothes, harvesting rice that shone like gold. These people were spirits of the dead. They invited him to go with them, and together they descended the hill on the other side, and came to another stream. The spirits crossed over, but he suddenly realized that to do so would bring him finally into the land of the dead. So he set his face away from the entrancing vision of the beautiful spirits and returned the way that he had come. Later he regained consciousness and, having passed the crisis of his illness, soon recovered.

Such is the Berawan notion of death. Physical death is usually referred to by the expression "to lose breath." But if the soul reaches the land of the dead at the moment of "losing breath," what is the ritual purpose of the rites of secondary treatment?

The journey of the soul: the death songs   Despite local variations in custom, for all Berawan the climax of the death rites is the singing of special songs. Following them, the bones may be taken to their final resting place in the monument prepared for them. But first the soul must be provided for, and the death songs sung on that last night give it very specific instructions as to how to make the journey to the land of the dead (Met-calf 1982a: 190–230).

The sequence from the village of Long Jegan will serve to illustrate the nature of the death songs of the last night of the "great feast."

The first to be sung has an important purpose, the recovery of any souls that may be tempted to wander off with that of the dead person, but it is sung in a lighthearted and playful manner. A verse is sung for every member of the community, and the soul of someone of the opposite sex is delegated to "pull" the soul home. This is an opportunity for rib-aldry and innuendo to which no one may object.

The most important of the death songs comes next, and it is sung in a formal and serious manner. The lead singer stands beside the coffin facing upriver. He takes up a large bamboo, the one that was used to bring water to wash the corpse at death, and which has been preserved near the coffin since then. Lightly but firmly, he strikes the coffin with the end of the bamboo, making a resonant noise. Simultaneously, he calls on the soul to prepare for the journey to the land of the dead. The song instructs the soul to go to the river to wash. Having returned, the soul is told to put on fine attire, as appropriate to the sex of the dead person. Now it is told to go out of the longhouse and, without so much as glan-cing backward, to descend to the canoe at the river's edge.

At this point, the format of the song changes. Now successive verses consist of questions posed by the journeying soul and answers provided by the living. The soul begins, through the voice of the lead singer: "What place is this, live ones?" The reply comes from the chorus: "The place of the longhouse, dead one." The soul is instructed to paddle upstream. Then it asks its whereabouts and is told that it is at a small stream that joins the main river, a short distance above the longhouse. So the song proceeds upriver, mentioning all the places where side streams, named or unnamed, join the main river. Each time the site of a previous Berawan longhouse is passed, it is mentioned specifically. Every three or four verses the soul is urged to paddle vigorously, making the spray fly up behind the canoe.

This recitation of place names makes up a large part of the death songs of the final evening. The journey of the soul has more cosmological sig-nificance than is at first apparent. The Berawan of Long Jegan have for several centuries been migrating away from an idyllic ancestral homeland in the interior, along the same river that the soul is now ascending.

The Living and the Dead

Berawan stories of migration move back in time to longhouse sites ever further upriver, and to hero figures who gradually become more stupendous, until a mythical time is reached when the living and the dead dwelt side by side. At the moment when this arrangement ceased, and humans were forever separated, the death rites were invented. It can thus be seen how fundamentally those rites are woven into Berawan ideas of what it is to be human. As the soul travels upriver, it not only travels toward the dead, but also backward in time. It moves from the larger-than-life heroes of a few generations ago, back past mythical ancestors that dug rivers and climbed the sky, to the creation itself. For the audience listening to them and participating in them, the death songs constitute an exposition of fundamental concepts of the Berawan worldview.

Eventually, in the song, the soul arrives at the mouth of a certain side stream, and instead of passing by, it is instructed to enter. This route brings it close to the highest point in the neighboring mountain range. In this region, the soul is told to get out of the canoe, and to search for the leaves used in chewing betel. At this juncture, the death song sequence of Long Jegan abruptly terminates. It is said that while the soul is searching for leaves it will be discovered by emissaries from the land of the dead, who will conduct it on the remaining part of the journey. The whole recital has lasted six to eight hours, and dawn is close.

But if the soul arrived in the land of the dead at the moment of "losing breath," is not this second journey redundant? It was necessary to press informants in order to get any answer to this question. They gave blank looks, or recapitulated data that were already familiar. Finally, a senior man of Long Jegan offered the following account.

The soul of a sick person wanders from the body of its owner. Prolonged absence causes serious illness, but the soul may wander far, into spirit worlds unknown to humans, without fatal results. Only if it should enter the land of the dead by some devious route will death ensue. Then the minimal connection of body and soul is severed and the lifeless body begins to decompose. The soul does not stay in the land of the dead; it continues to wander. But on returning finally to the body it discovers that decomposition has begun, and so it is unable to reenter the body. It cannot or will not reanimate the putrescent corpse. If it did so, a monster would result. But neither can the soul easily find its way back to the land of the dead, because it arrived there previously by accident and not by the direct route. Even if it can find its way there again, it will not be welcomed by the community of the dead because it has not yet become one of those beautiful spirits. So it must wander miserably in unfamiliar spirit regions, or enviously lurk in the environs of the long-house, near the corpse. At the "death feast," the dead are summoned to the festivities, and the soul is properly conducted to the land of the dead. This ensures its welcome there. In support of this account, the informant cited the practice of calling back the soul of the dead person on the first night of the ceremony, which may last as long as ten nights. The purpose of calling it back is to ensure that it is not wandering in some distant spirit world, and thus to prevent it from, literally, missing the boat. What is striking is the similarity that this indigenous exegesis bears to that of Hertz.

Both posit a period when the soul is homeless, miserable, and malicious. Both place a central emphasis on the decomposition of the corpse. In the native account, the soul is unable to reanimate the corpse because putrescence has already begun. To do so would be contrary to nature, and the result would be monstrous. Moreover, the fate of the soul is related to the fate of the corpse, because the soul needs time to convert itself into a spirit worthy of the land of the dead, even as the corpse needs time to become dry bones.

The ritual expression of Berawan eschatology Many practices lend substance to the informant's account. In the year or more before the soul's final release, dozens of small rituals woven into the funeral, or having to do with the mourning usages of the close kin of the deceased, draw attention in unmistakable ways to the continuing presence of both the corpse and the hovering soul, and to their ambivalent nature, both demanding care and inspiring fear at the same time. Here we give a few examples only.

The presence of the soul near the corpse is attested to by the practice of addressing it throughout the death rites. As relatives arrive after hearing news of the death, they immediately go to the corpse. Women mourners drop to their knees before the corpse and throw their long hair forward over the crowns of their heads so that it hides their faces. Amid tears and sobs, they produce a dramatic dirge, the main thrust of which is: "Why have you abandoned those that love you?" Such dirges are a vocal art form, but they are also the vehicle of intense emotion. Close female relatives may repeat the dirge daily, or even more frequently. Men express similar sentiments but they stand back dry-eyed.

A second practice with the same implications is the provision of food and tobacco for the corpse. This begins immediately after death. In the minutes after "loss of breath" has been confirmed, a complex and rapid series of rites are enacted on the corpse. Two of these concern us here. In one, the spouse and children of the dead person lie down in turn beside the corpse and puff on a cigarette of native manufacture. Then they sit up and offer it to the lips of the corpse. In the other rite, the corpse is carried into the kitchen and its hands are laid in the hearth. Simultaneously, a little cooked rice is pushed into its mouth. After the corpse is displayed on its special seat, a plate is hung before its face (see Figure 4). Each time the widow or widower is fed, a little of the same food is placed in the suspended plate. A cigarette is placed in the corpse's fingers. After the corpse is inserted in the coffin or jar, the plates are placed on top, and token quantities of food are placed there as before.

But the soul is not within the corpse, and this makes the body itself a source of intense danger, aside from the threat of the malicious soul. During the period before the corpse is removed from the house for temporary sepulture, a constant vigil is maintained over it. In the case of an adult, the spouse and at least the eldest child are near the corpse at all times. At night a large crowd collects near the coffin to talk, drink, and play games. Officially, no adult should sleep at night during funerals. In practice, it is sufficient if each family apartment sends one representative to attend the gathering. Toward morning many people are stretched out asleep on the mats around the coffin, but earlier in the night games are played and there is much joviality. Many of the death songs sung on these occasions resemble games more than somber dirges. Such levity is in accordance with one stated aim of the gathering, namely, to entertain the soul of the dead person, and make its last hours in the longhouse jolly.

The other aim of the vigil is to prevent harm from befalling the corpse. The noise of the crowd and the bright lights kept burning all night discourage the intrusion of evil spirits. Intense horror centers on the idea of the putrescent corpse becoming inspired by some demon. There is a particular spirit that attempts to gain control of fresh corpses, and if it should succeed, a monster results of superhuman strength and nightmarish mien that is invulnerable to human weapons. On one occasion, a

Figure 4. Corpse of a Berawan woman displayed on a special seat. The woman seated to the right of the picture is the daughter of the deceased. She is dressed in white mourning attire. The dead woman is decked in fine clothes and surrounded by valuables. Her hands rest in a bowl containing candy and money, and she holds a cigarette in her fingers. In front of her (partly obscured by the rich hangings) is hung a small bowl into which cooked food is placed from time to time. The deceased's husband is housed in a small cubicle of mats out of the picture to the left.

coffin resting on the longhouse veranda was heard to emit a mysterious knocking sound, as if there were something inside rapping on the lid. The noise may have been caused by contraction of the timbers of the longhouse in the cool of the late afternoon. But the women sitting casually nearby saw a different explanation. They fled carrying their children. Men came carrying weapons, which were waved above the coffin. Extra bands of rattan were tied around the coffin, so as to secure the lid more firmly, and magical plants intended to repel evil spirits were placed on top of it. Calm was not restored until the old shaman arrived, and declared that nothing was amiss with the corpse. Reassured, the crowd resumed its vigil.

The Living and the Dead

A further instance of the care taken with new corpses is the practice of hanging mats along the open side of the veranda. These mats are lowered an hour or so before sunset, and raised again during the early hours of the morning. Sunset is a dangerous time, when many evil spirits are abroad, and the corpse is best shielded from their view. Color symbolism is also involved in this fear: Berawan say the sunset is too full of threatening red hues.

The many privations visited upon a widow or widower during the funeral also express the theme of the danger of the corpse and soul. A widow suffers them in a particularly acute fashion. She is cooped up for as many as eleven days in a tiny cell made of mats, next to the corpse. She may not bathe, and must defecate through a hole in the floor, wear filthy clothes, and eat only the poorest of foods, which she "shares" with the deceased. These harsh prescriptions fit nicely with Hertz's suggestion that she partakes in the condition of the deceased. But we must be careful to observe in just what way she shares his condition. That the widow is not simply in "quarantine" so that she cannot spread her "pollution" is revealed by her purposely cramped quarters. It is hard to see how this prevents the spread of infection. She suffers not because of the *corpse*, but because of the *vengeful soul* of the deceased. Its envy of the living, caused by its own miserable state, is softened by the spectacle of the hardship visited on those it formerly loved. Nor are these practices intended punitively, but paradoxically, out of a concern for the widow's welfare. As the one closest to the deceased, she is most likely to have her soul stolen to keep him company. Only by suffering can she deflect his malice. Only by sharing his condition metaphorically can she avoid sharing it literally (Metcalf 1982a: 94–111).

The same ideas explain why a funeral, even the funeral of unimportant people within the longhouse, is an intensely communal affair. The widow, by her confinement, deflects the hostility of the vengeful soul. She thus performs a service for the entire community, and all its members have a reciprocal moral commitment to see to the workaday details of the rites. A widower is subjected to an identical restriction, and other close kin, although not physically confined, wear mourning attire, maintain somber disposition, and spend many hours sitting silently by the corpse. Consequently, the responsibility to feed guests or construct a suitable tomb is spread among more distant kin, and the cooperation enjoined at funeral rites has a powerful integrative function. There is no more binding duty on the longhouse resident than that of participation in death rites.

In the months following the funeral, the close kin, especially the widow or widower, observe many rites and restrictions. For instance, at each full moon a new widow addresses a dirge to the dead man. Kneeling alone in the moonlight, keening pitifully, she makes a dramatic figure.

All these practices lend credence to our informant's account of the nature of the deceased's existence in the months following death. The corpse and the soul are likewise the object of fear, and of solicitude. The corpse must be protected lest it become some terrible monster, and is feared for the same reason. The soul is pitied because of its discomfort, and feared because of what its discomfort might lead it to do. The double character of the funeral, half ordeal and half party, like the nature of the soul, both pitiful and dangerous, are alike consequences of the state of the corpse, which demands attention and repels it at the same time.

The nature of the abridged rites　　The metaphorical relationship that Hertz observed has enabled us to see a remarkable consistency in Berawan death rites. Both the overall format and the details of ritual express the same set of ideas.

However, a problem arises in connection with the abridged death rites. Not every corpse receives secondary treatment. In fact, it is a relatively rare event. The more common practice is to give the corpse the initial funeral rites, and then to store it permanently in the tomb. Hertz suggests that such abbreviated rites are the result of foreign influence (1960: 58). Douglas Miles (1965) makes a similar argument for societies of southern Borneo, but it is not convincing as applied to the Berawan. They claim that both a full and an abridged death ritual sequence have always been available, and the monuments in old graveyards bear out their statement. In the Berawan case, there is no evidence of devolution from an epoch when the full rites were performed for every corpse.

What concerns us here is the ritual significance of the abridged rites. The question is: Are the notions of the fate of the soul in death the same if only the abridged rites are performed? If so, how does the soul get to the land of the dead without the death songs? If not, why are some people, including those most respected in the community, made to suffer the horrible fate of the intermediary period? In some longhouses, the songs conveying the soul to the land of the dead are sung during the initial wake. At others, they are never sung at all. In communities of the first type, do they believe that the soul can be formally introduced to the ancestors after so brief a period? Our answer to all these questions is that even where the songs are sung early, basic notions of the fate of the soul in death remain identical to those revealed by the extended death rites. Many practices point to this conclusion.

First, despite the removal of the corpse from the longhouse, and its entombment in a permanent death monument, the soul is still talked to and fed. The most obvious occasion on which this occurs is a rite performed during the first full moon after the rice harvest subsequent to the death. A ritual apparatus is erected in the open space in front of the longhouse adjacent to the dead person's apartment. It consists of a bamboo pole, about fifteen feet tall, with ears of the new rice arranged in geometrical patterns around its top. This rice is the share offered to the dead person, who may have lent a hand in planting it. A time of full moon is chosen so as to be sure of encountering the dead person's ghost. If the deceased was male, his widow makes a dirge much as described above.

Second, the ghost is still feared, because it is still likely to be near the longhouse, and vindictive. Mourning continues after the removal of the corpse from the house, with a slow relaxation in severity. The privations visited upon the widow or widower are relaxed two days after the removal of the corpse from the longhouse. But mourning clothes and sobriety of living are prescribed for a full year. For months a widow will not go into any other family apartment than her own, even the adjacent ones that house her daughters and grandchildren. She will not sing or dance during that year. Close female relatives will observe the prohibition on dancing for several months. The widow cannot remarry for at least a year.

Certainly these mourning usages are observed partly from sorrow, but their function in placating the dead man is explicit. Any further deaths in the community are likely to be attributed to the vengeful soul. Particularly if there was some irregularity concerning the death or the funeral, an apprehensive period ensues. This period lasts about one year.

In Berawan thought, the soul of a dead person undergoes a protracted metamorphosis whether or not its corpse receives secondary treatment. If the death songs are sung too early, they serve to conduct the soul along the path to the land of the dead, but the soul still cannot gain admittance. This is why some communities dispense with them in the abridged rites.

We can now summarize Berawan eschatology and its relationship to funeral ritual. Their conception of dying is uniform from one longhouse to another, regardless of the particular ritual employed. The stability of these ideas is illustrated by the comment of a Berawan convert to Catholicism that purgatory is the place to which Christian souls went "until their bones are dry." He argued that it was a morally responsible act to convert because in purgatory God could keep an eye on the souls of the recently dead, and prevent them from bothering the living.

What is variable is the ritual expression of these beliefs. Different rites are observed in each of the four communities, and even within one longhouse at least two sequences are available, the abridged and the full. All of these ceremonies embody the recognition of the changing nature of the dead, but they do not do so equally. Only when the "great feast" is held are these conceptions given full expression. That is why its importance is out of all proportion to its frequency.

The "great feast" has the same relationship to spiritual maturation that a debutante ball has to puberty. On the one hand, those who do not receive the full rites are not excluded from the land of the dead; it is only that their arrival occasions no ceremony. On the other hand, the full rites are an honor, and not a punishment, because the soul of the recipient is given a moment of consummate glory. The rites of secondary treatment are celebratory in nature, rather than instrumental, and it is this feature that removes the paradox of their relative infrequency.

For the community as a whole, the "great feast" has another aspect; it provides an opportunity for renewed contact with the sacred dead. The ancestors are summoned to the festival, so that there is a movement reciprocal to the journey of the deceased toward the land of the dead. It is from the ancestors that good things come, and they are constantly invoked in prayer (Metcalf 1989: 61–69). Their presence in the longhouse is potentially rewarding and invigorating, but it is also dangerous. Any mishap could cause disaster. At the funeral, there is fear of the unquiet soul. During the "great feast" that threat is passed and there is genuine festivity, tempered, however, with great seriousness. The awesome sacredness of the "great feast" is another dimension of its uncommonness.

The Living and the Dead

Hertz was unable to appreciate the significance of diverse rites, no doubt because the sources that he had available to him report only the grandest ones. This leads him to incorrectly dismiss other kinds of rites as modern developments symptomatic of cultural impoverishment, and to arrive at a mechanistically instrumental view of the rituals. But these are minor quibbles. In general, Hertz's formulation succeeds admirably in unlocking the religious ideas that lie behind Berawan funerals.

VARIATIONS ON A THEME: MA'ANYAN, TORADJA, BALINESE, IBAN, AND MAMBAI

Needless to say, secondary treatment of the dead is not restricted to Borneo, nor are such rites elsewhere identical to those of the Berawan. Our next objective therefore is to examine briefly some variant forms, to see if the metaphor that Hertz isolated in the core of such rites can be discerned in them also.

Before beginning, it might be useful to review the elements that we expect to find together. The metaphor is that, where secondary treatment occurs, the fate of the corpse is a model for the fate of the nonmaterial component of the person. By secondary treatment, we mean the regular and socially sanctioned removal of the relics of some or all deceased persons from a place of temporary storage to a permanent resting place. "Temporary" storage means a period of a few months or years, but not a few days. At least two things follow in terms of ideology. First, that dying is a slow process of transition from one spiritual state to another. Second, the process of spiritual change is disagreeable, in the same way that the decomposition of the corpse is disagreeable. In addition to these minimal items, other beliefs that may be found include: an emphasis on decomposition in symbols or statements referring to the recently dead; a fear of the recently dead; a fear that corpses may be horrifically reanimated; an assumption that the malice of the recently dead will gradually wane, being replaced by the benign influence of the long dead, and also that the recently dead somehow hover near human habitation, whereas the long dead are removed and anonymous.

Other instances of secondary treatment from Indonesia: Ma'anyan, Toradja, and Balinese   Hertz principally bases his analysis on the peoples of southeast Borneo, whom he refers to collectively as the Olo Ngaju. This name means nothing more than "people from upriver," and disguises the fact that there is considerable cultural variation within the area of southern Borneo that has come to be designated by the term. However, in this he simply followed the usage of those who provided his sources (Braches 1882; Grabowsky 1884, 1889; Hardeland 1858; and others). More recent work has been done by Hans Schärer (1963) and Alfred Hudson (1966). We draw on Hudson's detailed account of the funeral rites of one particular ethnic group in the area, the Ma'anyan.

Ma'anyan mortuary practices involve temporary storage of the corpse in a coffin, which is buried in the graveyard. Instead of having a rite of secondary treatment for one person at a time, as in the Berawan case, corpses are allowed to accumulate over a matter of years, and then all of them receive these rites together. This community festival of the dead lasts over a week and attracts large crowds. At its climax, all the accumulated coffins that are sufficiently old are stacked on a grating and burned in relays of a dozen or so. After each firing, the ashes containing fragments of bone are collected. Later they are stored in a large raised wooden container in the graveyard, together with relics from former festivals (Hudson 1966: 361–98).

The nonmaterial component of a living person is called *amirue*. After death, it is no longer referred to by that name, but is called *adiau*. No ordinary shaman can aid or manipulate the *adiau*; instead, another ritual specialist must care for it. It is her job (they are always women) to guide the *adiau* to the land of the dead, and protect it on its journey by means of long ritual chants. These chants terminate on the day the coffin is burned, and simultaneously the *adiau* arrives at the land of the dead and reverts to being *amirue*.

The land of the dead is regarded as a pleasant place, although notions about it are vague compared to the elaborate seven-layer heavens described to Schärer by the Ngaju of the Katingan River (Schärer 1963: 157–8). Mourning usages are similar to those of the Berawan, with gradually decreasing severity after interment of the corpse. Of themselves, these usages are not evidence of a fear of the recently dead, since some kind of mourning is well nigh universal. It is the emphasis on deprivation that is indicative here. In particular, one close relative, often the mother of the deceased, is kept locked up in a room for seven days with only a very poor diet of water and cold cassava (Hudson 1966: 371). This is reminiscent of the privations visited on the widow in Berawan funerals. Also, food is taken regularly to the grave for as long as three years, unless secondary treatment occurs first.

Among the Ma'anyan, the intermediary period is even more clearly marked than among the Berawan, and the transition is similarly conceived. This is not surprising, given that the rites of the Ma'anyan and their neighbors were the ones that originally prompted Hertz's analysis. In addition, it is interesting to note how different are the Ma'anyan rites from those of the Berawan, although they express similar eschatological ideas. The scheduling of cremation is particularly instructive. It provides a final sterilization *after* bacterial decomposition is completed. Were it not for the notion that the corpse is associated with a transition of the soul, it would surely make more sense to cremate the corpse immediately after death, as is done in India.

In addition to southern Borneo, Hertz also made use of data from Celebes, but important material on the mortuary rites found there appeared shortly after his essay was completed. In 1912, Adriani and Kruyt published a three-volume account of the Bare'e-speaking Toradja of central Celebes. Their account is rich in detail but poorly organized, so that a more recent reanalysis of their data on Toradja religion is welcome (Downs 1956). Downs is careful to indicate the variation found among Toradja communities, and we summarize only general features here.

Corpses are stored after death in a rough hut, built some distance from the village. A slave is designated to stay with the corpse to mop it clean of liquids of decay and to protect it from being stolen by witches. Mourning usages are similar to those of the Berawan, particularly with regard to the widow, who is walled up in mats, deprived of good food, and forbidden to stretch out her legs. Every few years, a mass second funeral takes place for all the accumulated skeletons, but the ceremony may happen more frequently if epidemics break out, or if plagues of mice attack the rice crop. These disasters are attributed to the unquiet dead. At the second funeral, the bones are brought from their rough huts to the village wrapped in a cloth. The slave that kept the death watch is thereafter freed, but is shunned by other people. Sometimes the bundles of bones are made into small effigies of the deceased by the addition of a mask. When the ceremony is completed, the bone bundles are inserted in a small wooden box and stored finally in a cave together with those of their kin (Downs 1956: 78–91).

Death as Transition

Meanwhile, the fate of the nonmaterial component of the deceased is that it has changed from *tanoana* to *angga* immediately upon death. The *angga* of the recently dead are greatly feared. They persistently return from the underworld in all manner of fearful guises, and their presence can be detected by smells of decomposition or low grumbling sounds. Their touch burns the skin, their breath causes dizziness, and they frequently frighten people at night. Constant small rites are performed to try to get them to return to the underworld. At the second funeral, a shaman summons the *angga* from the underworld or wherever they may be and instructs them in a chant to wash and dress themselves preparatory to going on their last journey to the underworld. This they accomplish by climbing through a hole in the ground off to the west, and dropping into the upper branches of a betel nut palm whose roots grow in the underworld. Safely arrived in the underworld, they are reunited with their dead relatives, at the same time that their bones are inserted in the cave with those of their ancestors.

As to the nature of the underworld, there are inconsistencies in Adriani and Kruyt's account. Some references report that the underworld is somber, but that the dead are content there anyway. Others say that on the completion of the rites of secondary treatment, the dead are allowed to leave the underworld and proceed to a joyful existence in the upperworld. The confusion may originate with Adriani and Kruyt, but not necessarily so. As we have seen, inconsistencies of this kind often go unremarked by their propounders. After the dead are settled into their final worlds, they join the company of the "revered ancestors" and are thought to exercise a benign influence. In particular, distinguished ancestors are vaguely conceived as guardian spirits of the community (Downs 1956: 31–2).

Toradja mortuary rites exhibit all the features that we expected to find, and incorporate the symbolism of the decaying corpse even more specifically than Berawan or Ma'anyan practices. The Ma'anyan are satisfied to allow the corpse to rot in the graveyard, removed from people, until they are ready for secondary treatment. The Berawan usually follow the same course of action, although they occasionally keep the remains within the longhouse in a sealed container with a drain tube. But the Toradja provide for the corpse to be watched over during the entire process of decay. The slave must sleep in the hut and minister to the corpse, which is laid out directly on the floor. The task is important as well as repulsive, for the corpse must not be allowed to fall into the hands of witches. It possesses the dual nature that was so much a feature of Berawan funerals.

Turning to our next case, Hertz makes only passing reference to funeral rites on the island of Bali, which was not brought under Dutch control until 1906–8, just as the death essay was being written. Nevertheless, Balinese mortuary practices involve secondary treatment, by cremation, for those who can afford it. Others receive simple burial only. All mortuary sequences follow a similar ritual pattern, but those of noblemen are on a far grander scale, with all manner of artistic and ritual refinements. Corpses are generally buried without great show of emotion, in a simple earth grave and without a coffin. The cadavers of priests and very prestigious individuals are not buried, but retained within the compound of the house on a special platform (Wirz 1928: 13, 20). The corpses of rulers are laid out in a pavilion erected for the purpose within the palace grounds, and attended by a slave who collects the products of decomposition for burial. This slave earns his freedom by this duty, but is shunned by other people in a manner reminiscent of Toradja practice (Covarrubias 1937: 386). After a minimum of forty-two days, preparations may begin for the cremation. This is a briefer intermediary period than those prescribed among the Berawan, Ma'anyan, or Toradja, but few people can afford to proceed immediately, and even the rich have elaborate preparations to make, so that long delays are the rule. Moreover, the minimal period is specifically to allow the corruption of the corpse to be completed (Wirz 1928: 17).

When preparations for a mass cremation ceremony are completed, the graves of commoners are dug up and the earth is raked over for pieces of bone. No great effort is made to collect all the bones, and it is possible to proceed even if *no* bones are found. The bones that are found are laid out in roughly their correct relationship to one another, and a crude effigy is built around them with herbs and flowers. Later this is packed into a bundle. Next the essence of the deceased is ritually captured in another small effigy. After a noisy all-night gathering, both the effigy containing the bones and that containing the spiritual component are loaded into a tall elaborately decorated tower, and rushed to the cremation ground by the sea. Many diversions are taken to confuse the departing dead, and there is much jostling, including mock battles for the control of the remains. Arriving at the cremation grounds, the effigies are taken down, loaded into coffins shaped to represent various animals according to the caste of the deceased, and burned. Later the ashes are strewn on the sea (Wirz 1928: 51–105; Hooykaas 1973: 22–3).

It has often been remarked that the culture of Bali is an amalgam of indigenous and imported Hindu elements (Boon 1977: 18–19). In the death rituals, the Indic element is shown by the casualness with which the corpse is treated. Bits of bone are pulled haphazardly out of the grave, and remains are poked about and jokingly urged to burn rapidly. This is in accordance with Hindu dogma that the body is but a container of the soul, and of little significance. However, Indonesian elements are also conspicuous. Balinese cremation resembles Ma'anyan rather than Indian practices in one important particular: It generally occurs *after* corruption of the corpse. Also, the efforts made to confuse the skeleton in its final journey suggest fear of the returning spirit. A similar polarity occurs in beliefs about the afterlife. The Hindu-derived doctrines speak of progression through an elaborate hierarchy of heavens and reincarnations, but this is the stuff of the priestly caste. Popular belief is dominated by a concern to settle the ghosts of the recently dead, who lead a restless existence. They roam around the graveyards and are irritable because of not having reached their final stage. They require constant small offerings (Hooykaas 1973: 22). Swellengrebel (1969: 203) remarks that the recently dead are demonic and are entitled to sustenance and offerings by way of exorcism. But a completely different attitude applies to the purified dead, who are venerated in household and clan temples. Consequently, the close relatives are anxious to see their dead cremated, even in modest style, as soon as possible. In the courtly, Hindu-dominated rituals of Bali, the symbolic identification that Hertz pointed out can still be discerned.

Application of Hertz where secondary treatment is not found   Having examined four cases – the Berawan, Ma'anyan, Toradja, and Balinese – where secondary treatment is found, we may seem to have identified a universal Indonesian conception of dying. But this is not so. For example, let us look briefly at the eschatology of the Iban of Borneo. (The locations of ethnic groups discussed in this chapter are shown in Figure 5.) The Iban are neighbors of the Berawan to the south and share many cultural features, such as longhouse residence. But they are far more

Figure 5. Indonesia and Borneo, showing the locations of ethnic groups discussed in the text.

numerous, and, what is most significant from our point of view, they do not practice secondary treatment of the dead.

Nor do they share Berawan ideas about death; their eschatology is radically different. Iban funerals are extremely rapid. The corpse is hurried out of the house soon after death, certainly on the same day. The men carrying the corpse to the graveyard stop at some convenient point along the way and prepare a rough coffin from a log cut from a softwood tree. The corpse is stuffed inside, and the coffin is tied up with rattan. Arriving at the graveyard, the coffin is buried in a shallow grave. Various grave goods are left and a marker may be set up, and then the funeral party returns rapidly to the longhouse. The corpse is not tampered with again, and the graveyard is full of old bones dug from their shallow graves by wild pigs and other animals (Gomes 1911: 134–42; Jensen 1974: 93–4).

This disregard for the corpse and its fate is in striking contrast to the attitudes of the Berawan. Moreover, the Iban concept of dying is very different. Gomes (1911: 134) describes how the living and the dead are conceived of as engaged in a struggle for the dying person. The relatives cry "*Pulai!*" at the near-corpse ("come back!"), and consider that the spirits of the dead are close at hand, pulling their new companion away from the living. This is very different from the Berawan spirits of the dead, who, far from coming to capture the newly dead, are unwilling to receive them into their company. This proximity of the dead explains the haste with which the Iban wish to have done with the corpse once death is pronounced.

The Iban ceremony that formally introduces the newly dead person to the spirits of the dead occurs on the *third day* after burial. A bundle of offerings is prepared, dedicated to the dead, and thrown out of the longhouse. Sometimes a song is sung recounting how this food is taken to the country of the dead by a bird. When the offerings are presented to the dead, they are pleased and warmly welcome their new member. Thereafter, the ghost of the dead person is not expected to trouble people (Gomes 1911: 139–41).

One subgroup of Iban celebrates festivals of the dead called *gawai hantu*. There are many varieties of Iban *gawai: gawai batu*, the festival of the whetstones; *gawai benih*, the festival of the seeds; *gawai kenyalong*, the hornbill festival; and others. The festival of the dead is not different in format from these other *gawai* (Jensen 1974: 198), and they do not mark a change in status of those who died since the last celebration. They are an attempt to gain the supernatural aid of famous warrior ancestors regardless of when those ancestors died (Gomes 1911: 195–6; Perham 1896: 208–9).

The Iban case demonstrates that even within Indonesia ideas of the fate of the soul are found that are radically different from those expressed in Berawan, Toradja, and Balinese funerals. This would not have surprised Hertz, who warned against the overextension of his analysis. "We must beware of attributing to the various representations a generality and an explanatory value which they do not have" (Hertz 1960: 48). As we have already emphasized, not all the arguments that Hertz advances in his essay are of the same level of generality. The Iban funeral does not undermine his analysis of secondary burial rites; it simply provides a *negative case*, or control.

However, there are cases that present a more serious challenge for Hertz. In the Lesser Sunda Islands of eastern Indonesia, death rites are found that incorporate many of the symbolic elements that derive from the metaphor of corporeal dissolution, but nevertheless do not involve secondary treatment of the corpse as defined in the previous section. Examples of this kind are described by James J. Fox from Roti (1973,

1977) and David Hicks from the Tetum of Timor (1976). We draw on material from the Mambai of Timor, described by Elizabeth Traube (1986).

First, the rites. At death, a corpse is immediately removed to the cult house of its agnatic descent group, where it is laid out on a mat. The corpse is dressed in ritually appropriate clothes, but is not put into a coffin. It is allowed to remain there for several days while all close kin are summoned. When the stench of the corpse can no longer be tolerated by the mourners, it is rolled into its mat and buried in the dancing ground at the center of the village. Because the dancing ground is not large, the bones of previous burials are often turned up in digging a fresh grave, and no great respect is accorded to these relics. In a ritually unimportant village, corpses may be buried just outside its perimeter. However, there is a festival or series of festivals that follow many years later that is concerned with the dead. This festival is called *maeta*, which means simply "death" or "the dead" (Traube 1986: 200–36).

At death, the nonmaterial component of the living person (*smakan*) becomes *maet smakan* (*maet* = dead person), and is conceived of as making a journey to the mountain of the dead to the west of the Mambai country. A vertical pole is erected beside the corpse, so that the soul may exit through the roof rather than using the door. The afterlife is considered to be much like the life of the living, but less burdened with troubles. The journeys of the dead are accompanied by elaborate ritual chants that name the places on the route.

The format of the festival of the dead is a repetition of the funeral, using a number of props to represent the already rotted corpse. The festival is held at irregular intervals to honor all those who have died since the previous one. It begins with a mimed reenactment of the death of an individual, who is represented by a pestle and mortar. After the inevitability of death is announced by divination, the implements are dressed in the cloths and ornaments used for a corpse. The kin are then summoned, as at a funeral. For the interment, the dead are represented by the betel nut bags that they used in life and which have been kept hanging in the cult house. It is these bags that are buried in the dancing ground, in a metaphorical second burial. Sacrifices and other presentations are made to the dead, who are thereby rendered wealthy and favorably disposed to the living. In the closing ritual of the festival, the dead are sent to their final home in the sea, and the festival is also called "to send away the dead." If this final rite is not performed, the dead remain on the mountain, and may be enriched by yet another festival at a later date.

The journey of the dead to the sea is vaguely associated with their transition from the recently dead to the long dead. But the association is not important, and it lies on the hazy edges of Mambai dogma. Some people think that all the dead, recent and long dead, attend important rituals and influence the affairs of humans. Others consider that only the recent dead have this role. Nor is the afterlife in the sea clearly conceived, except as a reservoir from which they may be reborn into the living.

Sensu stricto, the Mambai festival of the dead, is not an instance of Hertz's "great feast," either in the rites that are performed or in what those rites are believed to accomplish. They can therefore be seen as simply a negative case like the Iban. No secondary treatment of bones occurs. No fundamental transformation of the soul is accomplished that is geared to the fate of the corpse. The soul is not regarded as vindictive and in a miserable state during the putrescence of its vacated body. There is no horror of reanimated corpses, nor pronounced fear of the dead. In theory, the festival of the dead may occur immediately after death, and frequently it does not happen for twenty years.

However, these distinctions have to be drawn with great exactitude. From a slightly wider perspective, it is the *similarities* that are noticeable between this festival and rites of secondary treatment found elsewhere. The schedule of events is very similar to the Ma'anyan case: Invariably, at least a year goes by before the festival is made for any particular dead person, and then all those that have accumulated in the interim are dealt with jointly. Moreover, there is a transition of the soul accomplished at the festival, though in a rather weaker form than that found in Berawan rites. In the Berawan case, the soul moves from near and dangerous to far and benign. For the Mambai, it proceeds from relatively far away and generally helpful, to very far away and irrelevant (except as a supply of souls). Among the Mambai, the ghosts of the recently dead are not routinely dreaded, yet they cause alarm if they are seen, and if their mortuary rites are too long delayed, they may cause sickness.

But most of all, it is the constant reiteration in ritual language of the motif of the decaying corpse that is so strongly reminiscent of Hertz. The significance of this motif relates directly to fundamental ideas of Mambai religion and cosmology. These ideas are expressed in the most sacred and

esoteric of their myths, which only the most knowledgeable ritual specialists know in its entirety. It is a creation myth. Impregnated by Father
Heaven, Earth Mother gives birth to the mountains, the trees, and the
first people. Having instructed her children about mortuary rituals, she
dies. But her body does not entirely decompose. An outer layer forms
the "black earth," but beneath this topsoil formed out of her own body
the Mother remains whole and pure, her white milk undiminished by
death and decay. From this milk plants draw life, and in turn men and
animals feed on the plants (Traube 1986: 38–40, 215–16).

The debt that humans owe to the Mother for the gift of life is the
underlying motivation behind Mambai death rituals. That debt must be
paid back with their bodies, which return to black earth again. Failure
to return the debt would throw the entire cosmos out of kilter; plants
would not grow to nourish humans, and children would not be born.

We have seen that attitudes to death and the decomposition of corpses
are not universally the same. For the Berawan, with their fluttering spirits, corruption is an ugly necessity; only through it can the soul be
released from the appalling bonds of the flesh. But for the Mambai, the
same process takes on a positive, life-renewing quality in and of itself.
Where the Borneans, as Hertz showed, equate the fate of the soul with
the fate of the corpse, the Mambai make an even stronger association.
For them, disposal of the corpse affects the fate of the whole world of
living things. The power of Hertz's approach remains plain. It explains
why the Berawan recover the bones of the deceased, and also why the
Mambai sit by and watch for as long as they can tolerate it, while the
corpses of their kin rot away.

5

DEATH RITUALS AND LIFE VALUES: RITES OF PASSAGE RECONSIDERED

LIFE THEMES IN DEATH

Death is a transition; but it is only the last in a long chain of transitions. The moment of death is related not only to the process of afterlife, but also to the process of living, aging, and producing progeny. Death relates to life: to the recent life of the deceased, and to the life he or she has procreated and now leaves behind. There is an eternity of sorts on either side of the line that divides the quick from the dead. Life continues generation after generation, and in many societies it is this continuity that is focused on and enhanced during the rituals surrounding a death. The continuity of the living is a more palpable reality than the continuity of the dead. Consequently, it is common for life values of sexuality and fertility to dominate the symbolism of funerals.

Let us carry our comparison of the variety of Southeast Asian funerals to the westward limits of the Malayo-Polynesian culture area: to the island of Madagascar (see Figure 6). The forebears of the Malagasy inhabitants of the island sailed their outrigger canoes from Borneo and Indonesia thousands of miles across the Indian Ocean more than a millennium ago. Over the centuries in Madagascar, these Indonesians mixed with peoples of Arab and African descent to form the unique Malagasy culture and language. Even after centuries of mixing and blending, and after long isolation from the East, the Indonesian and Bornean ele-

Figure 6. Countries bordering the Indian Ocean, showing as the shaded area the Malayo-Polynesian culture area.

ments still dominate Malagasy culture. The linguistic evidence suggests that the Malagasy are most closely related to the Ma'anyan of Borneo (Dahl 1951).

The cultural diversity within Madagascar is almost as great as that in island Southeast Asia. The variety of funeral rites and tomb design is also great; some people construct large showy tombs, where other groups dispose of their dead in secret and camouflaged caves. Yet, despite the variation among the eighteen major ethnic groups that comprise the Malagasy people, the ritual of exhumation and reburial is of great importance in almost all regions of the island. For instance, the Merina people open the family tomb ever few years, bring out the skeletons, rewrap them in new cloths, add the newly exhumed relics of those who have died since the last general tomb opening, and then replace all the relics and close the tomb. As the dominant ethnic group, the Merina have moved away from their homeland near the capital city and spread throughout the island. For these general exhumation ceremonies, kin from all regions converge on their ancestral hamlet as an expression of family solidarity and to arrange practical matters such as marriages (Bloch 1971). Among the Sakalava of the western region, only the relics of royalty receive this sort of periodic attention. The royal ancestors belong, in one sense, to everyone. Commoners do not exhume and rebury their own dead, but rather they attend the annual ritual treatment of the "national ancestors."

Death as Transition

Among the Bara people of the South, the focus of this chapter, everyone is eventually exhumed and placed in a family tomb. Details of secondary treatment of the dead are not available for all the Malagasy peoples, and so it is difficult to chart all the variations with accuracy. But it is clear that secondary treatment of the skeletal remains is an important custom that is called on to give expression to various social and political values among the different ethnic groups.

These funeral rituals are the most important cultural institutions in traditional Malagasy societies. The expenditures of time and resources for death rituals and the maintenance of tombs are considerable, especially in light of the often meager economic base. The conspicuous entombment of the dead is the central activity in Malagasy systems of religion, economics, and social prestige. Even a casual visitor to Madagascar quickly becomes aware of the large role burial customs play in the lives of the people. In many parts of the island, tombs, whose elaborate and solid construction far exceeds the care given to the houses of the living, dominate the landscape. During the cool season, one finds the roads full of people traveling to their family reburial ceremonies. Even in the taxicab on the way from the international airport, the visitor reads on the official list of cab fares that the rental rate for exhumations is negotiable.

Let us contemplate for a moment the implications of this centrality of death in Malagasy culture, for most of us belong to a society in which death is kept on the periphery of our experience. In order to begin to understand the death rituals of the Malagasy, or of many of the other peoples considered in this study, it is necessary to see that the social and cultural context of funerals is utterly different from that in our society. Death rituals, especially the seasonal reburials, are, in much of Madagascar, as normal and as pervasive as is Christmas or the Fourth of July in the United States. The Malagasy funeral-related institutions are both private and public affairs of religious as well as social significance, and they are a great expense to individual families and a stimulus to the general economy. These activities are closely associated with positive and central familial, social, and political structures, and their connection deprives them of that sense of abnormality and near indecency that seems to hover around funerals in most Western societies.

There is in most Malagasy funerals the sort of emphasis on life and vitality that Wilson described for the Nyakyusa, and which he suggested may be a universal aspect of death rituals. Certainly the themes of rebirth, love, and sexuality as symbols transcending death have been explored by countless poets and dramatists. If people feel the need to confront death with an emphasis on life, then, nonetheless, the theme will be uniquely implemented in societies that put death and the dead at the center of their social and moral system.

In our society, both sexuality and death belong somewhat outside the normative and public values pertaining to the family and the community. Hence love and death, sex and death, rebirth and death provide symbols whose great power is partly derived from the fact that they oppose everyday institutions. The relationships are very different in Madagascar, where death and funeral customs pertain to the ancestral order that is at the heart of the normative social system. Furthermore, this ancestral system directly requires the birth of new generations, and the ancestors themselves are seen as the most important agents encouraging virility and fertility. Funerals, social order, fertility, and all that these entail are naturally and positively related in Madagascar. The combination of themes of death and sexuality contains little of the antisocial power that these themes evoke in our cultural tradition.

PROBLEMS WITH THE APPROACHES OF HERTZ AND VAN GENNEP

Both Hertz and van Gennep were familiar with the funeral customs of Madagascar and both made important use of the Malagasy data in their studies (Hertz 1960: 47–8; van Gennep 1960: 148–9). Van Gennep in particular was a leading authority on the religion of Madagascar, and the author of a major monograph on the topic (1904). Although the examples he cites in *The Rites of Passage* have a worldwide distribution, the elaboration of his theory is strongly influenced by his long familiarity with Malagasy ethnography.

There are, however, problems in the application of the theories of van Gennep and Hertz to the ritual data of Madagascar. Both viewed such rituals as a symbolic representation of the ambiguous liminal state of the deceased while in passage from life toward some fixed eternal condition. But, in spite of the widespread custom of secondary treatment of the dead in Madagascar, the emphasis on beliefs about the afterworld present in our Indonesian examples is lacking in Madagascar. There are few concepts of a journey of the soul, or of a land of the dead off somewhere in the distance. The dead reside in the tomb. This is not to say that eschatological concepts are entirely lacking. It is just that they are not important enough, explicit enough, or central enough to the culture to provide a basis for such elaborate rites of burial and reburial. Bloch (1971) noted this difficulty in his study of the secondary burial rituals of the Merina. He asked about the world of the dead and received scant information.

Hertz identified a metaphorical relationship between corpse and soul that makes sense of the rituals, large and small, of death in Borneo. The same is not true in Madagascar. There, a different significance is placed on the separation of bone and flesh that is celebrated in the rites of secondary treatment. In view of the discussion of cultural universals in Chapter 3, it comes as no surprise that there are symbolic uses of the corpse that achieve considerable generality without becoming universal even within a particular culture area. How these differential symbolic elaborations arose is a matter for speculation. Meanwhile, it is interesting to note that there are echoes of Malagasy notions about death in Bornean funerals, just as eschatological ideas are not entirely absent in Madagascar.

Van Gennep's notion that a funeral ritual can be seen as a transition that begins with the separation of the deceased from life and ends with his or her incorporation into the world of the dead is merely a vague truism unless it is positively related to the values of the particular culture. The continued relevance of van Gennep's notion is not due to the tripartite analytical scheme itself, but to the creative way it can be combined with cultural values to grasp the conceptual vitality of each ritual. In following this theoretical approach, it is necessary not merely to apply an old formula to new rituals, but in a sense to create anew the rites of passage in a dynamic relationship among the logic of the schema (transitions need beginnings and ends), biological facts (corpses rot), and culturally specific symbolizations.

The most striking aspect of Malagasy funerals is the bawdy and drunken revelry enjoined on the guests. Malagasy participants state that these lively events are necessary because the deceased is in transition. He or she is isolated and lonely and needs to be amused and entertained. But such an explanation is obviously incomplete. It fails to tell us why these particular forms of entertainment are seen as the appropriate amusement for the spirit of a recently departed relative. Why drunkenness, sexual liaisons, and bawdy songs? Why not respectful hymns of praise or a decorous show of family morality and solidarity? To answer this, and provide an analysis of the specific symbolic content of Malagasy funerals, one must look away from beliefs about ghosts and the hereafter and examine basic values and concepts about the nature and meaning of life.

BARA LIFE VALUES:
ORDER AND VITALITY

We focus the rest of this chapter on one ethnic group of Madagascar, the Bara, sedentary pastoralists of the island's southern plains. Only by looking at one situation in some detail can we evaluate the several analytic aspects that have been discussed so far in this book. In a single case, we can view the complex interplay of the expression of emotion, ritual action, specific beliefs, the universal rite-of-passage schema, and the phoenix theme of rebirth with those basic values and categories that are pervasively important to Bara social life. The Bara, of course, cannot stand as a substitute for any other society either within or outside Madagascar. But they can stand as a demonstration of how people of one culture face squarely the fact of death.

A difficulty in the analysis of Bara funerals stems from the fact that although the rite-of-passage approach stresses the ambiguous and transitory aspect of dying, important Bara values stress that it is life that is transitory, and dying that is tragically unambiguous. In terms of the Bara phenomenology of the person, life is maintained by a tenuously balanced combination of what can be referred to as "order" and "vitality." As a biological being, a person is formed when the fertile blood of the mother's womb is ordered and arranged by the sperm of the father during sexual intercourse. To be socially and economically successful, an individual must balance out his or her relationships with his mother's and father's families. A person's life is seen as a journey leading gradually from mother's womb to father's tomb. Bara kin groups, if they are to maintain themselves, must balance their members' desire for agnatic solidarity against the need to maintain affinal alliances. Dying, tombs, ancestors, father, and social order are explicitly associated by the Bara. Keeping this in mind, we seek to explain Bara funeral behavior with the hypothesis that they view death as an excess of order upsetting the life-sustaining balance, and that much of the funeral behavior is an attempt to redress the imbalance through a symbolic increase in vitality.

By formalizing these Bara notions of order and vitality into a table of oppositions and extensions, it is possible to begin to understand how such conceptions articulate with the ritual behavior.

Order	Vitality
male	female
father	mother
semen	blood
bone	flesh
sterility	fecundity
dying	birth
tomb	womb

However, oppositions include relationships of many different natures.

Consider the pairs black and white, and odd and even. . . . The first pair admits intermediates (grey and other colors), but the second pair does not. It is not the case that all colors are either black or white, but every whole number is either odd or even. [Lloyd 1966: 87]

Additionally, some terms admit only one opposition, whereas others may be opposed to several terms. The obvious term to pair with "male" is "female"; but "father" can as easily be opposed to "son" or "mother's brother" as to "mother," depending on the context. By examining the list of opposed pairs in terms of the varying natures of the oppositions, it is possible to begin to see in what ways the notion of death as a transition relates specifically to Bara culture.

As one moves down the columns, the relationships of opposition become more and more extreme. The upper pairs are each complementary, with the two poles combining to produce viable existence (male/female, father/mother, semen/blood, bone/flesh). But for the other three pairs, this complementarity is replaced by a profound antagonism. In fact, this antagonism is so pronounced as to be almost inexpressible, for as the one column progresses toward the maximal order of the tomb, the other column progresses toward maximal vitality and chaos. We have

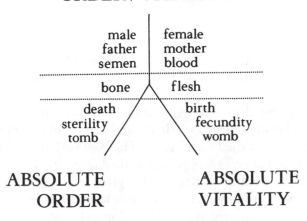

Figure 7. Bara concepts of the person.

used the terms "fecundity," "birth," and "womb" merely to indicate the sorts of attributes the Bara view in opposition to death. But actually, the opposite of pure order cannot be expressed in an orderly fashion. Reconsidering the list of symbolic oppositions and extensions, it is clear that there are two different relationships of opposition represented, one complementary and one antagonistic. The pair flesh/bone partakes of both these forms of opposition. Bone and flesh are complementary in the human body but become antagonistic when breath has ceased. The two columns of the list can be elaborated to express the change in the nature of the symbolic opposition that accompanies dying.

The corpse clearly occupies a liminal state between that conjunction of bone and flesh that is considered "life" and that separation of these substances that is considered "death." As Hertz and van Gennep explained long ago, an understanding of the liminal nature of the corpse does much to explain the rites of burial, exhumation, and reburial. The sexual aspects of these rituals relate to the mortal consequences of liminality: the dead, sterile order of bone takes dominion over the ebbing vitality of the decomposing flesh. A state of mediated equilibrium between order and vitality has become a state of pure, fatal order. This extreme aspect of order cannot be mediated, but can only be opposed by the most extreme aspects of vitality. The sex and sex-related activities of the funeral nights are symbolic ammunition in the open warfare between the extreme ends of the polar continuum of the human condition (see Figure 7).

THE BARA FUNERAL SEQUENCE:
BURIAL, GATHERING, REBURIAL

Let us bring this abstract interpretation down to earth and see how the opposition between male orderliness and female vitality is worked out in the activities of the funeral-goers. The Bara perform a series of three ceremonies in the process of providing final disposition for each person. There are (1) the burial, which takes place in the first few days after death; (2) the gathering, which is a great feast celebrated after the harvest following the death; and (3) the exhumation and reburial after the corpse has completely dried and the flesh rotted away. This is the sequence for the deceased, but the living experience these rituals somewhat differently. Death and burial are often shocking events that disrupt the normal flow of village activity. But the gathering and reburial events are experienced as an annual season of festivities during which families go first to one gathering, and then, perhaps the following week, to another, or to a nearby reburial celebration. It is partly in this sense that we suggested that funeral ritual in Madagascar is somewhat like Christmas to Western Christians. It is a seasonal event, which is highly sociable, but also deadly serious. We will consider these rites in order – burial, gathering, reburial – and, in so doing, we can observe the relevance of van Gennep and Hertz's insights.

Burial   The radical separation at death of the "male" and "female" components of the person is dramatically established in the first few moments after breath has ceased. The death is not immediately acknowledged or announced, but the preparation of the body and houses are quickly and silently begun. A male and a female house are selected. The corpse will rest in the female house for three days. Here women will gather and keep a long vigil punctuated with periods of loud ritual weeping. For this reason, the female house is also called "the house of many tears." In the "male house," the men of the stricken family will receive male visitors from whom they accept stylized expressions of condolence. The formality in the "male house" is striking with regard both to seating patterns and verbal exchanges. Here also the men will keep a vigil and organize the logistics of burial. At first, while these two houses are being cleared and arranged, all are enjoined to silence, and weeping is forbidden. The most important task is the preparation of the body. The eyelids and jaw are closed. The limbs are straightened and the body is placed on its back. The jaw and limbs may be tied in place until the postmortem stiffening sets in. Directly after breathing ceases, the person is divided in two, as it were. The male aspect, deriving from the soon-to-be-joined ancestors, is represented in one house, from which the burial is directed. Yet the corpse remains with the living, with the women, for a little longer.

The rigid separation of males and females is broken during the nighttime festivities. Girls must leave the "house of many tears" to sing and dance in the courtyard. The young men come out to watch, and gradually join in. Rum and food are served, a musician is hired, and, little by little, the funeral generates an orgy of sorts. These festivities exhibit a close, almost licentious relationship between males and females that is most unlike the normal cross-sex behavior patterns. All in all, the burial is a ritual of extremes. The sexes are almost absolutely separated by day and enjoined to an obscene, boisterous togetherness by night. There is also an extreme contrast in sound: Funeral activities are separated from the preceding normality by total silence at the time of death, which is then followed by loud wailing, singing, shouting, and gun shooting.

On the third day, the men enter the "house of many tears," put the body in a coffin, and take it outdoors over the tearful protests of the women. The coffin is covered with a cloth, which must be new and in an unsewn, unfinished state. At this point the coffin is carried around and around the "house of many tears" while unhusked, fertile rice is sprinkled in its wake. Several gunshots may be fired and the procession heads toward the burial mountain several miles away. The funeral procession stretches out over the countryside with the youths and young girls quickly leading the way with the coffin, followed at a distance by adult men, then women and children, and finally the family cattle herded at the rear. The youths with the coffin, the so-called "strong birds," pull farther and farther in advance, running all the way, carrying the coffin in relays. Only youths who have had sexual experience can take part in this episode, which is represented as a sexual contest between the girls and the boys for possession of the corpse.

Death as Transition

The procession halts and regroups at a prearranged place about halfway to the mountain. At this point, the cattle are brought up and stampeded around and around the coffin while the young men vie with one another in the somewhat risky sport of cattle wrestling, which consists of leaping up onto the hump of one of the members of the stampeding herd and holding on as long as possible. Finally, the young men and girls go on with the coffin to the burial cave, accompanied by two or three older men to ensure a proper burial. The remainder of the people sit and wait for the party's return.

At the tomb, an elder acting as "owner of the death" approaches, sprinkles rum on the entrance, and announces the presence of the mourners to the ancestors. The rocks sealing the cave entrance are taken away, and the principal workers are served rum. The coffin is slid head first into the small opening of the tomb-cave, but most of the assistants feel safer entering the tomb feet first, in contrast to the corpse. After the coffin is properly placed inside, and the assistants have come out, the entrance is carefully closed again. The elder then addresses the ancestors within:

> Here is your grandchild.
> Born here. Do not push him
> away, even from here.

Then the elder picks up a green branch and raps the entrance to the tomb several times, addressing the newly deceased:

> There you are, brother.
> If someone has bewitched you,
> then look for this tree.
> If it is God [Gods] who has taken you,
> who can command God, brother?
> But if it is merely a person
> who has bewitched you,
> Then you take him, you bewitch him.

People say that the branch is like the new corpse, cut off but still wet, and that before either is dry, the witch too will die.

Gathering   The gathering is the biggest, most important and most elaborate event in Bara social life. Whereas at the burial ceremony there may be 50 to 100 people, as many as 500 people may attend a gathering. Whole families walk ten, twenty, or thirty miles and then move into the host village for several days. A hundred liters of rum are considered very adequate for a burial ceremony, but at a gathering there are often 500 liters. Ten or twelve cattle are slaughtered, providing abundant beef for all. The gathering is essentially a conspicuous display of wealth. The rum is paraded before the people to be admired, and anticipated, likewise the cattle. Girls dressed in their finest clothes parade before the crowd. All expenditures are announced to the public: the fee for the dance specialists, the amounts of money given to the wrestlers and cattle riders, the number of slaughtered cattle, and most important, the amount of rum. Normally, the Bara are quite modest about their material success, and they never boast of, or even admit to, the size of their herds or the success of their harvests. But a gathering is not a time for modesty.

Although these activities are largely a grand extension of the earlier burial ceremony, the gathering does not exhibit the extreme polarities that characterize the burial. In particular, the relations between the sexes are more normal. There is a women's hut and a men's hut as at the burial, but now women and men often enter the opposite hut for a variety of reasons. The young men and girls dance together at night, form liaisons, and couple discreetly; but their public demeanor is somewhat reserved. Bawdy songs and sexual taunts are notably absent. Also, the paradox of extreme grief and great celebration is diminished with the passage of time. Death and burial are sudden, unplanned-for, shocking, events. Gatherings, on the other hand, are prepared, organized celebrations that occur each year at the same season. So, in spite of the huge consumption of resources and its association with the activities surrounding death, the gathering partakes of a regularity and normality that clearly distinguish it from the burial ceremony.

There is, however, a dark side to the gathering, which is due to the danger of witchcraft. A witch causes illness or death by deftly slipping a minute amount of evil medicine into rum or food while serving it to the victim. Rum is considered especially dangerous in this regard, and I have seen Bara order that a liter bottle of valuable rum be poured out because its cork seemed to have been disturbed. Also witchcraft medicine is transferred from one person to another by being placed on the genitals before sexual intercourse. In cases of adultery, incest, and witchcraft, the victim suffers from a similar malady: a grotesque and fatal swelling of the stomach. It is no wonder, given this analogy between witchcraft, sexual excess, and gluttony, that a ceremony at which hundreds of people eat, drink rum, and copulate should generate a degree of inquietude regarding witches. Additionally, it is the dry season; the "wet branch" and the corpse are drying out fast. If the man was killed by witchcraft, time is running out for the responsible party. A gathering, then, is particularly dangerous, both because it is a perfect opportunity for witches in general, and because it is seen as the logical time for specific witchcraft attacks in retaliation for the death that has already occurred.

In summary, the gathering is characterized by multiple but related dangers. The standard entertainments of wrestling, cattle riding, and specialized dancing are all believed to be dangerous to the practitioners, who must carry protective charms and observe numerous taboos. The risks of witchcraft, sex, incest, and adultery have already been explained. Rum is considered extremely dangerous, not only as a vehicle for witchcraft, but also because of its power of intoxication. I have seen gatherings that ended in large-scale fighting or individual hatchet attacks. Often, all the spears, clubs, walking sticks, and rifles, which Bara men always carry to these affairs, are collected and placed in a large pile some distance away before the rum is served. The occasion is beset by what a Western observer would classify as both natural and supernatural dangers, but the Bara do not seem to make such a distinction. They are concerned with the danger of unrestrained, excessive, and destructive vigor, whether it comes as a hatchet attack or a witchcraft attack.

Reburial   At the first burial ceremony, the deceased is placed in an individual coffin and put in the family tomb or in some other temporary location. After the flesh has decayed, the body is exhumed and the bones are cleaned and then put in the final resting place in the tomb. This reburial ceremony, which like the gathering takes place during the dry season following the harvest, is referred to by several names and euphemisms such as "doing the corpse," "dropping the tree or branch," and "moving the dried-out one." The rite lasts only one day and, although there is usually rum, beef, music, and dancing, it is a smaller affair than the gathering. It is, however, ritually more important than the gathering. Although reburial can be delayed for many years, it is an absolute obligation of the descendants toward the deceased.

Death Rituals and Life Values

Inside the tomb are numerous large, decorated, communal caskets, each containing the dried bones of perhaps ten persons. The number of caskets varies, but the tomb of a well-established family may contain between ten and fifteen of these caskets. To the north are grouped the caskets containing the bones of all the male ancestors. Each skeleton is placed in its rightful position with that of its father. At the south, by the door, are grouped the caskets holding the bones of the female agnates. The bones of a woman are grouped with those of her sister, father's sister, and brother's daughter. Also in the female casket are the bones of young children of female agnates. These skeletons properly belong to the tomb of the father, but are given to their mother's family as an affinal prestation. Women are always buried in the tomb of the father, never with the husband. This common custom, "dividing the children," is the only way a woman can be buried with immediate kin. Otherwise a woman is cut off in death from her father (with whom she shares a common tomb but not a common casket), mother, husband, and children. The male caskets embody a lineal order of grandfather, son, and grandson; the female caskets are like collection boxes for the skeletal residue of this agnatic system.

If a corpse is to be moved from another location to the official tomb, then the "strong birds" leave early in the morning to exhume the body. The composition of the group of "strong birds" is very much like that at the burial, but now there are more senior male relatives of the deceased. At the opening of the temporary tomb (usually another cave), the "strong birds" take care to announce themselves, sprinkle a little rum on the rocks, and then drink the remainder. The old coffin is pulled out and opened and then the bones are scraped clean, rubbed with cow grease, and placed in a new cloth. All signs of grief are forbidden during these preparations, just as they are forbidden during the preparations immediately following death. The return down the mountain is also much like the burial procession, with everyone running and the boys carrying the remains in relays. They do not return to the village, but join the rest of the people already gathered at a prearranged location out on the savannah. There is one last wailing scene with both male and female kin joining in, and then the "strong birds" pick up the remains, perhaps a new casket, as well as clothing for the deceased, and start on the merry run up to the final tomb.

The tomb is opened with the usual rum sprinkling and drinking; the remains and other objects are taken inside and arranged. At reburial, new clothing is placed near the corpse to replace the now rotted unfinished cloth in which he or she was originally buried. The clothes are his or her "best," and often include Western items such as long trousers, shoes, used military uniforms, and even an occasional umbrella. One additional item brought to the tomb is a pair of horns from a newly slaughtered ox to be placed with those from previous reburials. At some tombs, there are as many as 100 pairs of ox horns placed in front of the wall opposite where the male caskets are grouped. When these arrangements are completed, the "strong birds" rejoin the group down in the savannah for a celebration, with more beef and rum.

Bara reburial rites are much like the burial and gathering ceremonies. But in spite of the similarity of the feasting, drinking, dancing, running, and general merrymaking, there are important differences. The reburial activities take place entirely by day and entirely out of the village. There is little of the extreme polarity and paradox of the original burial, and little of the dangerous element so conspicuous at the gathering. Bawdy songs, professional dance troupes, wrestling matches, and cattle-riding contests would all be out of place at a reburial. Not surprisingly, the reburial signals a return to normality, one important aspect of which is that the deceased's spouse is finally free to remarry.

SYMBOLIC GENERATION OF "VITALITY"

The full funeral sequence is long and complex. Let us now focus our attention on the symbolism of one brief phase leading up to the initial burial. Dying, to the Bara, involves an imbalance in the components of human life. As we have indicated, the extreme and fatal dominion of "male" order must be countered by a radical increase of "female" vitality. Vitality is represented in songs, dances, and contests that express the interrelated themes of sex, birth, life, disorder, incest, danger, war, and fertility.

Songs   These powerful themes are most explicitly presented in the lyrics of the girls' songs that continue throughout the preburial nighttime festivities. New songs come into fashion every year and the most popular songs of even recent years are rarely heard. Like popular music in much of the world, new songs rapidly replace old, but the themes remain the same from year to year. The most popular funeral song of 1970 was a clever and rousing piece of ribald double entendre.

> Now hide it
> Now hide it, boys
> Now hide it because there is a death
> Together let us copulate
> Together let us copulate, boys
> Now hide it
> Now hide it because there is a death
>
> "Brroo" flies the quail
> To perch at the head of the *sely* tree
> The eye wants to sleep?
> They eye wants to copulate
>
> "Brroo" flies the quail
> To perch on a bump of a *sakoa* tree
> The eye wants to copulate
> The eye wants to ejaculate
>
> "Brroo" flies the quail
> To perch at the head of the mud
> Hide it!
> Hide it boys!
> Now hide it because there is a death
> Together let us copulate
> Together let us copulate
> Whether big
> Whether little
> Now hide it!

The onomatopoeic "brroo" of the quail is an expression commonly used to refer to ejaculation in sexual intercourse. The word for quail is also the word for belly. The word for eye also refers generally to any center, hole, circle, or vortex, in this case, the vagina. The vagina is also suggested by the word for mud, which refers generally to any wet slime or slipperiness. And the quail, according to the Bara, is quite incapable of perching either at the top or the lower branches of a tree. There is the suggestive image of the quivering quail looking for the appropriate place to hide. First it tries the head of a tree, then a lower knob, and finally settles into the stickiness below. The comparison between these Bara songs and the long funeral travelogues of the Berawan elders discussed in Chapter 4 is interesting. Playful sexual themes are also present in the Berawan song cycle, but they play a subordinate role to the songs pertaining to the land of the dead. By contrast, the sexual theme dominates all the funeral singing of the Bara.

Another popular funeral song takes up a serious related theme as the girls sing a lament on the difficulties of childbirth. This song, like all these funeral songs, is sung at funerals and at no other time.

> O bright red
> O I am hurting now
> O bright red
> I am hurting from this birth
> O bright red
> My breasts have fallen heavily
> O I hurt, mother
> Massage my stomach
> Make it easier

Energy   When referring to participation in these preburial vigils, the Bara say they are going to await *faha*. The word *faha* is difficult to translate, but its various usages and connotations include: nourishment, ration, a live prestation to a visitor, rifle cartridge, the winding of a clock, elasticity, rebound, resiliency, and energy. Bara most commonly use the word in referring to a thin cow (lacks *faha*) and as a name for those curing ceremonies that aim to strengthen one who has been weakened by illness. In general, *faha* signifies vitality, but the emphasis is on a potential, stored-up vitality rather than on the dissipation of energy in activity.

Here again there are parallels with Berawan practices. At Berawan funerals, there is an emphasis on lively, even tumultuous, socializing and play. In Chapter 3 we described several energetic games in connection with the making of noise. Horseplay among young people is common at funerals and is encouraged by the older folk. Frequently this involves an element of flirtation, as when a teenage girl attempts to rub pot black on the face of a young man. Often such ambushes result in chases up and down the longhouse, and melees involving dozens of people. During this skylarking more body contact between the sexes is allowed than would normally be tolerated, and young people think of funerals as an opportunity to initiate new sexual liaisons. Although themes of vitality play a less conspicuous part in Berawan than in Bara funerals, Berawan do express the sentiment that displays of exuberance are proper in order to offset the presence of death. The sleepy and the comatose are fair game for all manner of practical jokes.

Dance   The concept of storing up vitality is perhaps evident in the mode of dancing associated with Bara funeral activities. The meaning of a dance style is less explicit than that of the lyrics of a song and perhaps less amenable to analysis. However, there is a definite contrast in style between funeral dancing and all other Bara dancing. In addition to the three funeral ceremonies, Bara also dance at circumcision and spirit-possession ceremonies. On these occasions, the dancing is wild and unrestrained, with dancers individually showing off their skills. At funerals, the girls dance in a slow, tight circle in front of the "house of many tears." One by one, the boys join so that there are often two or three circles, one inside another. The dancers in the innermost circle move slowly forward, dancing in a tense double-time, while those in the larger outer ring come down hard on the beat. Often one or two preadolescent boys dance at a languid half-rhythm very quickly around the outside of the other circles. Each succeeding circle (from outside) is tighter, faster rhythmed, and slower moving. The dance gives the appearance of winding a human clock spring. It is this dancing combined with the girls running (while singing) around and around the hut containing the body that are seen by the Bara as the epitome of *faha*, vitality.

Cattle   Cattle play important roles in Bara funeral events in two ways. First, there is the little cattle wrestling at the burial and gathering ceremonies. This sport of stampeding the herd around and around resembles a bovine version of the funeral dances (see Figure 8). When describing the event, Bara boys always emphasize the snorting, panting, and bucking of the cattle as signs of intense vitality. This sport is practiced at only one other occasion and that is at the sowing of the rice fields when the trampling hooves perform a plowlike function. The association of cattle

Figure 8. Cattle wrestling at a Bara funeral.

with the fertility of the earth is also clear in a number of Bara legends. In one such tale, the cow states:

When I die do not bury me in a tomb but your stomachs shall be my tomb. My head you shall not eat. Bury it in the earth. After one week corn sprouts and rice, manioc, and sweet potatoes. And the herd too shall give you life. And this is why you must offer up the First Fruits in thanksgiving. [Faublée 1947: 381]

Another legend recounts how God was once about to give all the animals a potion of life so that death would be eradicated. The cow accidentally drank the entire supply and because there was no more to be had God advised the other animals to kill the cow during times of danger and eat of its flesh, which contains the force of life. This relates to the second role of cattle in the funeral events, namely the slaughter of numerous cattle to provide for the feasting. The killing of the cattle is done differently at funeral events than at all other ceremonies. Whereas in other ceremonies cattle are carefully sacrificed to facilitate communication with

126

the ancestors, at funerals cattle are slaughtered en masse so that the living can protect themselves by absorbing the force of life inherent in beef.

Chaos: incest and war   An important aspect of the representation of vitality is the idea that it is chaotic, as opposed to the order of the ancestor cult. In one of the songs, the girls call on the boys to act crazy, unrestrained, and shameless during the funeral fete. It is in this regard that rum takes on special significance. Rum is served not merely because intoxication is pleasant, but because disorderly conduct is essential.

The most dramatic aspect of the generation of disorder is manifest in the tolerance of incest. For the neighboring Betsileo funerals, Father Dubois describes what he considers "the moment of horror," when everyone copulates incognito with a total disregard for incest regulations (1938: 666). The Bara do not tolerate unexpiated incestuous intercourse, not even at funerals; but the songs, dances, and bawdy remarks exchanged among kin at a funeral would at any other time require the sacrifice of a cow in expiation. An actual attempt at intercourse with a relative at a funeral celebration constitutes a wrong and must be expiated. But the attitude of the Bara toward such incest is that it is an inevitable part of the funeral fetes and the offender should pay the penalty (one cow, bony) with good humor. The incestuous behavior of the participants in the burial and the gathering celebrations is in opposition to the fundamental Bara principle of moral and social order.

Dance troupes are also viewed as possessing dangerous and asocial qualities. They are hired for virtually every gathering and occasionally for a burial, if the family can afford it, but they are prohibited from singing or dancing at any other function. Should such performers sing to a sick person, it is said that the patient will die. At the gathering celebration, the dancers perform only during daylight to stimulate and amuse the guests. At night, with the occasional exception of early in the first evening, it is considered far too dangerous to have them performing. They may not enter the village before the start of the gathering celebration and must be out of the village before the final closing ceremony. They dress outrageously. The men wear their hair in long braids entwined with coins and bells. They are explicitly dressed in the symbols of warriorhood, and no dancer ever dances without his elaborate spear. The dancing is wild and sexual, with particularly energetic dances being done to entice even more money from members of the audience. The dancers do not merely have low status, but are seen as being, in a sense, outside the system of social and moral order.

RESOLUTION: INTERCOURSE AND REBIRTH

During the time following death, vitality is generated through the various excesses of the funeral celebration, in an effort to counterbalance the excessive order of death. The instability of the situation derives from the antagonism between the bone and the flesh of the corpse, the resolution depends on removing the corpse from the world of the living. For as long as the corpse, in which bone is taking dominion over flesh, remains in the village, the life-giving balance is impossible. In another Bara legend, a man with ten cows asks the king for advice because his cows are barren. The king says this is because the man did not bury his father, who died when he was young. The man then holds a funeral, builds a tomb, kills cattle, and buries his father. Soon there are many new calves and his wife also gives birth.

The actual burial takes the form of a double metaphor of sexual intercourse and birth. The funeral procession resembles a "burial by capture," as the men enter (for the first time) the "house of many tears" and take away the coffin over the tearful protests of the women. The young men then run, carrying the coffin in relays, toward the mountain of the ancestors. A group of young girls, often with their hair and clothes disheveled, run to catch up to the coffin bearers, and to distract and detain them from their task. Often the girls intervene physically to stop the journey to the tomb and there ensues a tug-of-war over the coffin as the girls try to pull it back to the village. When this fails, the girls may run ahead and line up across the boys' path. The boys then charge, using the coffin as a battering ram to penetrate this female barrier.

This sexual symbolism is continued at the tomb itself as the coffin is poked head first into the small hole at the mouth of the cave. But the symbolism shifts as attention focuses on the arrival of the deceased among his ancestors. The dominant theme becomes that of birth, with the deceased entering the world of the ancestors head first like a fetus. When asked to comment on the meaning of burial, the Bara invariably use the metaphor of birth. This theme is evident as well in the song cited earlier and in the tomb-side address to the ancestors: "Here is your grandchild, born here. Do not push him away, even from here." Just as one must be born into the world of the living, so must one also be born out of it and into the world of the dead.

Bara burial is indeed concerned with transition, but the Bara recognize only one mode of transition that is adequate for changing the state of being for a human: sexual intercourse and birth. Not unexpectedly, the process of being born into the world of the dead is the inverse of the process of entering the world of the living. Biological conception begins with the chaotic fecundity of the mother's womb and menstrual blood, to which must be added the ordering power of the father's semen. Order is added to fertile vitality. Entering the tomb, however, is quite the reverse. The cessation of life and breath in the deceased has created a situation of sterility, which must be offset to accomplish the difficult birth into the world of the ancestors. It is not enough merely to bury someone, merely to dispose of the body. The survivors must bring about the renewed conception and rebirth of their deceased kin into the world of the ancestors. This process is as difficult and risky as childbirth. Should it fail, the consequence is nothing short of catastrophic infertility, with the deceased remaining like a dead fetus in the womb of the survivors' world.

TRANSITION AND LIFE

Among the Bara, the familiar phases of the rite of passage are expressed through a unique configuration of values relating to the opposition between flesh and bone. Because the notions of flesh and bone are closely associated with ideas of male and female, father's line and mother's line, ancestors and affines, and the ultimate human problem of reconciling unchanging order with the disruption of necessary renewal, the corpse is a powerful symbol relating the fate of the individual to the ongoing moral order of society. The imbalance of the male and female components of the corpse threatens the balance of the very same components in the Bara social and moral universe, and only through their symbolic manipulation can the corpse be removed.

The burial is only the first rite, however. Each of the three Bara funeral ceremonies concentrates on liminality of a different sort. The burial is largely concerned with the transition of the corpse. The gathering is distinguished from the other ceremonies by the concern shown toward the reordering of social relationships that have been altered by the loss of a kinsman. This is manifest in the witchcraft fears and accusations that concern the settling of old scores, especially with regard to the death of the person in whose honor the gathering is held. The affair closes with the granting of new names to the deceased and to some of the living, followed by a short speech stating that it is time to leave off yearning for the departed.

The reburial focuses on the transition of the remains from the individual coffin to the final resting place in the communal coffin containing the bones of agnatic kin. The ritual itself is a miniature and subdued replication of the original burial. The exhumation is marked by the same mandatory silence and prohibition of weeping that mark the moment of death itself. There is a festive procession between the temporary burial place and the family tomb, ending with the placement of the bones in their proper place and the closing of the tomb. Separation, transition, incorporation. It is a rite of passage concerned with arranging the ambiguities that death creates in the organization of the ancestors. The proper relationship between the worlds of the ancestors and the living is reestablished.

Additionally, one can view the whole funeral sequence as a single rite of passage, seeing the original burial as a rite of separation, the gathering as a period of liminality, and the reburial as the ceremony of reintegration. It is a question of how wide a perspective one takes. There are transitions within transitions. For the Bara, all of life is ultimately a transition and only a perspective wide enough to include birth allows an understanding of death.

The deepest Bara value is vividly expressed in one of their legends about the origin of death. God gave the first man and woman a choice between two kinds of death. They could die like the moon, being reborn over and over. Or they could die like the tree, which puts forth new seeds and, although dying itself, lives on through its progeny. It was a difficult decision, but the first man and woman chose to have children even at the cost of their own lives. And which of us, asks the storyteller, would not make the same choice today?

PART III

THE ROYAL CORPSE
AND THE BODY POLITIC

6

THE DEAD KING

There is a paradox about death. On the one hand, it is the great leveler, badge of our common mortality. As Hamlet reflects:

> Alexander died, Alexander was buried, Alexander returneth
> to dust; the dust is earth; of earth we make loam;
> and why of that loam whereto he was
> converted might they not stop a beer barrel?
> Imperious Caesar, dead and turned to clay,
> Might stop a hole to keep the wind away.
> O, that that earth which kept the world in awe
> should patch a wall t'expel the winter's flaw!
>
> *(Hamlet, Act V, scene i)*

Yet, earlier in the play, the worldly Rosencrantz conveys a very different sentiment:

> The cess of majesty
> Dies not alone, but like a gulf doth draw
> What's near it with it; or 'tis like a massy wheel
> Fixed on the summit of the highest mount,
> To whose huge spokes ten thousand lesser things
> Are mortised and adjoined which when it falls,

Royal Corpse and Body Politic

Each small annexment, petty consequence,
Attends the boisterous ruin. Never alone
Did the king sigh, but with a general groan.
(*Hamlet, Act III, scene iii*)

It is to this latter theme that we attend in Part III of the book. We examine the funeral rites of great men in societies large and small: the Dinka "masters of the spear" and the pharaohs of Egypt; the chiefs of Borneo and the monarchs of Renaissance France. For present purposes, we stretch the word "king" to embrace them all.

In some of the stricter sects of Islam a conscious effort is made to stress the "leveling" aspect of death. So, for instance, the kings of Saudi Arabia are buried with spartan simplicity, their only monuments being rough piles of stones. They are the exception. More frequently, the death of a king sets off a tremor of ritual activity that climaxes in a display of national pomp unrivaled even by the coronation of a successor.

Royal death rites are special because they are part of a political drama in which many people have a stake. Especially in kingdoms in which the state was personified by the monarch, the king's funeral was an event that reverberated with far-reaching political and cosmological implications. Royal deaths often set in motion powerful ritual representations of unifying values designed to offset a blow that leaves society "stricken in the very principle of its life," to use Hertz's phrase. Moreover, for the citizens, the king-as-hero encounters a death that is the archetype of the end of Everyman.

Even in modern bureaucratic systems, the funerals of heads of state are often grand and highly politicized events, and their corpses subject to national cults. Consider Lenin in his glass coffin in Red Square. He has probably been seen by more people than any other leader in history. In his will, he asked to be buried simply, in accordance with his egalitarian principles. But he was overruled; his successors still needed him. Later, the corpse of Stalin came and then disappeared, according to political expediency. Another example concerns a counterestablishment figure, whose remains wandered about homelessly, in contrast to the solid permanence of Lenin. They were those of Eva Perón, wife of the Argentinian dictator. During her husband's period in power, she gained a saintly reputation among the working classes. After her death and his fall, her relics were shunted about two continents to serve as a rallying point for the Peronista faithful.

In this chapter, we look at royal funerals to see how they express and influence the social order. We focus on the corpse, seeing how it is manipulated to serve the ends of the living.

ROYAL FUNERALS IN THE INDIC STATES OF SOUTHEAST ASIA: THAILAND AND BALI

Royal rituals were extremely important in the numerous Indic states that rose and fell in Southeast Asia after the fourth century A.D. In several respects, these polities contradict our notion of the state. They did not so much possess territory as a center. Frequently, the names of the kingdoms were those of the capital city, which was conceived of as the pivot of a mandala, or set of concentric circles. At the very center lay the royal palace; outside that the city; then the royal realm; and beyond that lesser tributary polities in idealized patterns of eight, sixteen, or thirty-two units. This conceptual plan rendered the kingdom as a miniature reproduction of the cosmos. At the center, the palace represented Mount Meru, the pillar of the universe, and the king and his nobles the divine hierarchy.

We would be wrong to assume that these sublime associations translated into a totalitarian state. On the contrary, each tributary unit was based upon its own smaller-scale reproduction of the cosmic plan, and each operated with considerable autonomy within its own borders. As one traveled farther from the center, the authority of the king decreased, until one entered the periphery of some neighboring state. Moreover, these semiautonomous tributary units maintained pretensions of their own and were capable of becoming independent centers that, in time, might compete with their one-time suzerain or even absorb it. For these reasons, S. J. Tambiah, whose recent study we draw on, describes these polities as "pulsating" (Tambiah 1976: 102–9, 112–13).

The king was not only unable to administer his realm in any real sense, he was also hard pressed to extract agricultural produce from it with which to support his center. Even in relatively strong polities, the majority of the surplus extracted from the peasant producers was retained at successive local levels to support the courts of nobles. Though the gross amount collected was large, only a trickle arrived at the capital. The best the king could hope for was a large force of peasants for brief periods only, enough to attempt a prestige building project or a rapid military campaign. Nor could the peasants be too heavily exploited, because they would then be tempted to shift their allegiance to some other lord, or even another state. The only secure royal income was from the monopolistic control of trade (Tambiah 1976: 129).

It is within this framework of cosmic pretension and chronic competition that royal funerary rites in Southeast Asia must be seen. We examine them in two kingdoms that survived more or less intact into the twentieth century, and that have been the subject of recent studies.

Thailand: the enshrinement of royal relics   Over the several centuries of its existence, the Thai kingdom experienced variable fortunes. It engaged in constant warfare, not for land, which was plentiful, but for population. Whole villages were detached from neighboring states and resettled within the royal orbit. More debilitating were the frequent wars over succession. Because the Thai kings had many wives and concubines, as a device for establishing kinship links with influential families throughout their realms, there were always plenty of claimants to the throne. From the foundation of Ayutthaya, succession passed through younger brothers of the legal heir, uncles, half-brothers by royal concubines, minor members of the royal family, and downright usurpers (Smith 1967). It is here that mortuary rites become significant. This account comes from H. G. Quaritch Wales (1931), and mainly concerns nineteenth-century Thailand, although the rites have also been employed in this century.

After death is pronounced, the king's corpse is washed, dressed in fine clothes, and displayed briefly on a bier. Then it is folded with the knees drawn up under the chin, and inserted in a large golden urn. The urn is stored on a catafalque in a special hall of the palace for a minimum of 100 days, and usually much longer. Food is regularly placed before the king's urn. At the funeral of King Rama VI in 1925, the food was prepared by the king's own chef and served at his habitual mealtimes. The liquids of decomposition of the corpse are collected in a vase (also made of gold) below the urn (Wales 1931: 137–48).

These details strikingly recall Bornean practices described in Chapter 4. But secondary processing shows greater technical elaboration, involving cremation, the collection of bone fragments, and the storage of these relics in a shrine. Soon after the death of the king, work begins on the erection of the "funeral pyre," which is an imposing structure with a series of concentric terraces from which emerge four tall columns supporting a conical spire (see Figure 9). These columns are fashioned from massive teak trunks that were in past times as much as 250 feet in length and 12 feet in circumference. The cone atop the building represents the sacred mountain of Meru. The pyre proper is prepared on the top terrace, under the spire. The whole is magnificently carved and gilded (Wales 1931: 145).

After a suitable period has elapsed and preparations are complete, the urn containing the remains of the deceased king is brought to the pyre, the bones are removed from the urn, washed with scented water, anointed with perfumes by the new king, wrapped in a white cloth, and placed in a sandalwood box that in turn is placed atop the pyre. At sundown, the fire is lit, and it is carefully controlled all night to provide for complete combustion without the main structure catching fire. Spices are burnt in the fire to make a pleasant aroma.

In the morning, the fire is extinguished and the new king and members of the royal family search through the ashes for fragments of bone. Some fragments are given to the children of the dead monarch to be worn in gold lockets. The remaining relics are placed in a golden container and carried in state to the palace, where they comprise the focus of a royal cult. The ashes of the funeral pyre are stored in a monastery favored by the dead king (Wales 1931: 144–54).

Wales includes his discussion of cremation rites under the section of his book dealing with "Ceremonies of Installation." He explains this paradox in terms of the similarities between the coronation of a Thai king and his funeral, so that the cremation can be seen as a "Spiritual Coronation" (1931: 162). The scale of the mortuary rites is actually greater than that of the coronation.

Prior to insertion in the urn, the newly deceased king's body is dressed in embroidered silks, diamond-studded baldricks, gold shoes and epaulets, heavy gold bracelets and anklets, and a golden mask. The new king then places the late king's personal crown upon the head of the corpse, to which all present make obeisance. These accoutrements are richer than any worn by the king in life. They are retained in the urn during primary storage, and only removed immediately before cremation.

The procession of the urn to the pyre is stately. Excluding its

Figure 9. Funeral pyre of King Rama VI. The pyre proper was lit at the top of the staircase, under the roofed structure (from Wales 1931: 145).

The Dead King

contemporary military units, the funeral procession of King Rama VI in 1926 comprised:

troops

THE ROYAL FUNERAL PARTY

two three-tailed flags

160 red drums of victory

20 silver drums of victory

20 gold drums of victory

headmen of the pipe and war drum

20 blowers of the foreign bugles

28 blowers of the Siamese bugles

4 blowers of conch shells

2 seven tiered umbrellas, 6 five tiered, and four sunshades

3 sword bearers

a bearer of the priest's fan

royal car with a prince reading the scriptures

4 sword bearers

a royal umbrella, sunshade and fan

8 representatives of Indra with lances

8 representatives of Brahma with lances

civilian guards

umbrella bearers

6 sword bearers

THE GREAT FUNERAL CAR, bearing the urn, and drawn by

200 soldiers and six royal horses

a royal umbrella, sunshade and fan

16 representatives of Indra and Brahma bearing

silver and gold ornamental trees

2 seven tiered umbrellas, 10 five tiered and

8 sunshades

2 palace officials with personal effects

4 sword bearers

32 pages

4 chargers with grooms

KING PRAJADHIPOK'S PARTY

8 royal lictors

the Monkey Standard and the Garuda Standard

Royal Corpse and Body Politic

THE KING, walking
royal umbrella
10 aides-de-camp
princes of the royal household
representatives of foreign states
high government officials
military units with bands

This procession was similar to that for the coronation of King Prajadhipok some time before, and more splendid (Wales 1931: 108, 148–9). Both processions were loud with drums, bugles, and military bands.

Until recent times, during royal funerals the fields surrounding the pyre were alive with stalls providing free food and drink for commoners, stands for the sale of fireworks, and theatrical entertainments and side-shows of many kinds. It is clear that the cremation of kings is popularly regarded as a time for jubilation.

The ideology behind the similarity of funerals and coronations is compatible with both the Brahminic and Buddhist traditions represented in the Thai court. It conceives not of a single coronation, but of a series of ascending grades of anointment spread over the lifetime of the king – a periodic renewal of the divinity of the monarch. Wales mentions several of these (1931: 121–5), and for one of the most exalted a representation of the sacred mountain is prepared not unlike the one fashioned for the funeral pyre. The anointment of the king's bones with scented water and spices just before cremation is simply the last and most important in a series of anointments.

The political significance of these sumptuous rites was profound. First, and most important, they served to refocus attention on the center. Given the parameters reviewed above, it was crucial, even for a resilient and enduring state like that of the Thais, that the prestige of the royal court be maintained. Any tarnish on its claim to be the most sublime representation of the cosmos immediately translated into a diminished orbit of influence. Second, the mortuary rites not only provided a major opportunity, if not *the* major opportunity, for ritual display, they also occurred at a dangerous moment of transition. Even when struggles for the succession did not break out, or were rapidly stifled by a few deft assassinations, a certain period of vulnerability was inevitable. The format of the death rites provided an opportunity to combat this vulnerability, because of the way that the rites of succession were nested within them. Because the cremation of the old king must await the drying of his bones, the coronation of the new king preceded it. At the final rites, the new king was present for all to see. Paradoxically, the funeral could be used to express the continuity of kingship, and this is no doubt the reason why even usurpers found it expedient to give sumptuous cremations for their predecessors.

Third, the secondary treatment of the corpse resulted in the production of royal relics that reinforced the centripetal tendencies of the kingdom. Stored in the palace, they formed a kind of charismatic stockpile, distilled from the genius of ancient kings. The eighteenth-century king Boromakot seized the throne from a better-qualified heir by a daring military stroke, climaxing in a brisk fight for control of the palace. After the palace fell, the legal heir was slowly abandoned by his allies. As he moved away from the palace, his claim became steadily less credible, until he finally suffered the fate of unsuccessful competitors for the crown (Wood 1926: 231–3, 238–41).

Bali: royal cremations as public theater   On the island of Bali, much the same dynamic can be seen in funerary rites, if anything in even more pronounced form, as Clifford Geertz has shown (1980). He describes the several small states of nineteenth-century Bali, not as a neat set of well-demarcated realms, but as a highly complex web of dissimilar political ties thickening here and there into nodes of varying size, the centers of states and client nobles. Within the same village, there were peasants that owed allegiance to different lords through the intermediary of a host of seneschals. But the role of the lord was limited anyway. He played no part in the organization of agricultural production, or even in the administration of law in the village. The peasant was neither a tenant nor a serf. The duties that he owed to his lord were those having to do with support of the center – participation in ritual, and, secondarily, war. Although the threat of war was always present, other tools were preferred, such as cajolery, bluff, and alliance, because the prize was prestige, not territory. Geertz characterizes the role of the peasant, not as a subject, but as a stagehand or *claquer* in an endless pageant (1980: 65).

Mortuary rites figured largely in that pageant. In Chapter 4, we described the sequence of Balinese mortuary rites. For those of modest means, they involve primary interment in a simple grave, with the possibility of final cremation when funds become available or when an opportunity occurs to join the cremation ceremony of a kinsman or patron, perhaps many years later. For priests and nobles, burial is not appropriate. Their corpses are stored within the courtyard of the house or palace for at least forty-two days – the conventional time required for putrefaction to be completed. When the necessary resources have been assembled, the bones are lustrated a final time, carried to the cremation ground, and burnt. An identical religious significance informs every cremation, regardless of whether the individual participates as principal or client, and irrespective of the cost of the proceedings. However, the scale, elaboration, and drama of the rites vary widely. In the present context, it is only the most grandiose that concern us.

The cremation of an important man is an event that attracts people from all over the island, and nowadays even from overseas. The tower in which the bones are transported to the cremation ground amid milling crowds is a favorite topic of Balinese painters. The tower itself is a representation of the cosmos. Around its base, demons swirl in carved relief. In the middle, the world of men is represented by a little "house," in which the bones of the deceased are placed, and at the top are realms of the gods, symbolized in tiers of conical Meru roofs. The number of these roofs indicates the level of heaven to which the soul of the deceased aspires: the single one of the commoner, three or five for the lesser gentry, seven or nine for a lord, and eleven for a king of one of the major realms. Preceding the tower come orchestras, dancers, bearers of the animal-shaped coffin in which the bones are to be burnt (a different variety for each class), carriers of sandalwood, heirloom weapons, regalia, and trays of offerings. Then there are women carrying holy water, doll-like effigies of the dead, and offerings to the lords of hell; next, the high priest on his lotus chair, chanting mantras, and connected by a long cloth to the close relatives of the deceased and the tower. Behind the tower comes the palanquins of the wives of the dead king, who formerly might have chosen to sacrifice themselves in the flames of his pyre. Finally, a long trail of the towers of lesser people, who have awaited this opportunity to disinter their dead for their final rites (Wirz 1928: 86–99; Figure 10).

The height of the funeral tower, the fineness of its decoration, the number of people required to carry it, the number of attendants and towers of the commoners (often hundreds of them, with dozens of corpses to a tower) – all express the status of the deceased. But, as Geertz makes

The Dead King

Figure 10. Tall funeral towers stand beside the cremation ground in an elite Balinese rite. Later they will be torn apart by the crowd. The ashes of the funeral pyre are strewn upon the sea (from Covarrubias 1937, with the permission of Alfred A. Knopf, Inc.).

clear (1980: 98–120), more than counting and measuring are involved. The ceremony is also assessed in terms of its impact as drama. The principal actors must preserve a perfect serenity while an explosive burst of chaotic energy swirls around them. There are mock battles to delay the loading and unloading of the bones of the king, spinning of the tower to confuse bad spirits, scrambling for coins in the mud along the route, and plundering of the tower at the cremation site after the bones have been removed, all amid the clangor of war music.

Cremation is the largest and most expensive of royal rituals. According to Geertz (1980: 117), it is the rite most thoroughly dedicated to the aggressive assertion of status, a "headlong attack in a war of prestige" that pervades much of Balinese culture. Goris (1955: 126) compares it with a potlatch.

In Bali, numerous political units were engaged in constant rivalry to maintain their autonomy and extend their influence. What they competed for was not land but allegiance. The carefully staged cremations of kings were a principal weapon by which their successors maintained or advanced their standing.

LEGITIMIZATION THROUGH DEATH MONUMENTS: THE BERAWAN

The Berawan of Borneo comprise neither a populous centralized state like the Thais, nor a complex of highly stratified and competing realms like the Balinese. By comparison, Berawan society is small in scale, relatively egalitarian, and composed of a handful of autonomous ritual and political units – the separate longhouse communities. Nevertheless, extended death rites play an even more important part in its ongoing political process than in that of the Thai and Balinese states, because they affect the survival of the entire community.

In Chapter 4, we saw that, among the Berawan, secondary treatment is not extended to every corpse, and that an abridged ritual sequence is more common. The question raised there was the ideological rationale, or meaning, of the two types of funeral. We argued that they both reflect an identical eschatology. Now we take up a different question. Given the ritual equivalence of the two sequences, why are some individuals picked out for special attention? Complex considerations of prestige are involved. Though political and religious specialization and differences of wealth do not exist among the Berawan to anything like the degree that they are found among the Thais and Balinese, there *are* differences of status among the Berawan, and only those of supposedly superior rank merit the full sequence. Only for them can the necessary resources and support be mustered: rice to feed the large crowd of guests, to prepare rice wine for them to drink, and to feed the specialists working on the tomb; the social standing to attract the guests in the first place; and the solid support of the community so that its members are willing to fish, hunt, work on the tomb, and prepare food endlessly, in order to make the event a success reflecting credit on all concerned.

However, a problem arises in specifying the conditions making for nobility. Claims to high rank rest upon relationships to the great men of the past, whose names are frequently heard in prayers and whose spirits are thought of as protecting the community (Metcalf 1989). Often these great men are titled Penghulu (chief) or Orang Kaya (rich man). Penghulu is now employed by the Malaysian government to designate men selected to act as official chiefs. Previously, the British colonial administration used it, and the regime of Rajah Brooke before that. Before 1882, the Sultan of Brunei used both titles to honor upriver potentates who earned his favor. These two titles have been in use by the Berawan for more than a century and serve to denote undying reputation. But some individuals achieved the same level of immortality without outside recognition. The famous rebel chief Aban Jau caused much trouble to authorities on the coast and was never a candidate for honorific titles. Undismayed, he styled himself Rajah Ulu (king of the interior). His name still glitters in the genealogies of several important Berawan.

But these genealogical claims alone cannot explain differences in rank. In a small, largely endogamous community that recognizes all consanguineous links as equally valid without discrimination of sex or birth order, there is hardly a single person that cannot dredge up *some* link to a great man, even if sometimes obscure and of dubious validity, to back up a claim of high rank.

Part of the answer lies in residence. In each longhouse, one family apartment is designated as that of the chiefly family, the former residence of the last outstandingly prestigious man of the community. Because a new longhouse may well have been built in the interim, it is obviously not the physical structure that is referred to. Residential social units have an existence over time that outlasts the individual members, and indeed they are the only corporate groups of Berawan society of which this is true, apart from the longhouse community itself. They are, for example, the groups in which land rights are ultimately vested. A prestigious man will attempt to ensure the continued high rank of his residential unit by keeping the cleverest of his sons at home and importing a wife for him, *contra* the almost universal Berawan practice of uxorilocality. Such marriages require the payment of bride-price and in themselves confer status. Lacking sons, or able sons, the prestigious man will try to import a husband of known ability for his daughter. After the demise of the great man, the favored son, or the husband selected for the favored daughter, becomes head of the household. Such a household is often larger than other households in the community, having perhaps retained both sons and daughters and their spouses. When a new longhouse is constructed, the group may choose as a matter of convenience to split into several apartments in the new structure, but the one containing the chosen heir will be designated as the continuing residential group of the prestigious dead man, from which the others are offshoots. In this way, a chiefly apartment may persist over a period of time and through a succession of longhouses.

From this it will be seen that factors of noble birth are interwoven with personal achievement to create leaders. To maintain the advantage of high birth, the aspiring young man needs to demonstrate adeptness at cajoling or bullying the fellow members of his community; in short, he needs his own charisma. Berawan leaders are neither born nor created, but both.

High status is a prerequisite of extended mortuary rites. But there is no simple equation in this. A high-ranking person is also more likely to have on hand the stocks of rice necessary to proceed with a large-scale funeral immediately, within a framework of abridged death rites (Metcalf 1981). Far from connoting inferior status, such a procedure makes plain the wealth of the family, and may be preferred if death occurs soon after the harvest and if a suitable tomb is already available to house the deceased. If death occurs at an inconvenient moment or rice stocks are low, a secondary festival will be planned for a later date. One thing, however, makes selection of the extended sequence absolutely necessary, and that is the decision to build a new death edifice.

Berawan mausoleums vary considerably in style (Metcalf 1977). Some are single massive posts up to forty feet tall and four feet in diameter, with a small niche in the top to accommodate one small jar. Others have chambers varying in capacity from one to forty coffins or jars, supported six to thirty feet above the ground on one, two, four, five, six, or nine posts, or sitting on the ground, or even underground. The aboveground styles are frequently elaborately decorated with fine incised carving in floral, abstract, and anthropomorphic designs, filigree buttresses and ridgepoles, all highlighted in red, white, and black. Often they are decorated with expensive brassware or pottery. Invariably they are carved out of dense hardwoods (see Figure 11). Their construction requires considerable effort on the part of a community with a simple, shifting agricultural system and little specialization.

Such tombs are to be found in the graveyards adjacent to every long-

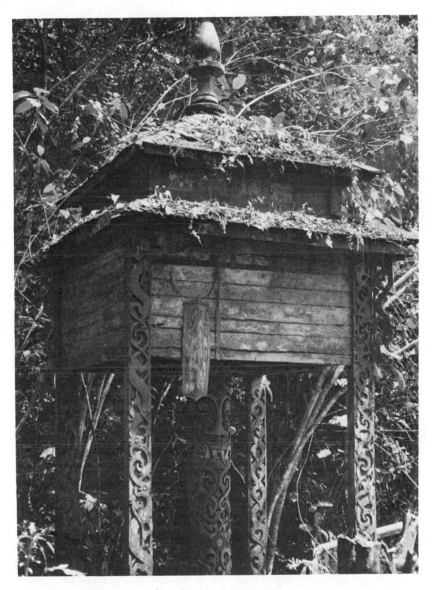

Figure 11. Finely carved Berawan mausoleum, with five supporting posts. It stands over thirty feet tall. Originally, it was painted with bold curlicue designs, which have now weathered.

house site occupied for any length of time. If one searches them out, as the anthropologist is wont to do, one finds them for the most part in twos and threes near the riverbank, spaced at irregular distances going upriver. This spacing is a consequence of Berawan migration over a prolonged period out of the hilly center of northern Borneo westward down major rivers toward the coast.

As the ancestors of the Berawan moved slowly downriver, they set aside a place for the building of tombs adjacent to each successive location. The wood from which the tombs were built is remarkably durable, and each former graveyard where their remains can be detected indicates a previous longhouse. Longhouses themselves tend to become dilapidated after twenty or thirty years, and then there is a strong tendency for people to spend more time at their farms, or even to fragment into smaller daughter longhouses consisting of a few households whose farms happen to be close together. These centrifugal forces are frequently exacerbated by factional quarrels and, if leadership is weak, the community can easily fall apart. In the last century when warfare was endemic in central northern Borneo, this situation was highly dangerous. A large war party could destroy a scattered population, whereas they would find a properly defended longhouse discouragingly formidable because of its greater manpower, solid construction, and elevation on massive piles – a veritable fortress, in fact.

Only when a new leader of exceptional ability appears can such incipient fission be reversed and the entire community cajoled into unified action. Because disunity was, in the last century, a matter of danger, so a supply of charismatic leaders able to overcome the egalitarian quarrelsomeness of individual Berawan was vital.

That this need was real is demonstrated by the fate of other small ethnic groups living in the Lower Baram in the nineteenth century, when large war parties swept downriver in search of plunder and slaves. The chaos that they caused is recorded in the journals of anxious European observers. These warlike expeditions originated from the relatively numerous Kayan and Kenyah folk who were newly arrived in the Baram watershed. In this situation, several of the small downriver groups moved farther toward the coast and put themselves under the protection of coastal Muslim peoples. Today these groups are assimilated into Malay culture. The Berawan gathered together in large fortified houses. At one point, the ancestors of three of the four present-day Berawan communities all lived together, along with some allied groups, in one heavily defended site. The remaining Berawan community was in a less-vulnerable location away from the major routes of travel of the war parties, but even so found it advisable to share a longhouse with another small non-Berawan group. The Tring – longtime rivals of the Berawan – neither fled toward the coast, nor allied themselves with other groups, nor even settled their own factional disputes. Instead, they relied on the infamous fierceness of their warriors. By the turn of the century, they were virtually extinct. A small remnant now lives absorbed into one of the Berawan villages.

What emerges is a model of the life cycle of the longhouse, related to the career of the great man associated with it. Construction or reconstruction begins as he first succeeds in commanding allegiance, and proceeds as he reaches his prime. During his vigor, the community is active and unified. After his death the house declines, matching its ruin to his.

It is within this historical process that the construction of mausoleums must be understood. The longhouse is itself a monument to the authority of its leaders. But the construction of a new longhouse may take many years. Each household bears primary responsibility for its own apartment, and some are slower to build than others. Moreover, it is the community as a unit that is emphasized. What the new leader requires to cement his position is a demonstration of community solidarity behind him personally.

The building of mausoleums provides an opportunity for such a demonstration. Funerals have an important integrative function. The obligation to assist in the funeral of a fellow community member is the most basic duty of longhouse residence. To fail consistently to do so is to break the link with the community. It is therefore a particularly appropriate duty to emphasize when unity is being consolidated. Even for a poor person, every household will try to provide a little assistance and will send a representative to keep the vigil each night that the corpse is in the house. For members of the most important family, more vigorous participation is prompted as a matter of pride, in view of the numerous visitors summoned from neighboring houses. The emergent leader must channel and build on these sentiments.

However, it would be unthinkable to prepare a mausoleum for someone not yet dead. Even the slightest preparation for death is proscribed among the Berawan. On the other hand, the emergent leader can hardly wait to aggrandize himself until after he dies. The solution is simple, and it explains a feature of the mausoleums that confused the ethnographer for some time. Mausoleums are known by the name of the person for whom they were prepared, and paradoxically these people often turn out to be nobodies. Further investigation reveals their special merit. They were relatives of emergent leaders (affines or consanguines, but residents of the same apartment) who happened to die at the right moment. In honoring them with a mausoleum the leader ennobled himself.

If the longhouse life cycle runs its course, the great man may himself occupy a humble grave, because the community is left disunited by his passing. The exceptions are cases where the important man shares the tomb he originally built for another, or where he succeeded in begetting, adopting, or recruiting a young man capable of commanding respect in a similar fashion. In this regard, the building of mausoleums is important because it ennobles the heir as it establishes the legatee.

There are several reasons, ideological, symbolic, and social, why mortuary rites are central to Berawan religion and society. But it is not hard to see why they are utilized by leaders to make a statement about their own positions. Weddings and other rites of passage also provide an opportunity for community cooperation and conspicuous consumption. The Kenyah have a more rigid system of prescribed rank than the Berawan, including endogamous class strata. For them it is possible to specify the status of a child in a way that it is not for the Berawan. They are accordingly less concerned with death rites. They do not practice secondary treatment.

The Berawan have no naming ceremonies comparable to Kenyah ones. They do appreciate the status implications of grand weddings. But when all the rice wine has been drunk, and the guests have shakily made their way home, what is there to keep a wedding in mind, to preserve it against the envious denigrations of rivals? The Berawan require something more concrete, and it is mortuary rites that provide it. Mausoleums are always built on the riverbank so that passersby can admire them and wonder at the power of their architects.

At the outset, we noted that only people of high rank can command the support required to conduct the full mortuary rite, or build a mausoleum. But we found it hard to define what rank is. We can now offer that definition by turning the original statement on its head: That person for whom the community can be fused together in coordinated action, that person *is* noble.

The Dead King

In this century, the role of the charismatic leader in Berawan society has changed. In the 1890s the Baram watershed, in which they live, was slowly brought under the control of the Sarawak government. The endemic and genocidal warfare that had raged throughout the area during the nineteenth century was checked, and then eradicated. As confidence in the new order grew, so also did trade. That there had for many centuries been a trickle of luxury goods into the interior is demonstrated by the fine old brasswear, beads, and Chinese pottery that can still be found there. But now the volume of this trade increased greatly.

Under these circumstances, the functions of leadership changed. Many of the old skills were still called for, however, revolving around the ability to cajole or bully people into corporate action, such as the collection of jungle produce, and expeditions to the coast to trade it for prestige goods. The military function of the longhouse declined, albeit warily, and the new type of leader may have been less prone to quixotic violence than his warlike forebears. But the necessity for community solidarity persisted, and indeed persists today in the need to protect land rights against encroachment.

In the new formula of power, legitimization through the construction of mortuary edifices still had an important part to play. In fact, a certain vying for elegance is noticeable. The tombs grow more lofty, delicate, and numerous. The Berawan themselves look back on the period from about 1900 to the arrival of the Japanese in 1941 as a golden age, a time of serenity and cultural florescence. They reminisce about the fabulous bridewealth paid by important men and the scale of ritual events. They compare it favorably with the tempestuous times before, when the disruption of headhunters made it hard to accumulate a surplus, and with the uncertainty of the modern era. The apogee of tomb construction reached in the 1920s and 1930s bears out their recollections.

In the rites of secondary treatment, the bones of distinguished Berawan are recovered and stored in tall tombs that cast a shadow down the generations. As the jungle creepers engulf and finally topple these structures, so their architects gradually fade from view. Monumentalization amplifies the equation that Hertz made between the fate of the body and the fate of the soul. The corpse, by association with its container, is made enduring and larger than life in order that its owner's name be the same.

Royal Corpse and Body Politic

PYRAMID BUILDING AND THE PHARAONIC STATE

The Berawan are not unique in the energies that they devote to the building of death edifices. On the contrary, there is hardly a region of the world that lacks examples of similar tendencies to monumentalism, and in each case we may be sure that the dynamics of power and legitimacy are somehow involved in their construction. But one example stands out above all others. For the title of *most* enduring and *most* imposing of death monuments there can be only one candidate: the Pyramids of Giza. It is indeed a far cry from the wooden tomb posts of Borneo to the artificial mountains of Egypt. They are separated by vast stretches of time and space. Nevertheless, useful insights may perhaps be gained by comparing one with the other (Hoffman 1979: 326–32). To do so constitutes an application of ethnographic analogy, as discussed in the Introduction.

Statistics hardly serve to express just how stupendous the Pyramids of Giza are. To say that they contain well over 20 million tons of stone makes little impression on the mind. They are still, 5,000 years after they were finished, far and away the biggest stone structures ever built. The cathedrals of Florence and Milan, Saint Peter's in Rome, and Saint Paul's Cathedral in London could all be grouped inside the base of the Great Pyramid of Khufu with room to spare.

Ever since Napoleon's Egyptian adventure thrust them into Western consciousness, the pyramids have inspired awe and bafflement. Who built them? When? How? Why? Such monumental mysteries have attracted serious scholars and crackpots with equal frequency over the last century and a half. The who and the when have been established. The question of how remains puzzling, although several interesting contributions have recently been made (Tellefsen 1975: Mendelssohn 1974).

For originality of theorizing, however, the most stimulating question has always been: Why? For what purpose were the pyramids built? It is self-evident that the construction of the pyramids cost their builders a vast effort. Their purpose must surely have been correspondingly important, their significance correspondingly timeless. It is the staggering size of the pyramids that makes all mundane explanations appear trivial and prompts some observers to see a Grander Design in them.

The Dead King

The originator of the theory of Divine Inspiration was a retired book publisher named John Taylor, who, in 1859, wrote the first of many books entitled *The Great Pyramid* (Riffert 1932). This fascination with the Great Pyramid and the folklore that it has spawned constitute a subject worthy of study in its own right. But it is not the subject that concerns us here. Divine prophecy aside, what other functions have been suggested for the pyramids? They cannot have been stellar observatories, for we know that Egyptian astronomy was not advanced, and that the stellar alignments found in the pyramids are few and simple. Despite a current fad attributing to the right-rectangular cone the ability to sharpen razor blades and reduce hypertension, there is no evidence to support the idea that the Pyramids of Giza were built with such functions in mind. Rather, it will be necessary to return to those purposes, rooted in the social and political circumstances of the Archaic Period of ancient Egypt, that at first sight appear so ephemeral compared to the great mass of the structures themselves.

In accordance with the findings of archaeology, we conclude that the pyramids are what they appear to be: tombs. Further, that the social factors that account for their construction are not entirely different from those that produce elaborate mausoleums in central Borneo.

An immediate difficulty appears with this notion. Of the ten major pyramids begun or completed during the height of the Pyramid Age, beginning with Zoser's and ending with Menkaure's, none contains irrefutable proof that a pharaoh was ever entombed in it. In fact, what evidence there is points in the opposite direction. Though the pattern varies from pyramid to pyramid, each one contains a number of passages, sometimes within the structure, and sometimes hewn out of the live rock below. Each tunnel system contains an inner chamber, heavily defended from intruders by sliding stone portcullises. In four cases these inner chambers contain massive, finely worked stone sarcophagi, which are, however, empty. Possibly the royal corpses were stolen by the graverobbers that are known to have entered the chambers in antiquity. Five other pyramids have no sarcophagi in them at all. Can it be that the robbers removed the heavy and essentially useless objects? How could they have moved them down the tiny corridors? (Evidently they were inserted during construction.) But the most difficult case is presented by the Step Pyramid of Sekhemket, the chamber of which was found intact. Inside was the expected sarcophagus, its opening still sealed with the original cement. Frustratingly for its excited discovers, it turned out to be completely empty (Edwards 1947: 83).

How is it possible that the pharaohs built themselves such impressive tombs and then failed to use them? The answer must be sought in the social, technical, and stylistic developments that led up to the Pyramid Age, and particularly in the burial edifices of the earliest pharaohs. In this context, the corpseless tomb is a recurring phenomenon.

For many years, the place of entombment of the pharaohs of the First and Second dynasties (the Archaic Period) has been controversial. The problem is not a lack of identifiable sites, but a plethora of them. In the opening years of this century Flinders Petrie, whose name figures so prominently in Egyptian archaeology, made a painstaking excavation at the plundered site of Abydos. He was able to identify there the tombs of eight pharaohs of the First Dynasty and two of the Second Dynasty, together with other royal graves. However, later, in the mid-thirties, Walter Emery excavated at Sakkara a series of tombs that turned out to be associated with the same roster of monarchs. Emery argued that the Sakkara tombs were the real ones, but despite the fact that they are larger and more impressive, the majority of experts now feel that it was the Abydos site that actually housed the royal corpses (Hoffman 1979: 267–75). For our purposes, it is enough to know that these kings each built two large tombs, provisioned them elaborately with food, luxury products, and valuables of all kinds, and surrounded them with the subsidiary graves of their courtiers or officials. We can only conclude that one of each king's tombs was designed from the outset to remain empty.

Why these ancient kings should have constructed dummy tombs is a question that leads us away from the hard data of archaeology. Despite several brilliant studies, of which those of James Breasted (1912), Henri Frankfort (1948), and John Wilson (1946) are the best known, many features of ancient Egyptian religion remain unclear.

Our uncertainty is most pronounced concerning the Archaic Period, from which no written records survive. The religious rationale that was used to justify the two tombs of the kings of the first dynasties is a matter for speculation. What is beyond doubt is the location of the two royal cemeteries. Abydos is in Upper Egypt, not far from some of the most ancient settlement sites in the area; Sakkara is in Lower Egypt, not far from the first capital of the unified country, Memphis. We have good archaeological data to show that predynastic Egypt had developed in two cohesive but distinct culture areas: the Nile Delta region, and the striplike floodplain of the Nile, that is, Lower and Upper Egypt, respectively. We know that the two regions were brought under unified rule sometime around 3100 B.C. by a king of Upper Egypt. It is likely that the dual tombs of the earliest pharaohs made a political statement in addition to any ritual justification they may have had.

This interpretation is rendered more likely by the many symbols of duality surrounding the institution of the pharaoh, several of them explicitly representing Upper and Lower Egypt. A common artistic motif is the lily of Upper Egypt intertwined or alternated with the papyrus of Lower Egypt. Often the gods Horus and Seth, themselves associated with the two regions, are shown in the act of binding the two plants together. Given the importance of mortuary ritual, an expression of the same duality in tomb structures is not surprising.

With the model of the Sakkara tombs before them, the pharaohs of the Pyramid Age may well have planned massive mausoleums that they did not intend to occupy. But why *so* massive? Again, an examination of the archaeological record reduces the singularity of the pyramids by revealing them as the climax of a long process of evolution.

Before 3000 B.C. Egypt suffered periods of decreasing rainfall. This brought on an ecological crisis, the effects of which are only now being worked out by archaeologists (Butzer 1976). One effect seems to have been an increase in status differentiation, due perhaps to competition for reduced areas of productive land and intensification of irrigation. The changes were particularly pronounced in Upper Egypt. The increasing stratification of society is reflected in a steady elaboration of grave furnishings and architecture.

In 1894, before his Abydos dig, Petrie explored an extensive necropolis at Naqada that had evidently been in use for a prolonged period in predynastic times. It contained more than 2,000 graves. The oldest, as dated by the seriation techniques pioneered by Petrie, consisted of shallow oval pits crudely roofed over and marked by small mounds. The body lay in a flexed position, and, even at this early date, was surrounded by a variety of grave goods. Later tombs consist of vaults lined with mud-brick masonry, are more carefully roofed, and presumably had larger mounds. Gradually, additional chambers were added to the main vault, and despite the depredations of grave robbers, who seem to have plied their trade from earliest times, it is clear that these chambers were filled with provisions and luxury goods of several kinds. Finally, at Naqada there are traces of a mysterious early step pyramid. Several features mark it out as an early experiment: its small size, crude use of the new medium of stone, and the inaccessibility of the simple vault in the rock below it. No tunnel led out of it, so that once the first course of the superstructure had been laid reentry was impossible. Significantly, the chamber was empty. It is not known whether its owner was a protodynastic or archaic potentate (Edwards 1947: 89).

The line of development begun at Naqada was continued at Abydos and Sakkara. Both sites contain a great number of tombs, often arranged in groups. The central edifice of such groups typically consists of many chambers, of which the central ones are usually subterranean. Their appearance above ground is of a low, rectangular building, as is suggested by the Arabic word used to describe them: *mastaba*, meaning "a bench." The walls were often vividly painted, and decorated with recessed paneling in the same way as palaces of the era, a resemblance marred only by the lack of internal connecting doors between the tomb chambers. Our greatest area of ignorance concerns the original superstructure of the mastabas. George Reisner (1936) believed that later tombs ascended in two or three steps to a summit much higher than now visible. Later commentators disagree, but the pyramid motif is presaged in other ways. The earlier tombs have a rectangular mound of sand cased in bricks directly above the burial vault, a feature, I. E. S. Edwards suggested (1947: 43), harking back to the mounds of sand atop predynastic graves (see Figure 12). Later tombs have a stepped central mound of larger proportions (see Figure 13). Although what now remains of these Archaic Period royal graves is less impressive than the monuments of the succeeding Pyramid Age, we should not underestimate the concentration of wealth and labor that their construction represents.

Architecturally, the largest single increase in scale of monuments takes place at the beginning of the Third Dynasty, with the construction of Zoser's Step Pyramid at Sakkara. That it was the first of its kind is revealed by the several changes in its design that were made as building progressed (Edwards 1947: 53–8). In the first design, the outline of a large stone mastaba can be made out, with subterranean vaults and tunnels of more complexity than hitherto seen. In a first extension, the mastaba was lengthened, and one end became the bottom stage of a four-step pyramid. Before a mortuary temple abutting it could be completed, the

Figure 12. A First-Dynasty mastaba (after Edwards 1947: 44).

Figure 13. A Second-Dynasty mastaba (after Emery 1961: 83).

Figure 14. A Third-Dynasty mortuary complex: Zoser's Step Pyramid (after Mendelssohn 1974: 41).

pyramid was extended to allow a six-step design. The result was the complex of buildings shown in Figure 14, in which the pyramid overshadows the original mastaba. During the Third Dynasty, several more step pyramids were begun, presaging the final developments in the Fourth Dynasty. The features of the Pyramids of Giza are too well known to need description here (see Figure 15). The Great Pyramid is more than twice as tall as Zoser's Step Pyramid and contains many times the volume of stone. Nevertheless, the family resemblance is unmistakable.

Having shown that the pyramids were the climax of a long process of escalating monumentalism in tomb design, we can now look at the timing of this escalation.

The most remarkable feature of the Pyramid Age is its brevity. At first sight, one might imagine that a pyramid was erected every few centuries as an expression of hubris on the part of particularly successful pharaohs. In fact, the five largest pyramids were all built within the space of one century. Shepseskaf, last pharaoh of the Fourth Dynasty, contented himself with a mastaba of Archaic Period type. Thereafter, pyramids were sometimes constructed, but they were invariably of inferior size and workmanship. Mud brick was substituted for limestone, and all that is left of them today are shapeless mounds. Between Shepseskaf and the legendary Menes, who first imposed his rule on a unified Egypt, lie little more than 500 years. It was during those centuries that the Egyptian state was welded together from the diverse traditions of predynastic times.

As Wilson has pointed out (1951: 44), we do not know if Menes was an actual historical figure or only a later composition of legend. We do not know if his "conquest" of Lower Egypt was effected at one blow or over several generations, nor if it involved a painful imposition of rule over a subjugated population or a popular movement toward unity. We

Figure 15. The classic pyramid complex of the Fourth Dynasty (after Mendelssohn 1974: 46).

do know that warfare was common at the time, that rivalries existed between different regions, and that the earliest representations of pharaoh figures, such as the palette of Narmer, show him wielding a club over the heads of captives.

We also know that on two occasions *after* the establishment of the state, during the episodes known as the first and second intermediate periods, centralized rule collapsed. For the first dynasties of pharaohs, these centrifugal forces must have been all the greater because a unified cultural tradition was lacking. They had to create that tradition and to place the institution of pharaoh at the center of it. What they needed were corporate projects that focused upon the person of the leader; the construction of mortuary edifices provided the opportunity for the pharaohs just as it did for aspiring Berawan aristocrats in nineteenth-century Borneo.

This is not an evolutionist argument. We do not imply that the Egyptian sequence of political evolution was in process of being repeated in

Borneo at the moment when Europeans arrived; nor that institutions found recently in Borneo are "survivals" of what was once practiced in Egypt. We employ the Berawan data only to suggest interpretations, the evidence for which must come from Egypt alone.

Like the mausoleums of Borneo, the important design feature of the pyramids was visibility. It was a matter of secondary interest who, if anyone, was entombed in them. The Berawan require a corpse before they can begin construction, so they honor their obscure relatives. The pharaohs evidently preferred simply to leave their mausoleums empty. Snofru, the greatest of all pyramid builders, actually constructed *three* (the Red and Bent pyramids and the ruined Meidum pyramid), a fact that A. Gardiner finds "unpalatable" because he cannot see why anyone would need three tombs (1961: 78).

Throughout the history of Egypt, the scale of royal mortuary ritual provides an index of the authority of central government. But in the first four dynasties it is particularly crucial. Wilson (1951: 44) characterizes the First and Second dynasties as a time of consolidation. Mortuary architecture reflects this in the elaboration of the mastaba form, a style of tomb carried over from predynastic times. Even so, the construction and provisioning of dual edifices (at Sakkara and Abydos) represents a considerable concentration of national effort. It we assume that labor-intensive phases of the construction went on during the off-season of the agricultural cycle, then the effort involved was largely one of coordination and organization, a task appropriate to nation building. In the Third and Fourth dynasties, according to Wilson, "The new state was stable and secure enough to express itself in a distinctively new and 'Egyptian' way" (1951: 44). In tomb construction, this new expression took the form of experimentation with, and perfection of, techniques for building in stone. Add to this a dramatic increase in scale, which in Zoser's Step Pyramid occurred in several jumps, and a need is apparent for yet further organization with emphasis on a range of new technical skills. The Fourth Dynasty began with Snofru and his three pyramids. His successor, Khufu, built the Great Pyramid. Djedefre built at some distance from Giza, and it is not known if he ever completed his pyramid. Khafre and Menkaure returned to Khufu's site and added theirs to make up the trio visible today. This concluded the Pyramid Age.

As to the religious innovations that accompanied the social changes implied by the construction of the pyramids, our information is once again incomplete. The end result, the cult of the god-king, is well known from the texts that begin to appear in the Pyramid Age. Its elaborate symbology is described in Wilson (1946: 71–86). But as Wilson remarks elsewhere, how the rulers of the First Dynasty were perceived by their subjects is not known. Cyril Aldred (1961: 157–8) sees the divine kingship as an ancient culture trait having its roots in the rainmakers of prehistoric tribal society, but this is guesswork. It seems more likely that the pharaoh as reincarnation of Horus was an ideological innovation. In perhaps the most complete study of Egyptian kingship, Frankfort consistently stresses its originality and uniqueness (Frankfort 1948: 15–35).

The mortuary edifices of the early pharaohs were the symbol and proof of royal authority. Though it would be absurd to suggest that they constituted the sole concern of rulers still in the process of building a complex state, they were a very large concern. The evidence for that stands in the desert to this day. Moreover, their fabrication must have called into being an organizational apparatus and a corporate awareness that made other state ventures possible, and further pyramid building unnecessary. As the pharaohs built the pyramids, so did the pyramids build Pharaonic civilization. And that, finally, is a purpose consonant with their vast bulk.

7

THE IMMORTAL
KINGSHIP

Western social thought has emphasized the importance of reason, law, and force in the evolution and maintenance of political institutions. Anthropologists, although not denying the role of these practical elements, focus on the crucial role of ritual for political integration. One anthropologist in particular, A. M. Hocart, stands out for his insistence on the primacy of the ritualized aspects of kingship in the development of early states (Needham 1970). Beginning with the striking suggestion that "the first kings must have been dead kings" (Hocart 1954), he went on in later works to outline the proposition that "modern" bureaucratic government actually began in a ritual organization and only later took on the administrative function (Hocart 1970). In Hocart's view, "government" formed around a ritual specialist involved in the propitiation of, as often as not, the ghosts of important men, and the evolution of the state is merely the unintentional by-product of the ritual attempt to secure life and well-being from supernatural powers.

We are not here concerned with the issue of the evolution of the state. Regardless of the origins of kingship, the symbolism surrounding the dead king remains crucial in many political structures. In Chapter 6, we looked at several instances in which the treatment of the royal remains figures prominently in the drama of royal succession and dynastic expansion. In this chapter, we examine specifically societies in which the person of the king, alive and dead, represents the prosperity and perpetuity of the political order. In this situation, the death of the king undermines the integrative symbol of political stability and makes all too palpable the danger of an outbreak of political violence. The decay of the royal corpse is often seen as participating in or even contributing to this dangerous situation. In many societies, the conception and representation of the "body politic" is intertwined in various ways with the body of the individual who is king, chief, or elder. The king's person is such a natural symbol of the authority and perpetuity of the political order that it becomes a problematic symbol once he dies and his body begins to rot. Royal death presents a major problem: Given the intimate relation between abstract concepts and the physical properties of the person through which they are expressed, what happens when the very symbol of permanence and high authority begins to sink rapidly into putrescence?

We shall explore a number of solutions to this issue, some cases that are prominent in anthropological theories of political symbolism, and other cases that speak more directly to the long development of the Western ideology of the state and its representations. One solution to the problem of the decaying symbol is to replace it with a more stable representation. In this regard, royal effigies allow a grand ritual representation of the immortal kingship and the body politic. Another solution is to have no royal corpse at all. Through traditions of ritual regicide and royal burial alive, the corpse simply disappears and is separated neatly from the task of representing the immortal kingship. Sensational as it may sound, the topic of ritualized royal murder is of solid importance to the anthropological study of political symbolism.

THE DIVINE KINGSHIP OF THE SHILLUK OF THE SUDAN

Perhaps the most famous case of divine kingship is that of the Shilluk who inhabit a stretch of the Upper Nile in Sudan. In Shilluk ideology, the person of the king represents the fertility and well-being of his entire nation, and for this reason no decay of his body can be tolerated. If the king dies, so does the land. Indeed, so direct is the connection between the king's well-being and that of the nation that not only is death a problem, but so are age, sickness, and especially decreased sexual potency.

None of those physical weaknesses, which the average man tolerates for long years before his eventual death, can be accepted in the king. The symbol of Shilluk unity and perpetuity cannot weaken. At the first evidence of lessening powers, the king is secretly suffocated and his body walled up in a mud hut. One moment, the king is strong and physically unimpaired, the next, he has vanished. Such are the customs of regicide reported for the Shilluk. They became famous through the writings of Sir James Frazer, whose magnum opus, *The Golden Bough* (1963), is a result of his decades-long quest for the meaning of ritual regicide.

Frazer was interested in collecting reports of the ritual murder of "priest-kings" because of the light that he thought such material would shed on the early eras of our own civilization. Myths suggested that such cults were widespread in the pre-Classical Mediterranean world. Unable to obtain any but shadowy evidence for the existence of these customs in Europe, Frazer searched the world for parallel customs that would confirm his hypothesis that such barbarous cults characterized a particular stage in human cultural evolution worldwide, a stage still in evidence outside Europe.

In his 1948 Frazer Memorial Lecture, E. E. Evans-Pritchard, appropriately, reanalyzes the divine kingship of the Shilluk, emphasizing the political context. He views customs of ritual regicide as a "problem in social structure," rather than of religion and magic. Even though the Shilluk king "reigns, but does not rule," even though he has almost no administrative, judicial, or military authority, nevertheless, he is the center of a political system. The beliefs in regicide and rituals of installation are best viewed as representing and contributing to the unity of the 100 or so separate Shilluk settlements along the West Bank of the Nile.

For this type of analysis, we must describe the Shilluk more specifically. In many respects, the social structure of the Shilluk is like that of their celebrated neighbors, the Nuer. They are patrilineal and their lineages are dispersed, so that each settlement contains homesteads of several lineages. As among the Nuer, certain lineages are politically associated with certain territories. In each village there is a dominant lineage and several others that are locally subordinate. What makes the Shilluk different from the Nuer is that all the Shilluk settlements compose a common polity united in the kingship. This difference is crucial, however, for if the Nuer are the ultimate example of political structure and process in an uncentralized, anarchic situation, then the Shilluk are an example of what must minimally be added to create a state. That minimal addition is a symbolic kingship, the nature of which is represented most clearly in the rituals surrounding the death and installation of the incumbents of the office.

The king sends his many wives, once they are pregnant, away from the royal capital to bear their children in their natal villages. Their sons, princes and potential successors, are raised by the village chief – often the brother or father of the prince's mother. Potential heirs, sons of the present king, are numerous, and each is allied and resident with an important commoner village chief who is a leader of his mother's family. Additionally, there are in most villages members of the royal lineage who are not contenders for the throne: the sons of those princes who did not become king. There are also various other groups affected by royal succession, such as the commoner clients of past kings. All in all, this kingship and its rule of succession have produced throughout the land a social hierarchy of royal house, nobility, and commoners. The king may come from a specific settlement, but he represents all the Shilluk. Furthermore, almost every settlement in the realm is closely allied to the current king and to a potential heir, and therefore has a stake in the maintenance of the kingship. Nonetheless, the kingship of the Shilluk is a rather tenuous institution in the face of the divisive and competitive nature of the segmentary system on which it rests.

The kingship is a symbol of the Shilluk people. The king is called *reth*, but it is not he who is said to reign, but Nyikang, the immortal culture hero of the Shilluk, the founder of the kingdom centuries ago. Nyikang, according to tradition, continues to reign through all his successors, who are mere receptacles of the one and only kingship – Nyikang. Nyikang, being immortal, is an abiding institution "which binds past and present and future generations" (Evans-Pritchard 1948: 200).

Nyikang, then, does not die, but the kings through whom he rules do. On the death of a king, his corpse is walled up for some months in a hut. Later, his bones are buried back in his natal settlement, but the rites are family and clan affairs carried out in privacy, bordering on secrecy. Once the king is dead, he ceases to be a symbol of national unity. His body, on whose physical condition the nation depended while he lived, is assiduously absent after death.

The king is dead, but what has become of the kingship? The answer is that the spirit of Nyikang is represented by an effigy that is kept in a shrine during each king's reign, only to be reanimated, so to speak, during each interregnum to participate in the installation of the next king.

The choosing and installation of a new king is an affair of the whole nation. The new king is chosen by the leading commoner chiefs of both northern and southern Shillukland. Consequently, the successor must have wide support. Because the effigy of Nyikang is kept in the North, it "leads" a long march upriver to the capital, picking up "warriors" and followers along the way at each settlement. Meanwhile, the king-elect joins a similar "army" from southern Shillukland and leads a march downriver. The two armies meet outside the capital and engage in a mock battle in which the army of Nyikang is victorious, defeating the army of the South and capturing the king-elect. Later, at the installation cer-emonies, the spirit of Nyikang leaves the effigy and enters the body of the new king, as in a spirit possession. The effigy is carted back to its shrine to await the return of the spirit of Nyikang at the death of the new incumbent.

The political unity of the Shilluk nation is primarily a ritual and dra-matic tour de force that focuses on the physical representation of the "body politic" in the perfect person of the king and in the unchanging effigy. In the representation of Nyikang, signs of decay and change are eliminated. The difficult problem of the royal corpse is solved by replac-ing it with an effigy. Evans-Pritchard suggests that, given the crucial importance of the symbol of kingship in a polity where the king had no real power and the government no administration, the symbol must be especially compelling. It is in this context that he wishes to explain the reports of regicide in the case of a failing monarch.

Evans-Pritchard emphasizes that it is the frightening idea of regicide that strengthens the kingship by its insistence on the extreme purity and potency of the monarch. There is power and utility in the *idea* of regicide, whether or not kings are ever actually murdered. Further-more, given the logic of belief, the idea of regicide could also serve to strengthen the position of a failing incumbent. Whatever strengthens the kingship is likely to strengthen the king. For if a weak incumbent has not yet been killed by those whose duty it is or by those who stand to gain by his death, then he must indeed still be the embodiment of the immortal Nyikang.

I have failed to find convincing evidence that any Shilluk king was put to death . . . although some of the kings must have qualified long before they died . . . and I am persuaded that the story of kings being walled up in a hut is a confusion arising from the usual walling up of the remains of a dead king, the bones being buried after decomposition of the flesh. In the absence of other than traditional evidence of royal executions in Shilluk history and in view of the contradictory accounts cited I conclude that the ceremonial putting to death of kings is probably a fiction. It possibly arises from the dual personality of the king, who is both himself and Nyikang, both an individual and an institution, which accounts also for the linguistic convention that a king does not die but disappears just as Nyikang is said not to have died but to have disappeared. [Evans-Pritchard 1948: 202]

Evans-Pritchard discusses the issue in terms that have a familiar ring to Western ears. Notions of the dual personality of the king (public-corporate vs. private-individual), of kings that "reign but do not rule," and of the problem of legitimate succession all relate as much to Western constitutional thought as they do to the concerns of a Nilotic kingdom. The problem of the immortal kingship and mortal kings is an old one in Europe. Frazer seems unaware of the way his chosen problem and illustrations resonate with important English concerns. Evans-Pritchard's approach is different. He not only renders the strange plausible to an English reader, but systematically relates the Shilluk customs to political concerns that are familiar and acceptable to his readers. If the Shilluk do not really kill their king, still the belief is a device that keeps the Shilluk monarchy functioning. It is representative of Evans-Pritchard's view of anthropology as a process of cultural translation to define the analytical parameters in terms of institutional arrangements in the West. In this case, the "political" aspect of the Shilluk material is related to the English institution of the king as a "corporation sole."

The problems of symbolism of the Shilluk kingship are so strikingly parallel to those of the traditional English and French political systems that one is prompted to look back at European doctrines of kingship. During the Renaissance devices of corporeal symbolism and funeral ritual were substantial factors in the development of the ideology of the modern state.

BODY POLITIC AND BODY NATURAL

To examine this issue, we turn to the work of historians, especially the now classic studies by Ernst Kantorowicz, *The King's Two Bodies* (1957), and by his student Ralph Giesey, *The Royal Funeral Ceremony in Renaissance France* (1960). These studies trace the secularization of various medieval theological notions as the English and French political systems developed. Subtle theological formulations pertaining to the duality of Christ and to the Holy Trinity were expropriated to create a "Christology" of European kingship. In England, generations of lawyers found it necessary to develop a complex legal fiction that the king had not one but two bodies. In France, the ambiguity about the dual nature of the king as political symbol was "resolved" not through law but through *pompes funèbres.*

Let us examine the English legalisms first. Kantorowicz offers as evidence the reports from a number of Tudor court cases regarding the status of transactions of deceased kings. Over and over, the jurists argue that their legal dealings are different from those of normal men:

For the king has in him two Bodies, *viz.* a Body natural and a Body politic. His Body natural (if it be considered in itself) is a Body mortal, subject to all Infirmities that come by Nature or Accident, to the Imbecility of Infancy or old Age, and to the like Defects that happen to the natural Bodies of other People. But his Body politic is a Body that cannot be seen or handled, consisting of Policy and Government, and constituted for the Direction of the People, and the Management of the public weal, and this Body is utterly void of Infancy, and old Age, and other natural Defects and Imbecilities, which the Body natural is subject to, and for this Cause, what the King does in his Body politic, cannot be invalidated or frustrated by any Disability in his natural Body. [Quoted in Kantorowicz 1957: 7]

One point about this English concept contrasts markedly with Shilluk notions; that is the dominance of the body politic over the body natural of the king. Whereas the senility of the body natural of the Shilluk *Reth* threatens the well-being of the kingdom, the imbecility or old age of an English monarch does not. Again Kantorowicz can offer us the jurists' reports:

His Body politic, which is annexed to his Body natural, takes away the imbecility of his Body natural, and draws the Body natural which is the lesser, and all the Effects thereof to itself, which is the greater. [Quoted in Kantorowicz 1957: 10]

The mysticism of the English formulation is striking in contrast to the Shilluk view. It seems quite reasonable and pragmatic that the aging or weakening of the human incumbent of the throne should weaken the kingship and endanger the polity. The Shilluk kingship at any moment is only as strong as the current king. However, the English view postulates an invisible body and attributes to it magical powers that remove mortal weakness from the king. The Western concept of the state, in the form that it took in late medieval and early Renaissance England, stressed the dominance of the abstraction (the state) over the individuals who composed the society, and even over that sole individual who represented the state in his person.

The nature of this English fiction of the king's two bodies, with the clear dominance of the body politic, avoids the Shilluk problem of the decay of the symbol of state either before or after the king's death. Royal death did create interesting problems for the jurists, however. During life, the two capacities of the king were distinct and separate, and yet at the same time formed a unity in which the political capacity dominated. This is a tricky intellectual position in itself, but it becomes more complex when, at the death of a monarch, the two bodies simply separate (see Figure 16).

. . . and this Body [politic] is not subject to passions as the other is, nor to Death, for as to this Body the King never dies, and his natural Death is not called in our Law . . . the Death of the King, but the Demise of the King, not signifying by the word (Demise) that the Body politic of the King is dead, but that there is a Separation of the two Bodies, and that the Body politic is transferred and conveyed over from the Body natural now dead, or now removed from the Dignity royal, to another Body natural. [Quoted in Kantorowicz 1957: 13]

But even after death, the dominance of the political capacity has its effects on the individual who was king. Not only does the *kingship* live on through successive kings, but also the individual king receives a legal immortality of sorts. For, as Plowden reports, legal contracts

Figure 16. This fifteenth-century tomb of the Earl of Arundel graphically contrasts the grandeur of office with the frailty of flesh, an idea
elaborated into the doctrine of the king's "two bodies" (from Kantorowicz 1957: Fig. 28, with the permission of the Warburg Institute).

made with King Henry VIII continue because "he as King never dies."
According to the ideology, the kingship separates and moves on (to
Edward VI). Henry Tudor is dead, but Henry VIII lives on (Kantorowicz
1957: 14).

Yet the Tudor jurists argued that every subject is sworn to the king in
the king's *natural* person rather than in his political capacity. This is
because the political capacity, being an abstraction, has no soul in the
specifically Christian sense and therefore cannot swear or be sworn to
in holy oath. Furthermore, treason is also against the king's body natural,
for the body politic, being immortal, cannot be threatened or killed. Regicide, then, in the English context bears a striking resemblance in its
conceived effects to the supposed regicide among the Shilluk. Indeed,
the dogmas of the royal jurists of the Tudor period provided the rationale
for the killing of Charles I in the English revolution of the mid-
seventeenth century. Parliament summoned, in the name and by the

authority of Charles I, king body politic, the armies that were to fight the same Charles I, king body natural. They succeeded in executing the king's body natural without doing serious harm to the king's body politic in Parliament (Kantorowicz 1957: 22).

The treatment of the royal corpse in medieval and Renaissance England reflects the logical gymnastics of the concept of the two bodies in a simple fashion. It became the practice, beginning with the funeral of Henry II in 1189 (Giesey 1960: 80), for the corpse of the deceased king to be publicly displayed during the funeral procession. The practice of evisceration allowed the reasonable preservation of the corpse for a few days. The heart and entrails of an English king usually received separate burial from the remainder of the corpse. Some monarchs generously had their remains distributed among three locales. Given the English notion of the separation of the king's two bodies at this "demise," the display of the corpse served a practical and quasi-legal purpose. All that was needed to validate (at least in a preliminary fashion) the authority of the new king was the obvious evidence that the body natural of the preceding king had come to its natural end. Again, we face the issue of the causal relation between beliefs and ritual action, and we note that styles of burial ritual developed gradually over the centuries, as did the legal concept of the two bodies. It seems, however, that ritual led the way, as usual, with the rationale following later.

The special circumstances of the death of Edward II in 1327 called for a practical innovation that later became important. Edward II was deposed in favor his son. When he died shortly afterward while under arrest, there were suspicions of foul play. Moreover, Edward III was far away and the funeral had to be delayed until the royal son could return and make a public show of filial piety. When the funeral procession took place, months later, a wooden effigy was substituted for the corpse. Whether this was done to cover possible evidence of murder or simply to allow Edward III to be present at a compensatorily grand funeral for the father he deposed, or for both reasons, is not certain (Giesey 1960: 81). But the innovation of the effigy did permit the staging of increasingly protracted and grand tributes to deceased English monarchs.

The use of effigies was adopted intermittently for a century and a half. The reasons for each use of, or failure to use, the effigy relate to practical political considerations, such as we discussed in the previous chapter. Although the first effigy was arranged for a deposed king, it was done by his son. Funeral effigies and the pomp they permitted seem not to have been provided for the several deposed or murdered English monarchs of the unstable fifteenth century: The funerals of Richard II, Henry VI, Edward V, and Richard III displayed neither corpse nor effigy. On the other hand, Edward III, Henry IV, Henry V, and Edward IV died naturally and were provided with effigies at their funerals (Giesey 1960: 80–5). Likewise, effigies were used for all the royal funerals during the dynastically stable Tudor era and for the funeral of the first Stuart king, James I. For his ill-fated son, Charles I, the concept of the king's two bodies had fatal implications, as we noted.

One can never separate fully the pragmatic from the symbolic. But it is intriguing to try to identify the meaning that the effigy held for those who used it. To what extent did the English royal effigy represent the immortal kingship and nation as the Shilluk effigy represented the timeless unity of Nyikang? Originally, it was the natural body of the deceased that was displayed, while the invisible body politic had shifted to the successor. The introduction of the effigy seems to have gradually brought about a subtle shift in meaning. For the effigy in royal garb was now visible in contrast to the invisible corpse in the casket. Kantorowicz (1957: 421) suggests that the funeral became a ritual inversion of the normal doctrine of the king's two bodies. Now the hitherto invisible body politic is made visible, and it is the body natural that can no longer be seen. Death may eventually separate the two bodies, but until burial they are not so much separated as inverted in their relationship.

However, the use of the royal effigy in England never completely loses its pragmatic aspect as substitute for the corpse (Giesey 1960: 85). There may be inversions of sorts, but the effigy remains with the casket, always proximally associated with the particular deceased monarch whose likeness it bears. It never represents the kingship or the total body politic of England. At most, it represents the perpetual royal dignity of the previous king. It relates to the jurists' explanation that King Henry VIII lives on after the death of Henry Tudor, separate from the kingship that passes to his son. Depending upon the times and circumstances of his assumption of royal authority, a successor may omit the tribute to the royal dignity of the dead king.

The Immortal Kingship

LE ROI EST MORT! VIVE LE ROI!

In French royal funerals, the effigy was not used until Henry V of England died in France in 1422. He was also heir presumptive of France according to the treaty that he had recently signed with Charles VI of France. Consequently, his funeral effigy was prominently displayed across France as his procession moved to Paris and finally to England. Within weeks, Charles VI also died, leaving the succession of the French throne in dispute between the young Henry VI and the Dauphin of France. The English regent for young Henry VI quickly arranged the funeral for the French king, including an English-style funeral effigy. This custom of royal funeral effigies was then continued for every French monarch until the death of Louis XIII and accession of Louis XIV. Whereas in England the practice of the effigy remained sporadic and its use and meaning peripheral to the funeral ceremony, in France the effigy quickly developed into the central symbol in an elaborate ritual allegory of the state.

The style of Renaissance French royal funerals relates to constitutional concepts and political institutions that differed markedly from English parliamentary traditions. The sovereignty of France became fused with a strong dynastic principle and the government of France moved steadily toward absolutism. The English legal fiction of the radical distinction between the king's two bodies did not apply to Continental political theory. In the context of the funeral, France was powerfully represented within the effigy of a particular monarch who was father (or brother) to the new king. Giesey suggests that it is no accident that the French custom of royal effigies died out with the accession of the "Sun King" and the establishment of Bourbon absolutism. Once the absolutism of Louis XIV's modern monarchic state had been achieved, the medieval and Renaissance notions expressed in the ritual of the effigy were no longer appropriate (Giesey 1960: 190–2). The state had come to be symbolized by the person of the *living* king and by the continuity of his family. Louis XIV's "L'état c'est moi" was no boastful invention, but the recognition of a state of affairs that had been slowly established and had been expressed through the elaboration of the royal funeral effigy.

It is interesting to consider some of the later implications of the French royal funeral symbolism and to compare the meaning of regicide in France with regicide in England. As we mentioned above, the radical

English distinction between the king and the king's body politic permitted the execution of Charles I while the king's body politic continued. The consequences of the eighteenth-century execution of Louis XVI were different. The killing of the king ended the monarchy and permanently altered the structure of European society and political thought (Kantorowicz 1957: 23).

This is not to attribute to ritual any necessary priority in the chain of political causality. Royal customs, such as the use of the funeral effigy, often begin in response to chance circumstances and practical considerations. But once performed, any part of a royal funeral ritual sets a precedent that may be repeated at the next kingly death. Once present, such an element accumulates meanings the way a ship accumulates barnacles. Over the centuries, practical precedents become powerful symbolic configurations that constrain and inspire the course of later political events.

In many respects, the meaning of the royal effigy in France was similar to the meaning of the Shilluk effigy in that it came to stand for the perpetuity of the kingship, and the French nation. Over the generations in France, the effigy and the corpse of the deceased monarch became spatially separated and ideologically juxtaposed in complex funeral rites that became expressive of great dyadic tension: the triumph of death versus the triumph over death, church ritual versus state ritual, grief versus joy, all revolving around the body of the mortal king and the effigy of the immortal royal dignity.

Following the death of one of the Renaissance French kings, the heir to the throne stayed discreetly out of the public eye during the long funeral arrangements and ceremonies, when all the pomp of royalty remained focused on the deceased monarch. Nonetheless, the heir to the throne actually ruled the land. From his seclusion, he issued edicts in his own name as king, and most importantly directed the complex preparations for his predecessor's funeral. The government of France continued in spite of the "mutation" of the reigning monarch.

The period immediately following the royal death was devoted to the preparation of the body and effigy for the grand ceremonies to follow. The heart and entrails were removed and each encoffined separately. The three coffins (corpse, heart, entrails) were then the objects of continuous high and low masses, night vigils, and services for the dead performed by members of the religious orders. After about a week, the heart and entrails received their final service and were put in a permanent resting place.

Meanwhile, the craftsmen were working to produce the effigy of the deceased king:

The Effigy was made with painstaking care to represent the king as closely as possible. . . . The trunk, arms and legs of the effigy were made of osier, and were completely covered by the vestments in which the effigy was dressed. The head and hands, however, were exposed, and it was to these that Clouet devoted most of his time. A model of potter's clay was made first, then a mold of plaster, and the final product of wax; the hair of the head and beard were attached with putty, and the whole visage very realistically painted. Two pairs of hands were made; one pair joined, as the effigy appeared on the bed of honor, the other pair separate to hold the sceptre and the hand of justice, as the effigy appeared in the procession in Paris.

The effigy was dressed in the following manner: a shirt of Dutch linen; a waist-coat of crimson satin; a blue satin tunic, with fleurs-de-lis, which extended to the elbow; the legs stockinged with fine linen interwoven with gold; the feet covered by red satin slippers; over all, a sleeveless royal mantle of purple, lined with white satin and sewn with fleurs-de-lis and having a collar of ermine; around the neck hung the collar of the Grand Order; on the head, over a small brownish-red bonnet, the imperial crown, studded with jewels. On the other side of the effigy, on pillows, lay the sceptre and the hand of justice. In short, the king in effigy appeared in the fullest majesty, in the robes he wore otherwise only at his coronation and at a lit de justice. [Giesey 1960: 4–5]

When all the preparations were ready, the focus of the ceremony shifted from the encoffined body to the lifelike representation of the deceased monarch. The great hall of the palace was lavishly decorated with tapestries in joyous blue velvet and gold cloth. At the front of the hall, high on his "bed of justice" or "bed of state," sat the effigy. Along the walls and throughout the hall, now called the "hall of honor," were benches for the bishops, cardinals, and nobles who attended the twice-daily ritual of the setting of the royal dinner table.

And in this state the effigy remained for eleven days. And it is to be understood and known that during the time the body was in the chamber next to the great hall, as well as while the effigy was in that hall, the forms and fashions of service were observed and kept just as was customary during the lifetime of the king:

the table being set by the officers of the commissary; the service carried by the gentlemen servants, the bread-carrier, the cup-bearer and the carver, with the usher marching before them and followed by the officers of the cupboard, who spread the table with the reverences and samplings that were customarily made. After the bread was broken and prepared, the meat and other courses were brought in by an usher, steward, bread-carrier, pages of the chamber, squire of the cuisine and garde-vaiselle. The napkin was presented by said steward to the most dignified person present, to wipe the hands of the Seigneur. The table was blessed by a Cardinal; the basins of water for washing the hands presented at the chair of the Seigneur, as if he had been living, and seated in it. The three courses of the meal were carried out with the same forms, ceremonies and samplings as they were wont to be during the life of the Seigneur, without forgetting those of the wine, with the presentation of the cup at the places and hours that the Seigneur had been accustomed to drink, two times at each of his meals. [Du Chastel, quoted in Giesey 1960: 5]

Then the mood suddenly changed. Overnight, all the blue and gold tapestries were removed and replaced with black mourning cloth. The "bed of state" and the effigy were replaced with the coffin under a large black canopy. All the attendants, who had been dressed in their finest robes, now changed into black mourning cloaks. The hall was no longer called the "hall of honor," but was henceforth referred to as the "hall of grief." It was in this "hall of grief" that the new king might make his only appearance during the funeral ceremonies. Seven weeks after the death of Francis I in 1547, his son and heir, Henry II, came to asperse the body of his father:

Even to call this ceremonial "official" is misleading. Henry II came not as *Roi de France*, but as *fils de Francois.* . . . Henry could not have appeared while the effigy was on display, else there would have occurred the simultaneous exposure to view of two kings of France – an impossible situation. So Henry waited until the effigy had been removed and the *salle d'honneur* converted into a *salle de deuil.* But to play the role of mourner was no less difficult for a king of France than to confront his predecessor's effigy. . . . So, when Henry II came to asperse his father's body, his great royal mourning cloak was purple in color, a darkening, as it were, of the royal scarlet, but not a blackening of it. . . . And when he left . . . Henry symbolically terminated his quasi-mourning by giving away the cloak. . . . [Giesey 1960: 7]

The Immortal Kingship

Let us consider the overall format of the ceremonies. Not surprisingly, the funeral reproduces a familiar tripartite structure. First, there are the "receptions" in the palace, which we have just described. Second, there is the procession into Paris to Notre Dame Cathedral and then out toward Saint-Denis. Finally, there is the burial at Saint-Denis. What could be a more poignant representation of separation than those last grand royal banquets with everything assiduously as it had been during Francis I's life, and then sharply reversed to portray a black and lugubrious mourning tableau? The parallels to the simple funeral from Madagascar are striking. For there, too, we have the symbolic pretense that the deceased is still with us while he remains in the women's house, the house of life, until suddenly the men come and wrench him away.

The procession through Paris is also reminiscent of the ambiguously joyful and irreverent funeral processions in Madagascar and elsewhere. Often the royal French funeral procession degenerated into "difference, combustions, and debates" as various participant groups forcefully disputed what they felt to be their ancient privileges regarding the order and rank of marching. The most important of these rights belonged to the presidents of Parlement. It was their privilege to carry the corners of the pall placed under the lifelike effigy and to wear red robes rather than black. This symbolized the perpetuity of French justice.

The procession itself can be divided into three parts. In the front was the chariot carrying the coffin accompanied by the "pieces of honor" such as the king's helmet, gloves, and shield. This part had the characteristics of a funeral for a knight, or a member of a sacred order. In the rear, representatives of the royal family marched in deep mourning. There one saw the characteristics of a private funeral for a kinsman (except for the assiduous absence of the son and heir). But in the center of the procession, near the effigy, there was no sign of a funeral. The effigy was the live king making his joyful and triumphant entry into Paris. Dressed in all the rich insignia of office and with features resembling those of the deceased, the effigy could not be distinguished from the real king by observers more than a few feet away.

Finally, the procession arrived at the church of Saint-Denis, the royal necropolis outside Paris. The church was draped in black. The effigy was for the first and only time placed directly on top of the coffin, where it remained throughout the final night of the ceremony. Giesey writes of Francis I's funeral:

An awe-inspiring and ghostly sight it must have been: in the center of the choir lay the effigy of the just-deceased King of France, shining in the light of a thousand candles which cast a soft glow roundabout on the figures of the host of his predecessors – sculptured in stone atop their tombs. Francis, too, was soon to be another of the *gisants* of Saint-Denis; but while his body was not yet entombed, and his effigy still displayed, the sovereign power inhered in him still. . . . [Giesey 1960: 15]

The two-month-long ceremonial concluded with the ensepulchering of the coffin and the pronouncement of the rebirth of the sovereignty of the French king. Although the famous pronouncement "The king is dead! Long live the king!" later became associated with the moment of death, during the Renaissance it was not uttered until the moment of burial many weeks after death.

The effigy was removed from the coffin, never to be seen again. The coffin was lowered into the vault and then all the royal insignia were placed on it by the heralds-at-arms, the Captains of the Swiss Guard, the One Hundred Archers, the Scots Guard, the One Hundred Gentlemen, and the knightly orders. They placed there the spurs, the gloves, the helmet, the shield, the coat of arms, the pennon, the crown, the *main de justice*, and the scepter. For the burial of Francis I:

. . . the Admiral d'Annebaut, acting as Grand Master, came to the edge of the grave, carrying the Banner of France. Too ill even to stand steadily, the venerable admiral had to sit on a chair at the edge of the vault as he dipped the flag till its tip touched the coffin. The symbols of sovereignty of France, which for weeks had adorned alternately the coffin and the effigy, followed Francis I even down into his grave. But only for a moment could they rest there, for the sovereign power is immortal, and must ever rise anew.

"Le Roy est mort!" cried Normandy three times, and the crowd moaned and wept. The admiral was so choked with tears he could not utter "Vive le Roy" as it was his office to do; Normandy came to the rescue by himself uttering the cry of the new sovereign: Vive le roy, vive Henri deuxième du nom par la grace de Dieu roy de France, a qui Dieu doint bonne vie.

With this cry, the banner and sword and baton were raised on high, and the various ensigns and coats of arms on the barrier around the grave recovered by the knights and heralds. The objects within the grave were not recovered until after the party had left, however, for the symbols of sovereignty belonging to the person of the king – the crown, sceptre, hand of justice, and the knightly pieces of honor – were not to be seen again until the coronation of Henry II at Reims. [Giesey 1960: 16–17]

We have noted the parallels between this royal ritual in France and the mortuary rites described in earlier chapters, for example, as regards the reverence toward ancestors. A deeper similarity relates to the dyadic tension expressed in them, and resolved through them. The royal funeral stresses a radical opposition between the two aspects of the king's person, not male bone and female flesh, but royal dignity versus personal mortality. At the beginning of the ceremonies, the symbolic opposition is most intense, with the coffin and effigy alternating their appearances, never appearing at the same place or time. During the procession through Paris, both the coffin and the effigy are present, although spatially and symbolically separated. In the last services at the church of Saint-Denis, the effigy is placed on top of the coffin. Finally, the burial recreates the unity of the two aspects of the king's person through the proclamation of Henry II as king of France.

REGICIDE

When one realizes the extent to which the symbolism of kingship is constructed on what might be termed fictions (the English king has two bodies, a wax effigy rules France, the Shilluk king is possessed by the spirit of Nyikang), the unimaginative realism of Frazer's "doctrine of survivals" becomes all the more obvious. Both the French and English royal funerals have their archaic qualities, and, as Giesey (1960: 190) points out, are, in their symbols and concepts, essentially medieval survivals in a later age. Nonetheless, these rituals continued during the Renaissance to play a dynamic and ever-changing role in the development of Western constitutional thought, and in political intrigues. Royal funeral practices, archaic or otherwise, are best explained as vital aspects of changing political systems as Kantorowicz, Giesey, and Evans-Pritchard have done. In each case, the ritual material is related to cultural ideas of the permanence of kingship and the political-moral order; to institutional structures; to changing historical circumstances; and to the maneuverings of people competing for power and prestige.

In addition to these political questions, there is the paradoxical nature of symbolism itself. By definition, any symbol must be both itself and something other. The cognitive qualities of both the "signifier" and that which is "signified" feed back on one another, simultaneously constraining and creating meaning. With any symbolic representation, there is a large measure of ambiguity, of as yet inchoate potential meaning, which, in a political context, provides the material for self-interested innovation and change.

Frazer placed his shocking subject matter, murder, in the wrong analytic context and provided a narrow, titillating, and self-serving explanation. It was Frazer's simplistic view that every representation suggesting regicide inevitably meant the former existence of the practice. Evans-Pritchard's view reverses the analysis, stressing (as does Wittgenstein, 1971) the power of the idea itself, and suggesting that the belief may be even more effective in strengthening the polity when the deed is not actually done. This approach stresses the similarities between the Shilluk kingship and our own institutions. By stressing the symbolic over the homicidal, Evans-Pritchard removes the imputation of savagery and primitiveness that Frazer had put to all such customs.

Regicide is a symbol, part of a complex set of symbols, pertaining to the death of the king and the perpetuity of kingship. But as Beattie (1966: 570–1) has pointed out, "Symbolism is no less symbolic (and no more pseudo- or proto-'scientific') when, as it often is, it is translated into action." Charles I and Louis XVI are cases in point. They certainly were executed, and largely because of their symbolic positions as king. In European history, in spite of the rationalizations of those responsible, regicide always carries the immoral tinge of rebellion. The original interest of the Shilluk custom to Westerners was that regicide is routinely put into the context of positive morality. That which is familiar in European custom, but rare and frightening, was reported to be common among the Shilluk, and morally proper.

Frazer had no real evidence to show that the Shilluk killed their kings, and Evans-Pritchard had no real evidence to show that they did not. The research that Frazer drew on was a survey rather than intensive field observation, and Evans-Pritchard admittedly never visited the Shilluk. We are fortunate, however, that in recent years two anthropologists have done major research on neighbors of the Shilluk, the Dinka, whose similar customs had also been cited in various editions of Frazer's *Golden Bough*. These recent studies address themselves to this issue of the positive morality of controlling the time, place, and means of death for the politico-religious leaders of the Dinka.

In negatively stressing the differences between our society and primitive peoples, Frazer focused on regicide and similar customs. Evans-Pritchard, in his emphasis on the *similarities* between the Shilluk institutions and our own, reacted to the Frazerian prejudice. This led him to deny the actual existence of regicide. In both analyses, there remains the implication that such customs would indicate a certain primitiveness. Two ethnographers of the Dinka, Francis Deng and Godfrey Lienhardt, are sensitive to the sensationalist aspects of such customs, and both are at pains to represent Dinka values clearly and accurately. Yet both are led to the conclusion that Dinka leaders often ended their careers by being voluntarily buried alive.

DINKA BURIAL ALIVE

The Dinka are a large ethnic group in the southern Sudan who today number almost 2 million. In contrast to their Shilluk neighbors, the Dinka have never been united into a single polity, and consequently their political traditions vary considerably from one region to another. In most Dinka tribes, leadership is diffusely shared among religious leaders known as "masters of the spear." The northernmost Dinka tribe, the Ngok, is the only group to have developed a centralized chieftaincy similar to that of the Shilluk.

Deng's study is particularly interesting on this topic, for the anthropologist is himself a Dinka, the son of the late paramount chief of the Ngok Dinka:

The principles and practices applicable to the death of a Chief are different from those applicable to an ordinary person. I have already pointed out the importance of the Chief to the spiritual and physical welfare of his society and how traditionally he was not supposed to wait until he was actually dead before burial, but would request that he be buried alive at the brink of death. This is a debated point among anthropologists. Some believe it was merely mythological and not real. Real or mythological, the Dinka believe that the custom pertained [sic] until it was prohibited by the British. My greatgrandfather was allegedly buried this way. According to the story he remarked: "Watch my eyes" as the grave was being filled in. Since the grave of a Chief is constructed in such a way as to leave a dirt-free space for his underground shelter, the possibility is not so absurd as it might sound. It is said that my grandfather, too, would have been buried alive had not government agents seen to it that this did not happen. [Deng 1972: 132]

Nor was Deng's father, Chief Deng Majok, buried alive, for he died in a Cairo hospital in 1969. At that time, the Ngok Dinka were caught in the midst of the long and brutal civil war between northern and southern Sudan. Deng Majok was chief from 1945 on; he was by all accounts a man of considerable vision and talent, who managed to mediate successfully between tradition and modernity, between Arabic north and African south. Ngok Dinka say that when his body arrived back home, many people were disappointed that he was already dead and hence could not be buried alive. We cannot interpret this to mean that, had he returned alive, his family or the authorities would have allowed that outcome. But such statements show the continued strength and immediacy of the belief.

Deng writes movingly of the events surrounding the death of his father:

The death of Deng Majok in August, 1969, was an unparalleled calamity for the Ngok and other Dinkas farther South. Ngokland suddenly ceased to be a secure bridge between the South and the North. The fear, despair, and surrender to the concept of a spoiled world that came with Deng Majok's death left no doubt in anybody's mind that a great leader and protector was dead.

We eyewitnessed this crucial phase in the history of the Ngok when we took his body from Cairo where he had died. . . . On landing at Abyei, we found a reign of terror. Deng Majok's absence had created a vacuum which the security forces were filling with arrests, torture, and murder. Just two nights before our arrival, they had shot and killed a brother of the Chief – a highly regarded and well-established person whom they had suspected of cooperation with the rebels. Among the many who had been tortured was the Chief's own sister because one of her sons was a rebel. Her arms had been rendered paralyzed. The Dinka, including their Chiefs and especially their educated, were under careful scrutiny and in constant apprehension. Abdalla Monyyak Deng, the son whom Chief Deng had left in charge and who was to succeed him, had tried to fill his father's position; but he had neither the legal authority nor as yet the personal influence to be effective. He was even suspected of cooperation with the rebels by the security forces. He succeeded his father without delusions about the size of the shoes he was inheriting. As though his father were to blame, he remarked with tears in his eyes, "We were all praying for him to return and bring an end to all this. Instead he returns as a corpse at the moment of our greatest need." [Deng 1972: 146]

It was the beginning of the end for the divine chieftaincy of the Ngok Dinka. Chief Abdalla Deng reportedly made some progress in becoming an effective leader and protector of his people under difficult circumstances. But then, one year later, he and several members of his family were assassinated by the police as they were strolling on the edge of the village. Where once the mark of chieftainship had been a calm and voluntary ritual death in old age, now a twenty-seven-year-old chief was shot in the back by a handful of security police.

The instrument of the modern state, which once reinforced the institution of chieftaincy, added to its traditional prominence, and made it pivotal, is now the instrument threatening its continuity. Chieftaincy being the backbone of Dinka society, its extinction also threatens the existence of that society. This is in essence the major crisis of the Ngok. [Deng 1972: 152]

Clearly, it has been many decades since an important Ngok leader has been buried alive. But the memory of the custom, the persistence of the belief, and all that it implies about the nature of Ngok chieftainship have implications for the death of every chief, however that death comes about; and the death of every chief has implications for the polity. One speculates that the Ngok chieftainship might have survived almost any emasculation of the authority of a living chief, but that the radical contrasts between each of these last two deaths and the ideal of chiefly death were decisive. For it is the contrived death that allows images of immortality, that associates the chief with divinity and with the will of his people. The last two chiefs of the Ngok surely died in ways that left little room for images of immortality: one of a slow emaciating disease in a sterile hospital in a foreign land; the other by being gunned down in his own village.

Even a brief examination of the traditional customs will show how very great is the disparity between these two deaths and the ideal. Lienhardt presents the following account from a Dinka who had witnessed in his youth two ritual deaths of masters of the spear:

Royal Corpse and Body Politic

The master of the fishing-spear Deng Deng was becoming very old, and when his years were finished and he was very old indeed, so that he could not see well and all his teeth had fallen out, he told his lineage that he wished to be buried alive, and that they should go and tell the people of the country and see if they agreed.

They prepared the ground for his burial at a very ancient cattle-camp site called Malwal, which was also hard by the homestead of Deng Deng and near his cattle-byre. So it was at his very own original home. . . . The clan which cleared and dug the ground was Padiangbar; it is that clan which buries a master of the fishing-spear alive in my country.

They dug a very big hole on the highest point of the cattle-camp site, in the middle of the cattle. Next to it were two bulls, a big white one and a red one. . . . When the hole had been dug, they made two platforms (frameworks) of *akoc* wood, which had been fetched by the young men of Padiangbar from far away in the forest, as much as a day's journey distant.

They worked for three days, and the old man was still above the ground. They honored the bulls with songs for two days, speaking invocations each day in the morning and the evening. Then the masters of the fishing-spear of Pakedang, along with those of Paketoi and Pagong, slit the throats of the bulls at about 10 o'clock. Deng Deng's mother was the daughter of a woman of Paketoi and his mother's father was of the clan Pagong. So they were all there together, to join together his father's and his maternal uncle's families.

Deng Deng made invocations over the bulls, and the horns of the first bull, the white one, sank forwards to the ground. When the bull had been killed, they took its skin and cut it into strips, and made a bed from it on the framework. And every day they made a feast and danced inside the cattle-byre during the daytime, and outside at night. And men slept in the byre with other men's wives, and everyone agreed to this (literally 'and there was no bad word').

They then placed a war-shield, made from the hide of a bull of the clan-divinity which had been killed in the past, on top of the bed. It was a war-shield which had for long been kept in the byre, and which the people had anointed with butter every spring and autumn, during the 'dividing months'. They placed Deng Deng on the shield and lowered him into the grave.

The red (brown) bull remained. When Deng Deng had been lowered into the hole, they made a platform over him, and so arranged it that the top of the platform was level with the surface of the ground. They sang hymns, and after the singing was finished, they made an enclosure of *dhot* wood around the grave. The enclosure was about twice the area of the surface of the grave, and of such a height that a man could just see over it if he tried. Then they took cattle-dung and partly covered over the top of the grave, leaving part uncovered so that his voice could be heard. From his grave, Deng Deng called the older men together outside the enclosure, and all the women and children, even his own wives, were sent away. . . .

Deng Deng had died at the time of the harvest. He said that in the following dry season, in the month of Akanythii, his tribe would fight with a neighboring tribe, and that he was distressed because his people were not brave enough in war.

Two months later, this fight took place, and eight of his people were killed and two from the neighboring tribe. That neighboring tribe soundly beat his tribe and drove them off as far as Agar Dinka country. Eventually, the Government forces came and prevented thefts of cattle. But even then that neighboring tribe made a feast near the river in the face of the dry-season pastures of his own tribe which had been so harried that they could do nothing about it.

While the master of the fishing-spear still speaks, they do not cover the grave with dung. But when he no longer replies when they address him, they heap up the dung over him. And when it has all sunk in, they make a shrine. Some people may then say "the master of the fishing-spear has died," but they will usually say "the master has been taken into the earth." And nobody will say, "Alas, he is dead!" They will say "It is very good." [Lienhardt 1961: 301–3, reprinted by permission, © Oxford University Press, 1961]

There are a number of other accounts reported by Lienhardt of the burial alive of masters of the fishing-spear and rainmakers among the various groups of the large and sprawling Dinka population. There are certain variations that correspond to region: The rituals of the northern groups tend to be more elaborate due in part to the proximity of the Shilluk and in part to more centralized social institutions. Otherwise, Lienhardt reports that the wide variation in practice is not regionally based, but that each "performance" creatively draws on a common fund of symbols and practices. The ritual, as an institution, was flexible to the desires of the master, his people, and to the demands of the times.

In spite of the variety of the customs, several important general points must be noted. First of all, burial was voluntarily initiated by the master himself when he was quite old and felt himself to be dying. The burial of a living master against his will is not unknown among the Dinka, but it is considered wrong. In legend, such is the fate only of an evil master of the spear. On the other hand, the volition of the master is limited by the fact that he is expected under certain circumstances to request the ritual, and he has lived much of his life with the knowledge that such would likely be his eventual end.

Second, the people must consent. In all the reports, the master requests that the elders consult with the people to see if they agree. The act of burial alive is a collective act; it is neither suicide nor regicide. It is performed by the master and people in concert, for the well-being of the community and the honor of the master.

Third, the master of the fishing-spear is believed to die. The ritual is not performed out of any unsophisticated belief on the part of the Dinka that their leader escapes death. The ritual is expressed in the idiom of immortality, to be sure, but we must be careful not to take their symbols more literally than do the Dinka themselves. Some expressions are clearly euphemisms that "replace the involuntary and passive connotations of the ordinary verb for 'to die' (*thou*) by expressions suggesting a positive act. Similarly . . . when we hear that the people bury their master of the fishing-spear it is as an alternative to 'letting him die'. In other words, the deliberately contrived death, though recognized as death, enables them to avoid admitting in this case the involuntary death which is the lot of ordinary men and beasts" (Lienhardt 1961: 314).

The fact that the Dinka actually did bury their leaders alive under certain circumstances does not eliminate the important role of symbolic fiction or artifice. The Dinka symbol of burial alive contains as much fiction as the English notion of the king's two bodies, the French royal effigy, or the Shilluk spirit of Nyikang. Lienhardt presents sound evidence that the Dinka recognized the metaphorical quality of the ritual. For example, the close kin of the deceased master were permitted and expected to mourn in recognition that, in spite of the idiom of renewed community vitality and joy, the death is real. "For the rest of the master's people . . . the human symbolic action involved in the artificial burial must be seen to transform the experience of a leader's death into a concentrated public experience of vitality and, in the Dinka world, aggressiveness" (Lienhardt 1961: 317).

Burial alive stresses the dual nature of the master's life force in a manner not unlike that of a European king of the Renaissance. The reality of the perpetual communal life that the master represents and to which his burial alive makes the decisive contribution is separable from his personal mortality. The immortal aspect of the master of the fishing-spear is the spirit of communal solidarity and experience created by the ritual.

Each of our "kings" – French, English, Shilluk, Dinka – possesses a certain duality by virtue of being a living symbol. The dualities are not entirely the same in every case, however. The English and Shilluk dualities make a radical distinction between the individual and corporate aspects of the leader and, as we noted above, ascribe contrasting weights to these aspects. The French and Dinka make a less clear-cut distinction, ritually mining the ambiguity of leadership. In these two cases, the corporate kingship is subsumed to a certain extent within the individual representative. Whereas the French kings used this ambiguity to create an absolute dynastic and personal rule, the Dinka masters of the fishing-spear weld themselves to the needs of the community and meet death in a way that is also a "social triumph over death" (Lienhardt 1961: 317). The power of the Dinka master is largely dependent on his personal morality and dignity. Such dignity in life implies personal dignity and unselfishness in the face of death, death which is as inevitable for him as it is for each Dinka. "Notions of individual personal immortality mean little to non-Christian Dinka, but the assertion of collective immortality means much, and it is this which they make in the funeral ceremonies of their religious leaders" (Lienhardt 1961: 319).

It seems that the most powerful natural symbol for the continuity of any community, large or small, simple or complex, is, by a strange and dynamic paradox, to be found in the death of its leader, and in the representation of that striking event. This would come as no surprise to Hertz, who drew attention to the fact that the most instructive illustrations of regular aspects of funeral behavior are often those pertaining to the special case of the succession of kings and chiefs:

The custom of not proclaiming the successor to a chief until the final ceremony . . . is reported from several peoples belonging to different ethnic groups. We may imagine the dangers of such an interregnum to the societies which are subjected to it. The death of a chief causes a deep disturbance in the social body which, especially if it is prolonged, has weighty consequences. It often seems that the blow which strikes the head of the community in the sacred person of the chief has the effect of suspending temporarily the moral and political laws and of setting free the passions which are normally kept in check by the social order. [Hertz 1960: 49]

Royal Corpse and Body Politic

Hertz's observation takes us beyond the political issues, beyond the corpse as symbol of the community. The death of a king or leader involves something more profound. Such an event becomes a symbolic paradigm for our own deaths and for the meaning of death itself. Whatever one may think of the leader's person or policies, one has a strong and vicarious personal identification with his death. Questions of political competition, social status, and constitutional stability aside, a royal funeral, effigy, or corpse becomes a highly condensed set of symbols directly representing every one of the deaths of all the people of the realm.

PART IV

SEEING OURSELVES
ANEW

8

AMERICAN DEATHWAYS

Taking our cue from Hertz, we have tried to unravel the ideological and sociological implications of funerary rites by focusing attention upon the fate of the corpse. Our comparative examples ranged from Europe to Asia, from predynastic Egypt to contemporary Africa, and from the simplest acephalous societies to complex states. But even so, our survey is far from exhaustive. This is for four reasons.

First, a world survey of mortuary customs, given the central importance that such rites often have, would amount almost to an encyclopedia of world cultures. Instead, we have drawn many of our examples from those areas that we know best, namely Africa and Southeast Asia. Second, we are conscious of the risk of overburdening the reader with descriptions of funerals to the point where they all begin to look alike. This is rendered all the more likely by the very similarities that it has been our purpose to identify. Third, we have chosen comparative examples from among the classics of anthropology; from the work of Durkheim, Evans-Pritchard, Frazer, Radcliffe-Brown, van Gennep, Wilson, and others. In this way, we have pointed out the importance of mortuary rites to the developing study of religion and society. Fourth, our emphasis on secondary treatment rites narrows the range of our examples.

Seeing Ourselves Anew

The justification for our initial emphasis on rites of secondary treatment is that it represents an attempt to *extend* Hertz's analysis. We first, in Chapters 2 and 3, discuss the attractiveness and difficulties of trying to explain certain seemingly universal psychological and symbolic features of funeral rituals. Chapter 4 provides a validation of Hertz's central equation of secondary burial, bodily decomposition, and certain beliefs about the afterlife. Chapter 5 extends this analysis and relates the practice of secondary burial to the issue of transition from life. In the chapters on royal funerals, we go beyond the topic of secondary treatment but continue to pay attention to the details of treatment of the corpse.

In so doing, we begin to explore traits that have little to do with secondary treatment per se, but that have a global distribution and a fascination of their own. Two examples of such traits are the use of effigies and mummification. The former, which we saw in connection with French royal rituals, is a recurring feature of funerals. In Bali, an effigy can be substituted for, or used in conjunction with, the corpse in the final cremation. In Malekula, New Hebrides Islands, life-size clay effigies are made, incorporating the skull of the deceased (Guiart 1963: 230, 240). One wonders whether these three cases share any other similarities than the use of effigies. In other parts of Melanesia, a seemingly related practice is found: the preservation of the corpse itself (Pretty 1969: 36–43). Many years ago, G. Elliot Smith (1915) showed that techniques of mummification have a worldwide distribution, and attributed this to diffusion from ancient Egypt. Few would now agree with his explanation, but an alternative has yet to be framed. These questions show that the impetus of Hertz's ideas is far from spent.

However, we pursue no further comparative material here – with one exception.

A justification that is often claimed for the study of societies remote from our own is that they permit a level of objectivity that cannot be achieved close to home. Armed, it is argued, with the insights that this objectivity provides, we return to our own society with new powers of observation. In our introduction, we pointed out just how odd American mortuary practices can be made to appear. Now we examine American funerals in more detail, asking ourselves what the approach through ritual can reveal about them.

American Deathways

PROBLEMS IN THE STUDY
OF AMERICAN DEATHWAYS

There are pitfalls in the way of the analysis of American mortuary rites. First, there is the problem of the comparability of our data. In contrast to many of the small-scale societies that we have discussed, America has a population of more than 200 million, and great cultural diversity. Does the United States provide us with one case or several? If more than one, how many? The second pitfall is superficiality, due, ironically, to lack of data. We have more descriptive material about funerals in Indonesia than in America. As David Sudnow remarked a decade ago: "Nowhere do we have an ethnography of death" (1967: 3).

These problems make it necessary to deal in generalities, creating a risk that a comparison with complex non-Western rituals will produce nothing more than a few bromides about the virtues or idiocies of American funerals. The risk is exacerbated by the literature on death in America, which is pervaded by value-laden and ethnocentric assessments. On the one hand are exposés of the American death industries, of which Jessica Mitford's *The American Way of Death* (1963) is the best known. An equally harsh critique, also of English origin, is Evelyn Waugh's satirical novel *The Loved One* (1948). On the other hand, there are numerous manuals combining, in different proportions, psychological insight with homely advice on how to approach one's own death and the deaths of those who are near and dear. A recent example is Elisabeth Kübler-Ross's *Death: The Final Stage of Growth* (1975). Dr. Kübler-Ross's title neatly conveys an areligious optimism appropriate to her profession as a psychiatrist. This partisan literature makes it hard to strike a balance between homily and sarcasm.

Our task is neither to criticize nor justify American deathways, but to interpret them as they exist. We begin by focusing on some illuminating paradoxes.

THE FIRST PARADOX: RITUAL UNIFORMITY
AND INDETERMINATE IDEOLOGY

Given the myriad variety of death rites throughout the world, and the cultural heterogeneity of American society, the expectation is that funeral practices will vary widely from one region, or social class, or ethnic group, to another. The odd fact is that they do not. The overall form of funerals is remarkably uniform from coast to coast. Its general features include: rapid removal of the corpse to a funeral parlor, embalming, institutionalized "viewing," and disposal by burial (see Figure 17).

According to a national census of morticians conducted by V. R. Pine, there are approximately 50,000 licensed funeral directors operating 22,000 funeral establishments, together taking care of "almost all" the dead in the United States (Pine 1975: 21). Embalming is nearly universal as a consequence of this reliance on death specialists. Contrary to common belief, embalming is not legally required, but funeral directors insist upon it on grounds of hygiene, in order to protect themselves (Pine 1975: 24). Even in rare cases where religious preferences disallow embalming, some other process of disinfection is substituted.

A study in Philadelphia revealed that 90 percent of burials were conducted directly from funeral homes. This does not mean that the participation of clergy has been eliminated, however, because the homes regularly provide their own interdenominational chapels (Dempsey 1975: 171). Regarding final disposal, more than 92 percent of deaths result in earth burial (Pine 1975: 22). Cremation has never been as popular in the United States as it is in Europe, and accounts for less than 4 percent of deaths annually (Dempsey 1975: 180). Finally, with regard to the public "viewing," it seems that there is more variability, but that display of the restored corpse is still clearly the norm. In his census, Pine asked funeral directors to state how many of the funerals that they conducted were what he refers to as "total funerals," that is, having a public viewing (and hence cosmetic restoration) and a religious service. Of his respondents, 78 percent reported that almost all their funerals were of this kind, 20 percent said that most were, and a mere 2 percent said that only some were (Pine 1975: 201).

This uniformity becomes all the more striking if we compare it to the variety found among the 2,000 Berawan of Borneo. They have two widely different death ritual cycles, an extended and an abbreviated one, plus a number of choices with regard to temporary storage, final storage, and processing of the corpse. As we saw, Berawan beliefs about the afterlife are at first sight inconsistent. A coherent eschatology only emerged after extended analysis. Because American funerary rituals are so much more uniform, one might reasonably assume that it would be

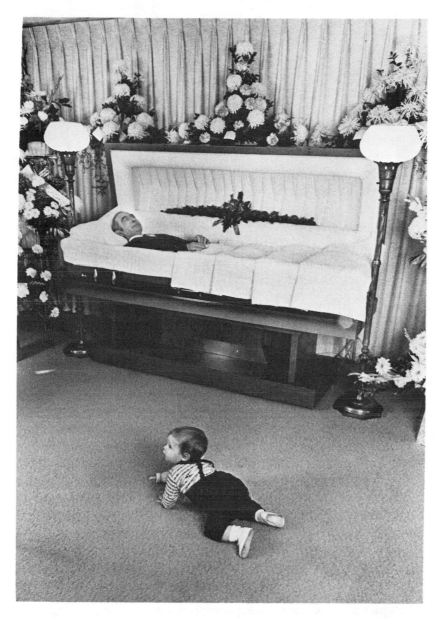

Figure 17. An embalmed corpse lies in an American funeral home. The photograph was taken by the grandson of the dead man, whose own child appears in the foreground (Mark Jury).

correspondingly easier to deduce the ideology underlying them. But this is not so.

In the first place, Americans claim adherence to a number of different denominations, whose formal doctrines on the fate of the soul in death are dissimilar. The Roman Catholic notion of purgatory is not shared by Protestants; Mormons are unique in believing that it is possible to arrange the salvation of unconverted kin who are long dead; and so on (Grollman 1974: 81–141). But these are formal doctrines – we know little about the degree of faith that ordinary practitioners have in them. Even more opaque are the views of those who claim no affiliation to any organized religious sect. We certainly cannot conclude that they totally lack ideas about the nature and meaning of death. Just how Americans conceive of death therefore remains a thorny issue. Few seem able to adopt a thoroughgoing agnosticism, and yet the majority seem shaky in their faith in a Christian afterlife.

In reviewing the customs of Borneo, we noted that it was frequently the case that the rituals of death are clearly set out and known to all, whereas their rationale is less explicit. American funerals present an even more extreme example of this phenomenon. We are left with two inter-related questions: What accounts for the uniformity in American death-ways? What do they express? At present, there are two sets of answers, both of which contain some truth, yet fail to provide a satisfying expla-nation for the form of the American funeral. The first relates to economic variables, the second to psychological.

CRITIQUES OF THE FUNERAL INDUSTRY

The economic explanation sees the uniformity of American deathways as a product of ruthless capitalism and their content as expressing only materialist values.

The emergence of the contemporary funeral parlor is the result of a process of accretion of functions over a period of two centuries. In colo-nial times, the undertaker was a part-time specialist only; his main skills were those of the carpenter. In addition to making coffins, he assisted in the laying out of the corpse. The first important abdication of function by church and congregation came about with the change in the location of graveyards. Partly as a result of increasing urbanization, and partly as a result of changing styles in mortuary architecture, the cemetery became separated from the church and was moved to an area peripheral to the residential area (Stannard 1974: 69–91). The undertaker now became a livery man as well, dealing in hired rigs. As factory-produced coffins became available, his premises also became a showroom.

Experiments with embalming began in the early part of the nineteenth century as a response to practical considerations. With the increasing mobility and spread of the population, it frequently became necessary to ship corpses long distances for burial by the close kin. During the Civil War, large numbers of young men died far from home, and professional embalmers appeared around the battlefields (Pine 1975: 16). At the conclusion of the war, the assassination of Lincoln brought further attention to the new techniques. The funeral cortege, with Lincoln's body on display, traveled from Washington across the Northeast and Midwest to Springfield, Illinois. In the 1880s methods of arterial injection were introduced, and for the first time effective cosmetic restoration became generally available; the funeral industry grew rapidly as a consequence (see Habenstein and Lamers 1955: 321–53, for a detailed account of developments in embalming).

The new techniques made possible the evolution of an old European institution, the wake, into a new and peculiarly American form. Traditionally, the wake occurs on the night immediately following death, when relatives and friends gather in the house where the corpse is laid out, either on a tabletop or in an open coffin. On the following morning, the sealed coffin is carried off for burial. Embalming allowed the period between death and burial to be extended, giving time for the deceased to journey home or for relatives to assemble. After restorative techniques were introduced, attention was focused on the display of the corpse and a more sumptuous setting was provided for it. In this way the old elements of the wake – a gathering in the presence of the body of the deceased – were reworked into a new complex.

These developments strengthened the role of the undertaker in several ways. First, in the beginning of the nineteenth century states began to enact legislation for the licensing of competent embalmers. This move, designed no doubt to protect the public from charlatans, created a controlling professional elite. Second, the technical apparatus required for embalming now rendered it impractical to perform the operation in the deceased's home, making it necessary for the undertaker to provide premises for the "viewing." This trend was encouraged by two features. Many houses, especially those of the less well-to-do, were too small to contain the crowds that now gathered for these occasions. Moreover, neither Jewish nor Roman Catholic practice allows the funeral service to be conducted with the coffin open, and most Protestant churches discourage the practice (Dempsey 1975: 177). In this way, the church or synagogue became removed from an important ritual phase of the funeral. The final step in this accretion of function was the addition of chapels to the proliferating mortuary complexes.

As the critics have shown, funeral directors have not failed to exploit their position in order to make a profit. Harmer (1963) and Mitford (1963) are full of examples of such opportunism. For example, Mitford describes how funeral directors regularly play on the emotional state of their customers to get them to purchase a more expensive coffin than they had intended. As she points out, the morticians' customers are almost by definition "impulse buyers." Again, cemetery landscapers are in a particularly favorable position vis-à-vis their customers. They collect payment on plots that they will not have to provide for perhaps many years, leaving themselves with interest-free capital in the interim (Mitford 1963: 97–118).

The National Funeral Directors Association has frequently exercised a powerful political influence. It maintains well-financed lobbies in Washington and the state capitals. Occasionally it has been able to secure legislation favorable to the business interests of its members. For instance, the association has steadily opposed cremation, and in some states has supported laws that make it unnecessarily expensive by requiring that a coffin be provided and burned up with the corpse (Dempsey 1975: 170).

However, in comparative perspective, the proportion of available resources committed to death ritual does not seem exceptional; certainly the Berawan and the Malagasy use up more. Moreover, the amount spent each year on funerals in the United States is considerably less than the amount spent on weddings, yet few condemn the materialism of weddings. Charges of exploitation are not leveled at the dressmaking industry or the Brewers' Association of America on the grounds that they make a profit out of these festive events (Fulton 1965: 104). Presumably this is because the critics regard weddings as socially useful and funerals as useless. But who is to judge the value of a ritual?

American Deathways

The same kind of overstatement has occurred in connection with conspicuous consumption at American funerals. Certainly, commercialism is noticeable, but it is not unlimited. For example, sumptuous flower arrangements surrounding the coffin are a feature of the "viewing," and it could be argued that the mourners compete to display their affluence in such gifts. However, very nice distinctions of status govern the size of floral tributes. It would be entirely tactless for a mere acquaintance or a distant relative to offer too large a wreath. In general, the impression is of a striving to find the *correct* level of expenditure in funeral accoutrements, rather than the most *impressive* (Crocker 1971: 123).

The same tendency is noticeable in the funeral cavalcade. Although it is common for close relatives to request that the hearse drive past the deceased's former residence or workplace, the display at such times is modest by comparison with, say, nineteenth-century England. Curl (1972) presents a remarkable photograph from England of a six-horse hearse, heavily draped in black crepe, the horses decorated with black-dyed ostrich feathers, and attended by a dozen or so equerries. The striking feature of the picture is the obvious poverty of the neighborhood to which this apparition has been summoned. By comparison, the dark American hearse and line of cars is positively spartan. In grave markers also, the prevalent trend is toward simple horizontal tablets. Clearly, wealth and social class *are* expressed in funerals, as they are in other phases of American culture, such as housing, clothing, and automobiles. However, there is little evidence of the manipulation of the dead for status-climbing purposes.

Considering the economic explanation as a whole, there is no doubt that the existence of a tightly organized group of specialists who control every phase of the disposal of corpses is the most significant single feature of American funerals. It explains why funerals cost what they do, and why nonspecialists, such as kin and clergy, appear only in passive roles.

But it does not explain everything about them. Why do they have the ritual form they do? There are other things that could be done to the corpse that would be just as expensive and therefore just as profitable. The very uniformity of funeral rites places limits on the economic explanation because merchandisers usually try continually to add new products to tickle the fancy of consumers. There has been, it is true, some gimmickry in the funeral industry – drive-in funeral parlors are a recent example – but the overall form of the rites has remained remarkably stable for several decades.

Moreover, it is clear that Americans are not just passive consumers of the only services available to them; they actively approve of them. A survey in several midwestern cities revealed that a majority of respondents felt that contemporary funerals are appropriate, and that the funeral director has an important role to play in comforting the bereaved (Kastenbaum and Aisenberg 1973: 213). Silverman (1974) reports that the widows she worked with in Boston received more help and comfort from the funeral director than from either physician or clergyman. This tacit approval is also manifest in the limited success of movements to reform funeral practices. Nonprofit funeral and memorial societies have had some success, and certainly provide much cheaper funerals, but their membership remains small. Some unions have established funeral plans for members, but their experience has been that the cheapest variety does not sell. Their blue-collar clientele still demands all the elements found in the commercial funeral (Dempsey 1975: 183, 187).

A final piece of evidence: Modern-style embalming, with its associated rites, has been practiced for nearly a century now. During that time, the United States has continued to receive immigrants from many different cultural backgrounds. The statistics quoted in the preceding section indicate that the majority have adopted American deathways, just as they have absorbed other aspects of national culture. Had it been otherwise, institutions would surely have sprung up to cater to their needs. This shows that funerals somehow fit into a peculiarly American ideology; that funerals express something. Economics is powerless to explain what.

FEAR AND GUILT: THE INADEQUACY
OF PSYCHOLOGY

The second type of explanation for the form of American funerals has the advantage that, unlike the economic explanation, it deals directly with the content of the rituals. It sees them as expressing deep currents of fear and guilt, and points to the uniformity of the rites as evidence of the prevalence of such emotions. The widest extension of the theory is found in Ernest Becker's influential book *The Denial of Death*, in which he argues that "the idea of death, the fear of it, haunts the human animal like nothing else; it is the mainspring of human activity" – presumably of funerals in particular (1973: ix). A more specific application of the theory to funerals is found in Bowman's *The American Funeral: A Study in Guilt, Extravagance, and Sublimity* (1964).

The strongest argument in support of these views is provided by the elaborate avoidance, both in word and deed, of the brute facts of death. The majority of deaths now occur in hospitals, where the fiction of probable recovery is often maintained until a person is near the point of death. The corpse is then promptly removed without the aid of the bereaved, who see it again only under very special circumstances, after it has been primped up to appear as if asleep. Coffins are selected for their superior padding, as if comfort mattered to the corpse. We speak of the deceased as having "passed on"; we describe the premises of the death specialist with the cozy-sounding terms "funeral parlor" or "funeral home"; we comment how "well" the embalmed corpse looks lying in the "slumber room"; and so on.

This endless shying away from confrontation with mortality is undeniably a marked feature of American culture. However, we cannot conclude that this is solely or exclusively the result of a pervasive fear of death. Other causes may be involved. For example, the professional titles used by undertakers have grown increasingly euphemistic: "mortician," reminiscent of such medical specialists as optician; "funeral director," suggestive of business or perhaps the stage; and most recently "grief counselor," a kind of terminal marriage counselor. As a result of participant observation research in a number of Chicago funeral parlors, Kaut (1952: 7–35) suggests that these euphemisms may have less to do with the insecurities of the public over mortality than with the insecurities of the specialists over their professional status. These titles represent a desire to shake off their pallid public image and acquire more of the éclat of the medical profession.

Similarly, the process of embalming itself represents more than an illusory negation of death. If Americans really associated preservation of the corpse with perpetuation of life, would there not be a demand for true mummification, as there was in ancient Egypt? Current embalming practices generally only impede decomposition by a few weeks, because the use of high concentrations of preservative fluids evidently makes it harder to produce a lifelike appearance for display purposes. The techniques exist to do a much more permanent job, but they are not in demand. In one instance, a funeral director was obliged to move a coffin to allow a road expansion a year or so after interment. The corpse turned out to be perfectly preserved, and the undertaker, proud of his handiwork, invited the close kin to come and inspect it. They emphatically refused (Kaut: personal communication). What this anecdote illustrates is that embalming is for a specific ritual purpose. Once the funeral was completed the family had no further desire to see or think about the lost member they had so carefully housed underground. The response of Americans to cryogenic suspension – the deep freezing of the body for later revival – validates the same point. It has now been available for a decade; it is promoted by an active Cryonics Youth Association; and it holds out the promise of a scientifically feasible immortality. Yet at the present time there is a grand total of just *fifteen* people in suspension (Dempsey 1975: 191).

What embalming clearly *does* prevent is the confrontation of the mourners with the processes of putrescence in the corpse. But this horror of corruption may be seen as a special case of the general aversion to body processes, of which the American stress on hygiene is a part. There are at least as many taboos on, and euphemisms for, defecation and copulation as there are on dying. In their horror of putrescence Americans resemble the Berawan of Borneo, but their reaction is different. The Berawan try to hasten the completion of the process; Americans try to halt it.

The avoidance of death may have several contributing factors other than fear. There is also a difficulty in specifying what exactly is feared. Jacques Choron (1964: 73–84) deals with this problem at some length. He shows that "fear of death" may be several things: fear of what happens after death, fear of the event itself, or fear of ceasing to be. It may even be the fear of being *unable* to die. Choron quotes the case of a young woman who found terrifying the idea of living with herself forever: "She worried most about it at the age of ten, but at twenty, she heard an address on immortality, and the feeling of unbearableness returned: it was as if she simply could not endure it – better total annihilation, anything, than this continual going on and on" (Choron 1964: 18). If there are all these different *kinds* of fear, and if the fear of death conditions the rituals of death, should there not be a corresponding variety of rituals?

American Deathways

This indeterminacy about the nature of the fear of death may explain the contradictory results obtained in psychological tests. In a volume edited by Robert Fulton (1965) is a series of articles exploring unconscious attitudes to death among various populations, such as students, the aged, and the mentally ill, employing a variety of verbal and projective tests. As the editor points out (1965: 80), the results are confusing: Swenson reports an inverse correlation between fear of death and religiosity, whereas Christ finds no connection between the two. Rhudick and Dibner find that people in good health are more likely to have a "positive attitude" toward death, whereas Swenson reports that the healthy are more "evasive or defensive" on the topic than the sick. The researchers also differed on what influence an unstable ego structure had on morbid fears.

We do not doubt that morbid anxiety forms an important force in the psychodynamics of the individual, in our society and in others, as Becker has argued. But these private fears cannot provide us with a theory of public ritual. If the fear of death is indeed universal (and the anthropologist invariably views such claims with narrowed eyes), then it cannot explain the *variation* of mortuary rites from one place to another. The general cannot be used to explain the particular. To salvage the hypothesis, it must be argued that all funerals express fear of death, but that American ones do so more than others because Americans are more fearful than other people. This heightened fearfulness is usually attributed to the decline of organized religion in the West, with a consequent loss of faith in the old certitudes (Becker 1973: ix). But the problem of exceptions remains. In Britain church attendance has declined even more markedly, yet British funerals lack many of the death-denying rites found in American ones, notably embalming and public viewing. Attempts to market these services in Britain have largely failed (Mitford 1963: 161–76).

These are the hazards of reductionism. In Chapter 2, we showed how variable are the emotions, or more precisely the emotional expressions, that different societies regard as appropriate toward death. These differing views on what is proper do not control the feelings of the individual, which are sovereign. But conventions condition feelings and provide a setting for them. Between ritual and emotion there is a subtle feedback, so that it is difficult at any moment to say whether the emotions are propelling the ritual or vice versa. In this circumstance, it becomes necessary to follow Emile Durkheim's precept: The determining cause of a social fact should be sought among the social facts preceding it and not among the states of the individual consciousness (1938: 110).

COLLECTIVE REPRESENTATIONS
OF DEATH IN AMERICA

That the practices of embalming, display of the corpse, and earth burial are social facts is easy to demonstrate. The mourners do not think of themselves as inventing anew the rite of embalming to express or relieve their guilts and fears. Instead, they do what they think is proper, what is socially prescribed. Proponents of the economic explanation might argue that they only do what they must. But, as we have shown, the bereaved *do* have other alternatives if they truly consider that the standard rites lack moral authority. The fact that people are so easily led to believe that embalming is legally required – all the funeral directors have to do is fail to inform their customers otherwise – is interesting in itself. Americans feel that it is the sort of thing that *ought* to be enforced by law.

But these main elements of the ritual sequence are only the most obvious social facts governing the funeral, only the tip of the iceberg. American deathways comprise an extensive complex of collective representations. There are many other items of behavior or expression associated with death and funerals that turn out to be subtly governed by notions of propriety, notions that ordinary people are not in the habit of formulating in words yet that they regularly put into action in moments of crisis. For examples we turn to Sudnow (1967), whose own work in two large hospitals in California goes a long way toward alleviating that lack of an "ethnography of death" that he pointed out.

The first example concerns rules governing the transmission of the news of death. These cover both the *way* that people are told, and the *order* in which they are told. The immediate family has the right to know within minutes or hours, and expect to be informed in person or over the telephone. In choosing between these two, the greater speed of the telephone must be taken into account if there is a risk that the person will learn of the death in an improper way. The physician is often the first to know, and will try to impede the spread of the news until he or she has talked to those entitled to learn it directly. Other visitors who happen to be at the hospital are only told if the doctor is confident that they cannot "leak" it to close kin. Sometimes this requires delicate maneuvering. Thereafter, people should ideally learn from someone who stood in approximately the same degree of intimacy to the deceased, and in rough order of intimacy. Some little discussion is often necessary to decide who should telephone whom, as the urgency, or lack of it, with which the close kin contact friends and relatives constitutes an evaluation of the importance of the person in the life of the deceased and in the estimation of the survivors (Sudnow 1967: 154–5, 158–63).

After news of the death has spread, a second set of representations is called into play, having to do with the timing of encounters between sympathizers and the immediate family. Normal rules governing the privacy of the bereaved family are put aside, and new ones substituted during the course of the *rite de passage* that are both more and less restrictive than normal. Those less closely related to the deceased are embarrassed to offer their condolences too soon after the death occurs. Information is sought as to the propriety of a visit, to make sure of not intruding on an intimate family scene. On the other hand, the family, out of respect for the intent of such sympathizers, cannot reject them or show irritation. They are therefore open to receiving relative strangers as well as close friends in a more intimate and less controllable way than they normally would. This open-door accessibility is institutionalized in the Jewish custom of *shiva*, but is evidently found in many American communities. Under these circumstances, an organizer often emerges who is able to decide matters of protocol; someone close enough to the family to be aware of their desires, but no so close as to be more properly concerned in active grieving (Sudnow 1967: 156–7).

A third example concerns the obligation not only to view the corpse, but also to say the correct things about it. Friends and relatives of the deceased mingle freely at the viewing, and often there is considerable sociability. But, on entering, the mourner must first approach the coffin. There is little show of emotion, but afterward it is appropriate to make some brief remark about how well the deceased looks. This pattern is established with the immediate family, who are the first to view the restored corpse. Generally the reaction is relief and muted admiration. If the reaction of some close relative is other than expected, particularly if someone so forgets themselves as to comment that the deceased looks dead, they will be gently coaxed by the funeral director. Often, he or she will ask the family to leave the viewing room while adjustments are made. It is hard to do much to the corpse at this stage, so the real changes are minimal. Yet when the family returns, they almost invariably say something to the effect: "That's just perfect now." Those less emotionally involved conform more easily (Pine 1975: 95–6).

These usages are rapidly acquired, even by those who have not had occasion to employ them previously, because they conform to collective representations that are found in everyday contexts, and not just in the situation of the funeral. That a close relationship exists between death-ways and other ideological and social systems in a society is easily demonstrated by tracing the changes that occur in each over time. Even a casual glance at the history of funerals in the West suffices to reveal a complex and sometimes remarkably rapid evolution in style. There is variation in the pace and direction of innovation from one country to another, indicating a dynamic interaction with other changing social factors. Interestingly enough, variation in the form of the death rites between classes within one nation (aside from sheer cost) is less noticeable than variation from country to country. This relative uniformity may indicate that, insofar as the nation is a solidary community, it needs to share a system of beliefs and practices concerning death.

The detailed history of Western deathways has yet to be written, although some interesting beginnings have been made, notably in the essays of David Ariès (1967, 1974a) and in those contained in Stannard (1974). Ariès provides an overview of funerals in Europe from the Middle Ages to the present and shows that the medieval pattern has haltingly, and with occasional reversals, been made over into its complete opposite.

THE SECOND PARADOX: PUPPET DEATH

Ariès's argument is a striking one: Contemporary French and English people have been deprived of their own deaths, and of the right to mourn the deaths of others.

In the Middle Ages, people were expected to detect the imminence of their death. If they failed to do so, it was the duty of a friend to point it out so that they could prepare themselves. The preparations involved were partly spiritual and partly social, and on both counts the sick were well aware of what was expected of them. The drama took place in a room crowded with people – kin, workmates, neighbors, even casual passers-by. The dying person played the central role, striving for the same dignity that he or she had previously witnessed at similar scenes. Each visitor was bade adieu, asked for his or her forgiveness, and given a blessing. Final instructions were given with the authority that death invested, and the sacraments were taken. After the event, the close kin gave themselves over to uninhibited grief. With this cathartic release, they soon returned to normal life (Ariès 1974b: 3–4).

Today, the physician and the family conspire to keep all knowledge of impending death from the sick person. The truth is also kept from children, and indeed the terminally ill are reduced to the status of minors. Should they suspect the truth, they keep quiet about their fears so that the survivors can have the comfort of saying to themselves: "At least, he never knew." The doctor presides over the deathbed. Afterward displays of emotion are kept to an absolute minimum, and those who, it is feared, will "break down" in public are avoided. Such intense embarrassment surrounds loss of control that widows or widowers will often stay away from the funeral rather than risk it, thereby giving up whatever comfort they might have obtained from an extremely brief and otiose ritual (Ariès 1974b: 8–11).

As he himself notes, Ariès's account of contemporary practices mainly applies to Europe. In America developments have taken a somewhat different turn, not in terms of the secrecy about impending death, which Americans share, but in terms of the response when death has occurred. Let us compare the ritual sequence of medieval Europe with that of contemporary America, which is as much a derivation of European models as is that of present-day France and England.

The medieval sequence began with the deathbed scene that Ariès describes so movingly, and which is often portrayed in pictures of the epoch. It continued with the wake – indeed the wake was virtually a continuation of the deathbed gathering because it occurred in the same building as the death (if not in the same room), it involved the same people or a group much like them, and it was held on the evening following the death. The corpse was removed to the church for the funeral service the next day, or at most a day later, and buried nearby.

In the contemporary American sequence, the deathbed scene has all but been eliminated. Sudnow (1967: 85) reports that relatives were infrequently present when death occurred in the large county hospital that he studied, and very seldom asked to see the corpse before removal to the funeral home. Even when they are present near death, no moral authority is invested in the dying person. The wake, however, has increased in duration and function. Usually it extends over about three days, although even longer periods were common a few decades ago. Funeral directors have attempted to establish the norm that shorter wakes are sufficient, using the rationale that transport is now rapid enough that a mourner can arrive from any part of the country within a couple of days. Visiting is light during the morning, but heavy in the late afternoon and evening. Often close members of the family are there many hours a day, and sometimes wish to stay all night, although this practice was already declining in the early 1950s (Kaut 1952: 51). The funeral service, meanwhile, has become fused with the wake, because it is often held on the same premises. Displays of emotion within the funeral parlor are perfectly permissible, and appear to have a cathartic effect. The wake or funeral is rarely held in the absence of the close kin, as happens in England; this is resented by the funeral director when it occurs because it compromises his position (Pine 1975: 99). The burial is not an important phase of the ritual. The close family may attend only briefly at the graveside and leave before interment occurs.

The comparison reveals a number of ironies. In contrast to medieval Europe, the nuclear family in America has been invested with enormous sentiment that was formerly dispersed over a wider group. Yet, in the country where "togetherness" is a national fetish, no phase of the most severe crisis of the family's existence takes place at home. The oddest feature is that a society that provided harsh living conditions and little chance of mobility for its members stressed a positive role for them in death, whereas a country that emphasizes individual achievement allows only a passive role to the dying.

Since the fifteenth century, there has been in the West a continuous tradition of literature on how to die. The *Ars moriendi* instructed the individual on how to shrive his or her soul in preparation for death, and how to meet social obligations to achieve a "proper death" (Boase 1972: 119–20). A seventeenth-century version, Menston's *The Art to Dye Well*, is phrased in equally muscular terms. But recent editions, such as *The Art of Dying* by Robert Neale (1973), stress an almost Buddhist resignation in the face of one's own death and the deaths of others. The earlier volumes urge that the sinner "look on death" in order to wake the fires of conscience; the latest writers advise a sidelong glance to avoid psychological maladjustment. In the Middle Ages, men and women made themselves masters of their own deaths. In America, the archetypal land of enterprise, self-made men are reduced to puppets.

AN INDIGENOUS AMERICAN RELIGION

The historical comparisons that we make here are crude, and the opportunity exists for more delicate analysis. For example, Ann Douglas (1974: 49–68) describes a remarkable religious movement in mid-nineteenth-century America that (for social reasons that she convincingly explains) sought to promote a homely, even domestic, view of the world to come. This movement produced some of the most detailed eschatology on record, with descriptions of the "eating habits, occupations, lifestyles, methods of childcare and courtship current in Heaven" (Douglas 1974: 63). How, one wonders, did such views relate to ritual practice?

Ariès's own explanation for the inversion of death since the Middle Ages turns on the increasing sentimentalization of the nuclear family during that period, with a consequent loss of individuality. However, the inversion of ritual is less complete in the United States, where the process of sentimentalization is most advanced. Ariès accounts for this by positing a rediscovery or continuation in America of the "tone and style of the Age of Enlightenment" (1974b: 17). This is a difficult assertion to test, but we can perhaps break it down into more tangible variables.

Though it is not easy to specify how Americans conceive of their fate after death, there are attitudes toward death that are strongly held by them, and which distinguish their views from those of societies in other times and places. As Sudnow's work suggests, the place to begin looking for these attitudes is not in the representations of organized religion, but in something more pervasive – medicine. Americans have vast faith in medicine, a faith that is certainly in tune with the Enlightenment values of progress and humanism. The development of powerful new drugs, and of reliable and safe surgical techniques, together with improvements in diet, have enabled the "inevitability" of death to be redefined. Formerly, for instance in medieval times, death was every-where, in all its ugliness and suffering. It might pick out anyone. In con-temporary America it is removed to the hospital, or the television screen, so that it is sometimes suggested that Americans are simply "soft" and unable to face reality. But *reality* has changed. Modern medicine has not greatly increased the maximum lifespan that a person can hope for, but it has greatly improved the chances of reaching that age. Moreover, it has the power to alleviate pain, even in the incurably ill. With the exception of the specter of cancer, it is strongly felt that death is only a matter of resignation in the geriatric, and suffering never (Parsons 1963: 61–3).

These attitudes toward death frame a view of the proper life that con-founds the medieval view of a proper death. The key notion is fulfillment. The life of the individual should rise in an arc through brassy youth to fruitful middle years, and then decline gently toward a death that is acceptable as well as inevitable. The practices of embalming and viewing express these collective representations. The point is to reveal the dead at peace. Because the last hours or days preceding death may have been marred with pain, which is inadmissible, the restored body provides a truer image of death. Because heavy sedation may have been necessary to alleviate suffering, deathbed scenes are precluded. Controversy has resolved around whether the viewing of the embalmed corpse helps the bereaved to recover from their grief by providing them with a pleasant "memory picture," as the Funeral Directors Association would have us believe. Psychiatric opinion is divided (Dempsey 1975: 175–8). What is clear is why the main actor in the rituals is dramaturgically passive (our "puppet death"), because peace and fulfillment are conceived of as passive conditions.

Views about the worth of medicine figure prominently in these atti-tudes toward death. But these views in turn derive from a worldview that predates the rather sudden rise to efficacy of modern medicine in the last century. This worldview is expressed in the Constitution, in concepts of the nature of social class, in aesthetic predilections, and in much else that is peculiarly American. Were an anthropologist from Borneo or Madagascar to visit the United States, we have no doubt that he or she would have little trouble in identifying a "solidary system of beliefs and practices relative to sacred things" (Durkheim 1965: 62) that constitute an indigenous American religion.

American Deathways

Robert Bellah highlights the public component of this religion in his essay *Civil Religion in America*:

While some have argued that Christianity is the national faith, and others that church and synagogue celebrate only the generalized religion of "the American Way of Life," few have realized that there actually exists alongside of and rather clearly differentiated from the churches an elaborate and well-institutionalized civil religion in America. This article argues not only that there is such a thing, but also that this religion . . . has its own seriousness and integrity and requires the same care in understanding that any other religion does. [Bellah 1967: 1]

Bellah explores the dimensions of this civil religion in the area of national politics by analyzing the religiously charged language of presidential inaugural addresses – which constitute a major rite of the national religion. He outlines the changes that have occurred in these collective representations during the two centuries of the nation's existence and what symbols have been mobilized to express them. He shows that the trauma of the Civil War introduced new themes of death, sacrifice, and rebirth into the civil religion. Abraham Lincoln came not only to express these themes, but through his martyrdom to embody them in his own person (see Figure 18).

In addition to the great rituals of state that Bellah points to, there is another aspect of the civil religion, a domestic aspect, which our study of funerals brings into focus. Here too, the death of Lincoln was a highly significant event. His assassination riveted public attention; his funeral continued to hold it. Lincoln's body was returned to Springfield by almost the same route that he had taken to Washington four years previously as president-elect. At towns and cities along the way, the funeral procession was repeated, amid crowds straining to catch a last glimpse of the man that they now called "the Saviour of the Union." An observer wrote:

I saw him in his coffin. The face was the same as in life. Death had not changed the kindly countenance in any line. There was upon it the same sad look that it had worn always, though not so intensely sad as it had been in life. It was as if the spirit had come back to the poor clay, reshaped the wonderfully sweet face, and given it an expression of gladness. . . . It was the look of a worn man suddenly relieved. [Quoted in Hamilton and Ostendorf 1963: 234]

In humbler rites across the country, a nation still grieving its war dead

Figure 18. Apotheosis picture of Lincoln. The martyred president is shown ascending to Heaven, assisted by Washington. This carte-de-visite is a composite of a photograph and a painting. Such mementos helped turn Lincoln into an American folk hero, and hardly a parlor in the North was without one in the post-Civil War period (Library of Congress).

tried to capture in their funerals something of the peace written upon Lincoln's face. In this way, public attitudes were made ready to accept the new techniques of embalming then being perfected.

It would be wrong to suggest that funerals comprise the entirety of the domestic civil religion. There are numerous other family and community rites, of which Christmas, Halloween, and Thanksgiving are the most obvious. Nevertheless, since the Civil War, the standard rituals of burial have taken on the power of collective representations for all Americans, regardless of religious affiliation.

It may seem surprising that such a system of beliefs and practices exists alongside Christianity, to which a majority of Americans give at least nominal adherence. But this duality is nothing new. For centuries, Christianity in Europe rubbed shoulders with the vestiges of tribal religions. It is often remarked that many of the trappings of Christmas are pagan in origin. Ariès cites a nice example from medieval Europe. The public gathering around a dying person was not a pious practice imposed by the church. In fact, priests frowned on it, because they saw it as distracting from the spiritual preparations and from their own role. Pious individuals sometimes took the church's advice and spent their last moments alone. More frequently, however, they responded to a different and independent set of mores, the power of which is demonstrated by the custom that anyone seeing a priest carrying viaticum should follow him to the dying person's bedside, even if that person were a stranger (Ariès 1974b: 4).

The only novel feature of the American situation is that the national religion germinated and grew under the nose, as it were, of a religious establishment that already commanded wide respect. What this demonstrates is the hardiness of such growths. It may be that no nation can emerge or persist without a belief system that encroaches to some extent on the terrain of world religions.

Even allowing for the undoubted influence of the funeral industry, it is in the last analysis the existence of the civil religion that explains the uniformity of American death rites, and enables us to discuss them in general terms. Paradoxically, it is a death-centered religion. This is indicated by the sacred quality of funerals compared to that of other life crises, such as weddings. Marriages are often solemnized in registry offices without the attentions of a religious specialist. But death demands a full religious service, with clergyman and congregation, even for those with only nominal church affiliation, or even none at all. Despite the obligatory presence of an officiant of some organized religious group, the usual setting of the service is carefully interdenominational. Many take place in the chapel attached to the funeral parlor, which lacks all but the most generalized insignia. The most extended and important rite is the wake. The wake is largely social in content, emphasizing that the loss is a unit event, a happening of the group (Sudnow 1967: 165). Its most important icon, the embalmed corpse, presides in impassive benevolence.

The civil religion of America operates on every level between the state and the family. The national religion focuses on the rituals of the presidency. Its hagiography features past presidents, such as the martyred Abraham Lincoln. As we have seen, it has a powerful effect on other phases of the civil religion, and may itself achieve poignancy by the borrowing of some small domestic rite. Another phase of the indigenous religion pervades the life of towns and cities. In *The Living and the Dead: A Study of the Symbolic Life of Americans*, W. Lloyd Warner emphasizes that the local center of community ritual is the graveyard. In the New England town that Warner studied, Memorial Day is a solidary tribute to ancestors, with its parade to the cemetery, speeches, floral tributes, and gunshot salutes. It is the one event that unites all the residents of the town. We have stressed the most personal, though still social, level of the civil religion, which receives its most telling representation in the funeral of the average citizen. In the funeral parlor, basic values of life are condensed into the peaceful image of the embalmed body.

BIBLIOGRAPHY

Abinal, R. P., and Malzac, R. P. 1888. *Dictionnaire Malagache-Français*. Paris: Editions Maritimes et Coloniales.

Abrahamsson, H. 1951. *The Origins of Death: Studies in African Mythology*. Uppsala: Studia Ethnographica Upsaliensia 3.

Adams, M. J. 1971. "Work Patterns and Symbolic Structures in a Village Culture, East Sumba, Indonesia." *Southeast Asia* 1(4): 320–34.

　　1977. "Style in Southeast Asian Materials Processing: Some implications for Ritual and Art." In H. Lechtman and R. Merrill (eds.). *Material Culture: Studies, Organization, and Dynamics of Technology*. Pp. 21–52. St. Paul: West Publishing.

Adas, M. 1989. *Machines as the Measure of Men: Science, Technology, and Ideologies of Western Dominance*. Ithaca: Cornell University Press.

Adriani, N., and Kruyt, Alb. C. 1912–14. *Der Baré'e Sprekende Toradja's van Midden Celebes*. Batavia: Landsdrukkerij.

Ahern, E. 1973. *The Cult of the Dead in a Chinese Village*. Stanford: Stanford University Press.

Aldred, C. 1961. *The Egyptians*. New York: Praeger.

Alexiou, M. 1974. *The Ritual Lament in Greek Tradition*. Cambridge: Cambridge University Press.

Althabe, G. 1969. *Oppression et libération dans l'imaginaire*. Paris: François Maspero.

Anderson, G. 1991. *A Time to Mourn, a Time to Dance: The Expression of Grief*

Bibliography

and Joy in Israelite Religion. University Park: Pennsylvania State University Press.

Århem, K. 1988. "Into the Realm of the Sacred: An Interpretation of Khasi Funerary Ritual." In S. Cederroth, C. Corlin, and J. Lindström (eds.). *On the Meaning of Death.* Pp. 257–300. Stockholm: Almqvist & Wiksell.

Ariès, P. 1967. "La mort inversée: Le changement des attitudes devant la mort dans les sociétés occidentales." *Archives Européenes de sociologie* 8: 169–95.

1974a. *Western Attitudes towards Death from the Middle Ages to the Present.* Baltimore: Johns Hopkins University Press.

1974b. "Death inside Out." *Hastings Center Studies* 2: 3–18.

1978. *L'Homme devant la mort.* Paris: Editions du Seuil.

1981. *The Hour of Our Death.* Translated from the French by Helen Weaver. New York: Random House.

Barley, N. 1981. "The Dowayo Dance of Death." In S. Humphreys and H. King (eds.). *Mortality and Immortality.* Pp. 149–60. London: Academic.

Barnes, R., de Coppet, D., and Parkin, R. 1985. *Contexts and Levels: Anthropological Essays on Hierarchy.* Oxford: Anthropological Society of Oxford.

Barnes, R. H. 1974. *Kedang: A Study of the Collective Thought of an Eastern Indonesian People.* Oxford: Clarendon.

Beattie, J. 1966. "Comment" on E. Leach. "The Founding Fathers." *Current Anthropology* 7(5): 570–1.

Becker, E. 1973. *The Denial of Death.* New York: Free Press.

Beidelman, T. O. 1966. "Swazi Royal Ritual." *Africa* 36: 373–405.

1974. *W. Robertson Smith and the Sociological Study of Religion.* Chicago: Chicago University Press.

Bellah, R. N. 1967. "Civil Religion in America." *Daedelus* 96: 1–22.

Belmont, N. 1974. *Arnold van Gennep: Créateur de l'ethnographie française.* Paris: Petite Bibliothèque Payot.

Binford, L. R. 1967. "Smudge Pits and Hide Smoking: The Uses of Analogy in Archeological Reasoning." *American Antiquity* 32: 1–12.

1971. "Mortuary Practices: Their Study and Potential." In J. A. Brown (ed.). *Approaches to the Social Dimensions of Mortuary Practices.* Pp. 6–21. Memoirs of the Society for American Archaeology, no. 25.

Binford, S. 1968. "A Structural Comparison of Disposal of the Dead in the Mousterian and the Upper Paleolithic." *Southwestern Journal of Anthropology* 24: 139–54.

Bloch, M. 1971. *Placing the Dead: Tombs, Ancestral Villages, and Kinship Organisation in Madagascar.* London: Seminar.

Bloch, M. and Parry, J. (eds.). 1982. *Death and the Regeneration of Life.* Cambridge: Cambridge University Press.

Boase, T. S. R. 1972. *Death in the Middle Ages.* London: Thames & Hudson.

Bibliography

Boon, J. 1977. *The Anthropological Romance of Bali, 1597–1972*. Cambridge: Cambridge University Press.

Bowman, L. 1964. *The American Funeral: A Study in Guilt, Extravagance and Sublimity*. New York: Paperback Library.

Braches, S. 1882. "Sandong Raung." *Jahresberichte der Rheinischen Mission*. Barmen: D. B. Wieman.

Braudel, F. 1980 (orig. 1969). *On History*. Chicago: Chicago University Press.

Breasted, J. 1912. *The Development of Religious Thought in Ancient Egypt*. New York: Scribners.

Budge, E. A. W. 1973 (orig. 1911). *Osiris and the Egyptian Resurrection*. New York: Dover Press.

Bühler, A. 1972. "Hanfverarbeitung und batik bei den Meau in Nord-Thailand." *Ethnologische Zeitschrift* 1: 61–81.

Butzer, K. W. 1976. *Early Hydraulic Civilization in Egypt: A Study in Cultural Ecology*. Chicago: University of Chicago Press.

Cannon, A. 1989. "The Historical Dimension in Mortuary Expression of Status and Sentiment." *Current Anthropology* 30: 437–58.

Cederroth, S., Corlin, C., and Lindström, J. (eds.). 1988. *On the Meaning of Death: Essays on Mortuary Rituals and Eschatological Beliefs*. Uppsala Studies in Cultural Anthropology 8. Stockholm: Almqvist & Wiksell.

Chapman, R. 1987. "Mortuary Practices: Society, Theory Building and Archaeology." In A. Boddington, A. Garland, and R. Janaway (eds.). *Death, Decay and Reconstruction: Approaches to Archaeology and Forensic Science*. Manchester: Manchester University Press.

Chapman, R., Kinnes, I., and Randsborg, K. (eds.). 1981. *The Archaeology of Death*. Cambridge: Cambridge University Press.

Chaunu, P. 1978. *La mort à Paris: 16e, 17e, 18e siècles*. Paris: Librairie Arthème Fayard.

Cherry, C. 1986. "Near-Death Experiences and the Problem of Evidence for Survival after Death." *Religious Studies* 22: 397–406.

Chidester, D. 1990. *Patterns of Transcendence: Religion, Death, and Dying*. Belmont, Calif.: Wadsworth.

Choron, J. 1964. *Death and the Modern Man*. New York: Collier Books.

Clark, S. 1985. "The Annales Historians." In Q. Skinner (ed.). *The Return of Grand Theory in the Human Sciences*. Cambridge: Cambridge University Press.

Collier, J., and Yanagisako, S. 1987. *Gender and Kinship: Essays towards a Unified Analysis*. Stanford: Stanford University Press.

Covarrubias, M. 1937. *Island of Bali*. New York: Knopf.

Crawley, A. E. 1912. "Drums and Cymbals." *Encyclopedia of Religious Ethics* 5: 89–94.

Bibliography

Crocker, J. C. 1971. "The Southern Way of Death." In J. K. Morland (ed.). *The Not-so-Solid South.* Pp. 114–29. Athens, Georgia: Southern Anthropological Society.

— 1977. "The Mirrored Self: Identity and Ritual Inversion among the Eastern Bororo." *Ethnology* 16(2): 129–45.

Cunnington, P. 1977. *Costume for Births, Marriages, and Deaths.* New York: Humanities Press.

Curl, J. S. 1972. *The Victorian Celebration of Death.* London: David & Charles.

Dahl, O. C. 1951. *Malagache et Maanjan: Une comparaison linguistique.* Oslo: Studies of the Egede Instituttet 3.

Damon, F. and Wagner, R. 1989. *Death Rituals and Life in the Societies of the Kula Ring.* DeKalb: Northern Illinois University Press.

Danforth, L. 1982. *The Death Rituals of Rural Greece.* With photographs by Alexander Tsiaras. Princeton: Princeton University Press.

Decary, R. 1958. *La Mort et les coutumes funéraires à Madagascar.* Paris: Maisonneuve et Larose.

de Coppet, D. 1981. "The Life-giving Death." In S. Humphreys and H. King (eds.). *Mortality and Immortality.* Pp. 175–204. London: Academic.

Delvert, J. 1961. *Le Paysan Cambodgien.* The Hague: Mouton.

Dempsey, D. 1975. *The Way We Die: An Investigation of Death and Dying in America Today.* New York: McGraw-Hill.

Deng, F. M. 1972. *The Dinka of the Sudan.* New York: Holt, Rinehart & Winston.

Douglas, A. 1974. "Heaven Our Home: Consolation Literature in the Northern United States, 1830–1880." In D. Stannard (ed.). *Death in America.* Pp. 49–68. Philadelphia: University of Pennsylvania Press.

Douglas, M. 1966. *Purity and Danger: An Analysis of Concepts of Pollution and Taboo.* New York: Praeger.

— 1970. *Natural Symbols: Explorations in Cosmology.* London: Barrie & Rockliff.

Douglass, W. A. 1969. *Death in Murelaga: Funerary Ritual in a Spanish Basque Village.* Seattle: University of Washington Press.

Downs, R. E. 1956. *The Religion of the Baré'e-speaking Toradja of Central Celebes.* The Hague: Excelsior.

Driver, H. 1961. *Indians of North America.* Chicago: University of Chicago Press.

Dubois, H. 1938. *Monographie des Betsileo.* Paris: Institut d'Ethnologie.

Dumont, L. 1978. "La communauté anthropologique et l'idéologie." *L'Homme* 18: 83–110.

— 1986. *Essays on Individualism: Modern Ideology in Anthropological Perspective.* Chicago: University of Chicago Press.

Bibliography

Durkheim, E. 1938 (orig. 1895). *The Rules of the Sociological Method.* Translated from the French by S. Solovay and J. Mueller. New York: Free Press.

  1965 (orig. 1912). *The Elementary Forms of the Religious Life.* Translated by Joseph Ward Swain. New York: Free Press.

Durkheim, E., and Mauss, M. 1963 (orig. 1903). *Primitive Classification.* Translated and edited by R. Needham. Chicago: University of Chicago Press.

Dworakowska, M. 1938. "The Origin of Bell and Drum." *Prace etnologiczne 5.* Warsaw: Nakladem Towarzystwa Naukowego Waszawkiego.

Ebersole, G. 1989. *Ritual Poetry and the Politics of Death in Early Japan.* Princeton: Princeton University Press.

Eckhardt, A. R. 1973. "Death in the Judaic and Christian Traditions." In A. Mack (ed.). *Death in American Experience.* Pp. 123–48. New York: Schocken.

Edwards, I. E. S. 1947. *The Pyramids of Egypt.* London: Penguin.

Emery, W. B. 1961. *Archaic Egypt.* London: Penguin.

Evans-Pritchard, E. E. 1948. *The Divine Kingship of the Shilluk of the Nilotic Sudan.* Cambridge: Cambridge University Press.

Fabian, J. 1973. "How Others Die: Reflections on the Anthropology of Death." In A. Mack (ed.). *Death in American Experience.* Pp. 177–201. New York: Schocken.

  1983. *Time and the Other: How Anthropology Makes Its Object.* New York: Columbia University Press.

Farrell, J. 1980. *Inventing the American Way of Death, 1830–1920.* Philadelphia: Temple University Press.

Faublée, J. 1947. *Récits Bara.* Paris: Institut d'Ethnologie.

  1954. *La Cohésion des sociétés Bara.* Paris: Presses Universitaire de France.

Favre, R. 1978. *La Mort dans la littérature et la pensée Françaises au siècle des lumières.* Lyon: Presses Universitaire de Lyon.

Feifel, H. (ed.). 1959. *The Meaning of Death.* New York: McGraw-Hill.

Firth, R. 1967. *Tikopia Ritual and Belief.* Boston: Beacon Press.

Forman, S. 1980. "Descent, Alliance, and Exchange Ideology among the Makassae of East Timor." In J. J. Fox (ed.). *The Flow of Life: Essays on Eastern Indonesia.* Pp. 152–77. Cambridge: Harvard University Press.

Fortune, R. 1965. *Manus Religion.* Lincoln: University of Nebraska Press.

Fox, J. J. 1973. "On Bad Death and the Left Hand: A Study of Rotinese Symbolic Inversions." In R. Needham (ed.). *Right and Left.* Pp. 342–68. Chicago: University of Chicago Press.

  1977. "Chicken Bones and Buffalo Sinews." Unpublished ms.

  (ed.). 1980. *The Flow of Life: Essays on Eastern Indonesia.* Cambridge: Harvard University Press.

Frankfort, H. 1948. *Kingship and the Gods.* Chicago: University of Chicago Press.

Bibliography

Frazer, J. G. 1963 (orig. 1890). *The Golden Bough*. New York: Macmillan.

French, S. 1974. "The Cemetery as Cultural Institution: The Establishment of Mount Auburn and the 'Rural Cemetery' Movement." In D. Stannard (ed.). *Death in America*. Pp. 69–91. Philadelphia: University of Pennsylvania Press.

Fulton, R. (ed.). 1965. *Death and Identity*. New York: Wiley.

Fulton, R., and Geis, G. 1965. "Death and Social Values." In R. Fulton (ed.). *Death and Identity*. Pp. 67–75. New York: Wiley.

Gardiner, A. 1961. *Egypt of the Pharoahs*. Oxford: Clarendon.

Garland, R. 1985. *The Greek Way of Death*. London: Duckworth.

Geertz, C. 1960. *The Religion of Java*. New York: Free Press.

1980. *Negara: The Theatre State in Nineteenth-Century Bali*. Princeton: Princeton University Press.

Genet, J. 1969. *Funeral Rites*. New York: Grove Press.

Gervais, K. G. 1986. *Redefining Death*. New Haven: Yale University Press.

Giesey, R. E. 1960. *The Royal Funeral Ceremony in Renaissance France*. Geneva: Librairie E. Droz.

Gittings, C. 1984. *Death, Burial and the Individual in Early Modern England*. London: Croom Helm.

Gluckman, M. 1937. "Mortuary Customs and Belief in Survival after Death among the Southeastern Bantu." *Bantu Studies* 11: 117–36.

1954. *Rituals of Rebellion in South-east Africa*. Manchester: University of Manchester Press.

Gomes, E. H. 1911. *Seventeen Years among the Seas Dayaks of Borneo*. Philadelphia: Lippincott.

Goody, J. 1962. *Death, Property and the Ancestors*. Stanford: Stanford University Press.

Gorer, G. 1965. *Death, Grief and Mourning*. New York: Doubleday.

Goris, R., and Dronkers, P. 1955. *Atlas Kebudajan*. Jakarta: Ministry of Culture.

Grabowsky, F. 1884. "Der distrikt Dusun-Timor in Süd-Ost Borneo und seiner bewohner." *Ausland* 57: 444–9, 469–75.

1889. "Der tod, das begräbnis, das tiwah oder totenfest bei den Dajaken." *International Archives of Ethnography* 2: 177–204. Leiden.

Grollman, E. A. 1974. *Concerning Death: A Practical Guide for the Living*. Boston: Beacon Press.

Guiart, J. 1963. *The Arts of the South Pacific*. New York: Golden Press.

Habenstein, R. W., and Lamers, W. M. 1955. *History of American Funeral Directing*. Milwaukee: Bulfin Press.

Haddon, A. C. (ed.). 1908. *Report of the Cambridge Anthropological Expedition to the Torres Straits*. Cambridge: Cambridge University Press.

Bibliography

Hall, D. G. E. 1981. *A History of South-East Asia.* Fourth edition. New York: St. Martin's Press.

Hamilton, C., and Ostendorf, L. 1963. *Lincoln in Photographs: An Album of Every Known Pose.* Norman: University of Oklahoma Press.

Hantman, J. L. 1990. "Between Powhatan and Quirank: Reconstructing Monacan Culture and History in the Context of Jamestown." *American Anthropologist* 92: 676–90.

Hardeland, A. 1858. *Versuch einer Grammatik der Dajakschen Sprache.* Amsterdam: F. Muller.

Harmer, R. M. 1963. *The High Cost of Dying.* New York: Crowell-Collier.

Harris, O. 1982. "The Dead and the Devils among the Bolivian Laymi." In M. Bloch and J. Parry (eds.). *Death and the Regeneration of Life.* Pp. 45–73. Cambridge: Cambridge University Press.

Harrison, T. 1962. "Borneo Death." *Bijdragen Tot de Taal-, Land-, en Volkenkunde* 118: 1–41.

Heelas, P., and Lock, A. 1981. *Indigenous Psychologies: The Anthropology of the Self.* London: Academic.

Helander, B. 1988. "Death and the End of Society: Official Ideology and Ritual Communication in the Somali Funeral." In S. Cederroth, C. Corlin, and J. Lindström (eds.). *On the Meaning of Death.* Pp. 113–36. Stockholm: Almqvist & Wiksell.

Hertz, R. 1907. "Contribution à une étude sur la représentation collective de la mort." *Année sociologique* 10: 48–137.

1909. "Le Prééminence de la main droite: Etude sur la polarité religieuse." *Revue philosophique* 68: 553–80.

1922. "La péché et l'expiation dans les sociétés primitives." Edited by M. Mauss. *Revue de l'histoire des religions* 86: 5–53.

1928. *Mélanges de sociologie et de folklore.* Edited by M. Mauss. Paris: Alcan.

1960. "A Contribution to the Study of the Collective Representation of Death." In *Death and the Right Hand.* Translated by R. Needham and C. Needham. New York: Free Press.

Hicks, D. 1976. *Tetum Ghosts and Kin.* Palo Alto: Mayfield.

Hocart, A. M. 1952. *The Life Giving Myth.* London: Methuen.

1954. *Social Origins.* London: Watts.

1970 (orig. 1936). *Kings and Councillors: An Essay in the Comparative Anatomy of Human Society.* Edited by R. Needham. Chicago: University of Chicago Press.

Hodder, I. 1982. *Symbolic and Structural Archaeology.* Cambridge: Cambridge University Press.

1984. "Burials, Houses, Women and Men in the European Neolithic." In

Bibliography

D. Miller and C. Tilley (eds.). *Ideology, Power and Prehistory*. Cambridge: Cambridge University Press.

Hoffman, M. 1979. *Egypt before the Pharoahs*. New York: Knopf.

Hooykaas, C. 1973. *Religion in Bali*. Leiden: Brill.

Howell, S. 1990. "On Persons and Things: Exchange and Valuables among the Lio of Eastern Indonesia." *Man* 24: 419–38.

Hubert, H., and Mauss, M. 1899. "Essai sur le nature et la fonction du sacrifice." *Année sociologique* 2: 29–138.

1964. *Sacrifice: Its Nature and Function*. Translated by W. D. Halls. Chicago: University of Chicago Press.

Hudson, A. B. 1966. "Death Ceremonies of the Padju Epat Ma'anyan Dayaks." *Sarawak Museum Journal* 13: 341–416.

Humphreys, S. C., and King, H. (eds.). 1981. *Mortality and Immortality: The Anthropology and Archaeology of Death*. London: Academic.

Huntington, R. 1973. "Death and the Social Order: Bara Funeral Customs (Madagascar)." *African Studies* 32(2): 65–84.

1978. "Bara Endogamy and Incest Prohibition." *Bijdragen Tot de Taal-, Land-, en Volkenkunde* 136: 30–62.

1987. *Gender and Social Structure in Madagascar*. Bloomington: Indiana University Press.

Jackson, C. O. (ed.). 1977. *Passing: The Vision of Death in America*. Westport: Greenwood.

Jensen, E. 1974. *The Iban and Their Religion*. Oxford: Clarendon.

Jung, C. 1964. *Man and His Symbols*. New York: Doubleday.

Kalish, R., and Reynolds, D. 1976. *Death and Ethnicity: A Psychocultural Study*. Los Angeles: University of Southern California Press.

Kantorowicz, E. 1957. *The King's Two Bodies: A Study in Mediaeval Political Theory*. Princeton: Princeton University Press.

Kastenbaum, R., and Aisenberg, R. 1973. *The Psychology of Death*. New York: Springer.

Kaut, C. 1952. "The Treatment of the Dead Body in Contemporary American Society." Unpublished ms.

Kopytoff, I. 1971. "Ancestors as Elders in Africa." *Africa* 41(2): 129–42.

Kruyt, A. C. 1906. *Het Animisme in den Indischen Archipel*. 's-Gravenhage: Mouton.

Kübler-Ross, E. 1975. *Death: The Final Stage of Growth*. Englewood Cliffs, N.J.: Prentice-Hall.

Kurtz, D. C., and Broadman, J. 1971. *Greek Burial Customs*. London: Thames & Hudson.

Kutscher, A. H., et al. (eds.). 1983. *Hospice U.S.A.* New York: Columbia University Press.

Bibliography

Lamb, D. 1985. *Death, Brain Death, and Ethics*. Albany: State University of New York Press.

Leach, E. 1958. "Magical Hair." *Journal of the Royal Anthropological Institute* 88(2): 149–64.

1961. "Golden Bough or Gilded Twig?" *Daedelus* 90(2): 371–87.

1966. "On the Founding Fathers." *Current Anthropology* 7(5): 560–7.

Lebrun, F. 1971. *Les hommes et la mort en Anjou au 17e et 18e siècles: Essai de démographie et de psychologie historiques*. Paris: Plon.

LeGoff, J. 1984. *The Birth of Purgatory*. Translated by Arthur Goldhammer. Chicago: Chicago University Press.

Leone, M. (ed.). 1972. *Contemporary Archaeology: A Guide to Theory and Contributions*. London: Feffer & Simons.

Lévi-Strauss, C. 1963. *Totemism*. Boston: Beacon Press.

1969. *The Raw and the Cooked*. New York: Harper & Row.

1973. *From Honey to Ashes*. New York: Harper & Row.

Lienhardt, R. G. 1954. "The Shilluk of the Upper Nile." In C. Forde (ed.). *African Worlds: Studies in the Cosmological Ideas and Social Values of African Peoples*. Pp. 138–63. Oxford: Oxford University Press.

1961. *Divinity and Experience: The Religion of the Dinka*. Oxford: Clarendon Press.

1966. *Social Anthropology*. Oxford: Oxford University Press.

1970. "The Situation of Death: An Aspect of Anuak Philosophy." In M. Douglas (ed.). *Witchcraft Confessions and Accusations*. Pp. 279–92. London: Tavistock.

Lloyd, G. E. 1966. *Polarity and Analogy in Early Greek Thought*. Cambridge: Cambridge University Press.

Lopatin, I. 1960. *The Cult of the Dead among the Natives of the Amur Basin*. The Hague: Mouton.

Lutz, C. 1988. *Unnatural Emotions: Everyday Sentiments on a Micronesian Atoll and Their Challenge to Western Theory*. Chicago: University of Chicago Press.

MacCormack, C. P. 1980. "Nature, Culture and Gender: A Critique." In C. MacCormack and M. Strathern (eds.). *Nature, Culture and Gender*. Cambridge: Cambridge University Press.

Macintyre, M. 1989. "The Triumph of the Susu: Mortuary Exchanges on Tubetube." In F. Damon and R. Wagner (eds.). *Death Rituals and Life in the Societies of the Kula Ring*. Pp. 133–52. DeKalb: Northern Illinois University Press.

Mack, A. (ed.). 1973. *Death in American Experience*. New York: Schocken.

McLennan, J. 1970 (orig. 1865). *Primitive Marriage: An Inquiry into the Origin and Form of Capture in Marriage Ceremonies.* Chicago: University of Chicago Press.

McLeod, N. 1964. "The Status of Musical Specialists in Madagascar." *Ethnomusicology* 7(3): 278–389.

McManners, J. 1981. "Death and the French Historians." In J. Whaley (ed.). *Mirrors of Mortality: Studies in the Social History of Death.* Pp. 106–30. London: Europa.

1985. *Death and the Enlightenment: Changing Attitudes to Death among Christians and Unbelievers in Eighteenth-Century France.* Oxford: Oxford University Press.

Mainfort, R. 1989. "Adena Chiefdoms? Evidence from the Wright Mounds." *Midcontinental Journal of Archaeology* 14: 164–79.

Malinowski, B. 1929. *The Sexual Life of Savages in North-Western Melanesia.* New York: Harcourt Brace Jovanovich.

1954 (orig. 1916). "Baloma: The Spirits of the Dead in the Trobriand Islands." In B. Malinowski. *Magic, Science and Religion and Other Essays.* New York: Doubleday.

Marcus, G., and Fischer, M. 1986. *Anthropology as Cultural Critique: An Experimental Moment in the Human Sciences.* Chicago: University of Chicago Press.

Mauss, M. 1921. "L'expression obligatoire des sentiments (Rituels oraux funéraires Australiens)." *Journal de psychologie* 18: 425–34.

1922. "Introduction à Robert Hertz: Le péché et l'expiation dans les sociétés primitives." *Revue de l'histoire des religions* 86: 1–4.

1926. "Effet physique chez l'individuel de l'idée de mort suggérée par la collectivité (Austrialie, Nouvelle Zélande)." *Journal de psychologie* 23: 653–69. Reprinted in M. Mauss. 1960. *Sociologie et anthropologie.* Paris: Presses Universitaires de France.

1938. "Une catégorie de l'esprit humain: La notion de personne, celle de 'moi': Un plan de travail." *Journal of the Royal Anthropological Institute* 68: 263–81.

Mendelssohn, K. 1974. *The Riddle of the Pyramids.* London: Thames & Hudson.

Metcalf, P. 1977. "Berawan Mausoleums." *Sarawak Museum Journal* 24: 121–36.

1978. "Death Be Not Strange." *Natural History* 87: 6–12. Reprinted in A. Lehman and J. Myers (eds.). 1985. *Magic, Witchcraft and Religion: An Anthropological Study of the Supernatural.* Pp. 332–35. New York: Holt, Rinehart & Winston.

1981. "Meaning and Materialism: The Ritual Economy of Death." *Man* 16: 563–78.

1982a. *A Borneo Journey into Death: Berawan Eschatology from Its Rituals.* Philadelphia: University of Pennsylvania Press.

Bibliography

1982b. "Supernatural Etiologies of Illness in Central Northern Borneo." *Journal of the Malaysian Branch of the Royal Asiatic Society* LV(2): 115–25.

1987. "Wine of the Corpse: Endocannibalism and the Great Feast of the Dead in Borneo." *Representations* 17: 96–109.

1989. *Where Are You/Spirits: Style and Theme in Berawan Prayer.* Washington, D.C.: Smithsonian Press.

Meyers, E. 1971. *Jewish Ossuaries: Reburial and Rebirth.* Rome: Biblican Institute Press. Biblica et Orientalia, no. 24.

Miles, D. J. 1965. "Socio-Economic Aspects of Secondary Burial." *Oceania* 35(3): 161–74.

Miller, D., and Tilley, C. (eds.). 1984. *Ideology, Power and Prehistory.* Cambridge: Cambridge University Press.

Mitford, J. 1963. *The American Way of Death.* New York: Simon & Schuster.

Moody, R. A. 1975. *Life after Life.* New York: Bantam.

Moore, S. F. 1981. "Chagga 'Customary' Law and the Property of the Dead." In S. Humphrey and H. King (eds.). *Mortality and Immortality.* London: Academic.

Morley, J. 1971. *Death, Heaven and the Victorians.* Pittsburgh: University of Pittsburgh Press.

Morris, I. 1987. *Burial and Ancient Society: The Rise of the Greek City-State.* Cambridge: Cambridge University Press.

Neale, R. 1973. *The Art of Dying.* New York: Harper & Row.

Needham, R. 1964. "Blood, Thunder, and the Mockery of Animals." *Sociologus* 14: 136–49.

1967. "Percussion and Transition." *Man* N.S. 2: 606–14.

1970. "Editor's Introduction." In A. M. Hocart. *Kings and Councillors: An Essay in the Comparative Anatomy of Human Society.* Pp. xii–xcix. Chicago: Chicago University Press.

1973 (ed.). *Right and Left: Essays on Dual Classification.* Chicago: University of Chicago Press.

1976. "Skulls and Causality." *Man* 11: 71–8.

1987. *Counterpoints.* Berkeley: University of California Press.

Neher, A. 1962. "A Physiological Explanation of Unusual Behaviour in Ceremonies Involving Drums." *Human Biology* 34: 151–9.

Okely, J. 1979. "An Anthropological Contribution to the History and Archaeology of an Ethnic Group." In B. C. Burnham and J. Kingsbury (eds.). *Space, Hierarchy, and Society.* Pp. 81–92. Oxford: British Archaeological Reports.

O'Shea, J. 1984. *Mortuary Variability: An Archaeological Investigation.* New York: Academic.

Bibliography

Overing, J. 1986. "Men Control Women? The 'Catch 22' in the Analysis of Gender." *International Journal of Moral and Social Studies* 1: 135–56.

Parker-Pearson, M. 1982. "Mortuary Practices, Society, and Ideology: An Ethnoarchaeological Study." In I. Hodder (ed.). *Symbolic and Structural Archaeology*. Pp. 99–113. Cambridge: Cambridge University Press.

Parry, J. 1982. "Sacrificial death and the Necrophagous Ascetic." In M. Bloch and J. Parry (eds.). *Death and the Regeneration of Life*. Pp. 74–110. Cambridge: Cambridge University Press.

Parsons, T. 1963. "Death in American Society – A Brief Working Paper." *American Behavioural Scientist* 6: 61–5.

1968. *The Structure of Social Action*. New York: Free Press.

Pelzer, K. J. 1945. *Pioneer Settlement in the Asiatic Tropics*. New York: American Geographical Society.

Perham, J. 1896. "Iban Religion." In H. L. Roth (ed.). *The Natives of Sarawak and British North Borneo*. Pp. 168–213. London: Truslove & Hansen.

Pine, V. R. 1975. *Caretaker of the Dead: The American Funeral Director*. New York: Wiley.

Pretty, G. 1969. "The Macleay Museum Mummy from Torres Straits: A Postscript to Elliot Smith and the Diffusion Controversy." *Man* 4: 24–43.

Rabibhadana, A. 1969. *The Organisation of Thai Society in the Early Bangkok Period, 1783–1873*. Cornell University Southeast Asia Program Data Paper, no. 74.

Radcliffe-Brown, A. R. 1964. *The Andaman Islanders*. New York: Free Press.

Ragon, M. 1983. *The Space of Death: A Study of Funerary Architecture, Decoration, and Urbanism*. Charlottesville: University of Virginia Press.

Randsborg, K. 1980. *The Viking Age in Denmark*. London: Duckworth.

Reisner, A. 1936. *The Development of Egyptian Tombs to the Accession of Cheops*. Cambridge: Cambridge University Press.

Renault, M. 1958. *The King Must Die*. New York: Pantheon.

Riffert, G. R. 1932. *Great Pyramid: Proof of God*. Haverhill, Mass.: Destiny Publishers.

Ring, K. 1984. *Heading towards Omega: In Search of the Meaning of the Near-Death Experience*. New York: Norton.

Rivers, W. H. R. 1926. *Psychology and Ethnology*. London: Kegan Paul.

Rosaldo, M. 1980. *Knowledge and Passion: Ilongot Notions of Self and Social Life*. Cambridge: Cambridge University Press.

Rosaldo, R. 1984. "Grief and the Headhunter's Rage: On the Cultural Force of Emotions." In E. Bruner (ed.). *Text, Play and Story: The Construction and Reconstruction of Self and Society*. Washington, D.C.: American Ethnological Society.

Bibliography

1989. *Culture and Truth: The Remaking of Social Analysis.* Boston: Beacon Press.

Rosenblatt, P. C., Walsh, R., and Jackson, A. 1976. *Grief and Mourning in Cross-Cultural Perspective.* New Haven: Human Relations Area File.

Saum, L. 1974. "Death in the Popular Mind of Pre-Civil War America." In D. Stannard (ed.). *Death in America.* Pp. 30–48. Philadelphia: University of Pennsylvania Press.

Saxe, A. A. 1968. "Explaining Variability in the Disposal of the Dead: Social Relationship Factors." Paper presented to the Annual Meeting of the Society for American Archaeology.

1971. "Social Dimensions of Mortuary Practices in a Mesolithic Population from Wadi Halfa, Sudan." In J. A. Brown (ed.). *Approaches to the Social Dimensions of Mortuary Practices.* Memoirs of the Society for American Archaeology, no. 25.

Schärer, H. 1963 (orig. 1946). *Ngaju Religion: The Conception of God among a South Borneo People.* Translated by Rodney Needham. The Hague: Martinus Nijhoff.

Schebesta, P. 1929. *Among the Forest Dwarfs of Malaya.* Translated by A. Chambers. London: Hutchinson.

Shanks, M., and Tilley, C. 1987. *Re-constructing Archaeology: Theory and Practice.* Cambridge: Cambridge University Press.

Shilts, R. 1987. *And the Band Played On: Politics, People, and the AIDS Epidemic.* New York: St. Martin's Press.

Shyrock, A. J. 1987. "The Wright Mound Reexamined: Generative Structures and the Political Economy of a Simple Chiefdom." *Midcontinental Journal of Archaeology* 12: 243–68.

Silverman, P. 1974. "Another Look at the Role of the Funeral Director." Paper presented to the meeting of the Foundation of Thanatology. March.

Smith, G. E. 1929 (orig. 1915). *The Migrations of Early Cultures.* Manchester: Manchester University Press.

Smith, R. B. 1967. *Siam; or the History of the Thais from 1569 A.D. to 1828 A.D.* Bethesda, Md.: Decatur Press.

Smith, W. R. 1889. *Lectures on the Religion of the Semites.* Edinburgh: A. & C. Black.

Stannard, D. W. (ed.). 1974. *Death in America.* Philadelphia: University of Pennsylvania Press.

1977. *The Puritan Way of Death: A Study in Religion, Culture and Social Change.* New York: Oxford University Press.

Steiner, F. 1967. *Taboo.* Harmondsworth: Penguin.

Strathern, A. 1981. "Death as Exchange: Two Melanesian Cases." In S. Hum-

Bibliography

phrey and H. King (eds.). *Mortality and Immortality: The Anthropology and Archaeology of Death.* London: Academic.

Sudnow, D. 1967. *Passing On: The Social Organization of Dying.* Englewood Cliffs, N.J.: Prentice-Hall.

Swellengrebel, J. L. 1969. *Bali: Further Studies in Life, Thought, and Ritual.* The Hague: Van Hoeve.

Tambiah, S. J. 1970. *Buddhism and the Spirit Cults in North East Thailand.* Cambridge: Cambridge University Press.

　　1976. *World Conqueror and World Renouncer: A Study of Buddhism and the Polity in Thailand against a Historical Background.* Cambridge: Cambridge University Press.

Tellefsen, O. 1975. "A New Theory of Pyramid Building." In D. Hunter and P. Whitten. *Anthropology: A Contemporary Perspective.* Pp. 151–6. Boston: Little, Brown.

Templer, D. I., and Lonetto, R. 1986. *Death Anxiety.* Washington, D.C.: Hemisphere.

Thomas, L. V. 1968. *Cinq essais sur la mort Africaine.* Dakar: Université de Dakar.

　　1975. *Anthropologie de la mort.* Paris: Payot.

Thomas, L. V., and Trink van Thao. 1977. *La mort aujourd'hui.* Amiens: Centre Universitaire de recherche sociologique.

Toynbee, J. M. C. 1971. *Death and Burial in the Roman World.* London: Thames & Hudson.

Traube, E. 1986. *Cosmology and Social Life: Ritual Exchange among the Mambai of East Timor.* Chicago: Chicago University Press.

Turner, V. 1953. *Lunda Rites and Ceremonies.* Occasional Papers of the Rhodes-Livingstone Museum, no. 10.

　　1957. *Schism and Continuity in an African Society: A Study of Ndembu Village Life.* Manchester: Manchester University Press.

　　1967. *The Forest of Symbols.* Ithaca: Cornell University Press.

　　1968. *The Drums of Affliction.* Oxford: Clarendon.

　　1969. *The Ritual Process.* Chicago: Aldine.

　　1975. "Death and the Dead in the Pilgrimage Process." In M. West and M. Whisson (eds.). *Religion and Social Change in Southern Africa.* Pp. 107–27. Capetown: David Phillip.

Tuzin, D. 1975. "The Breath of a Ghost: Dreams and the Fear of the Dead." *Ethos* 3: 555–75.

Tylor, E. B. 1964 (orig. 1878). *Researches into the Early History of Mankind and the Development of Civilisation.* Chicago: Chicago University Press.

van Gennep, A. 1904. *Tabou et totemisme à Madagascar.* Paris: Ernest Leroux.

　　1909. *Les rites de passage.* Paris: Emile Nourry.

Bibliography

1960. *The Rites of Passage*. Translated by M. Vicedom and S. Kimball. Chicago: University of Chicago Press.

Vicedom, M. 1976. *Rites and Relationships: Rites of Passage and Contemporary Anthropology*. Beverly Hills: Sage.

Vovelle, M. 1976. "Les attitudes devant la morte, problèmes de méthode, approches et lectures différentes." *Annales E.S.C.* 31: 120–32.

Wagner, R. 1972. *Habu: The Innovation of Meaning in Daribi Religion*. Chicago: University of Chicago Press.

Wales, H. G. Q. 1931. *Siamese State Ceremonies: Their History and Function*. London: Bernard Quaritch.

Warner, W. L. 1959. *The Living and the Dead: A Study of the Symbolic Life of Americans*. New Haven: Yale University Press.

Watson, J. 1982. "Of Flesh and Bones: The Management of Death Pollution in Cantonese Society." In M. Bloch and J. Parry (eds.). *Death and the Regeneration of Life*. Pp. 155–86. Cambridge: Cambridge University Press.

Watson, J., and Rawski, E. (eds.). 1988. *Death Ritual in Late Imperial and Modern China*. Berkeley: University of California Press.

Waugh, E. 1948. *The Loved One*. Boston: Little, Brown.

Weiner, A. 1976. *Women of Value, Men of Renown*. Austin: University of Texas Press.

1980. "Reproduction: A Replacement for Reciprocity." *American Ethnologist* 7: 71–85.

Westermann, D. 1912. *The Shilluk People: Their Language and Folklore*. Philadelphia: United Presbyterian Church of North America.

Whaley, J. 1981. *Mirrors of Mortality: Studies in the Social History of Death*. London: Europa.

Wilson, G. 1939. "Nyakyusa Conventions of Burial." *Bantu Studies* 13: 1–31.

Wilson, J. 1946. "Egypt." In H. Frankfort, J. Wilson, T. Jacobson, and W. Irwin. *The Intellectual Adventure of Ancient Man*. Pp. 31–123. Chicago: University of Chicago Press.

1951. *The Burden of Egypt*. Chicago: University of Chicago Press.

Wilson, M. 1951. *Good Company: A Study of Nyakyusa Age Villages*. Oxford: Oxford University Press.

1957. *Rituals of Kinship among the Nyakyusa*. Oxford: Oxford University Press.

Wirz, P. 1928. *Der Totenkult auf Bali*. Stuttgart: Strocker & Shroder.

Wittgenstein, L. 1971. "Remarks on Frazer's 'Golden Bough.'" *Human World* 3: 18–41.

Wolf, A. P. 1970. "Chinese Kinship and Mourning Dress." In M. Freedman (ed.). *Family and Kinship in Chinese Society*. Pp. 190–207. Stanford: Stanford University Press.

Bibliography

Wood, W. A. 1926. *A History of Siam from the Earliest Times to the Year* A.D. *1781.* Bangkok: Government Printing Office.

Zandee, J. 1960. *Death as the Enemy, According to Ancient Egyptian Conceptions.* Translated by W. F. Klasens. Leiden: Brill.

INDEX

aborigines, Australian, 3, 48–52, 61
Adams, Marie Jeanne, 68–9, 72
Adas, Michael, 9
Adriani, N., 99–100
afterlife. *See* eschatology; land of the dead
AIDS, 22
alliance. *See* exchange
American funeral rites, 16, 22–3, 25, 26–7, 39, 46, 191–214
  collective representations concerning, 204–6, 213
  funeral directors, 22, 194, 196–201, 204, 208, 210
  wake and viewing, 22, 205, 208, 210, 214
  see also corpse, display of; embalming
ancestors, 96, 100, 104, 109, 117, 118, 128–30, 148, 178–9. *See also* eschatology; land of the dead; soul, spirits of the dead
Andaman Islanders, 44–7, 61
Année sociologique, 3, 36, 79
archaeology, 1, 14–9, 27, 153–61

Århem, Kaj, 13
Ariès, Philippe, 20–1, 26, 206, 209, 213

Bali, 6, 101 2, 141–4
Bara, 7–9, 12, 113–30
  compared to Berawan, 12, 124, 125
  death rites, 116–22, 130
  generation of vitality, 7–9, 122 8
  legends, 126, 128, 130
  life as transition, 113, 128–30
  notions of conception, 113, 124
  sexual license, 117, 124–5, 127
Barley, Nigel, 11
Becker, Ernest, 201, 203
Bellah, Robert, 211
Berawan, 64–6, 73, 85–97, 107, 144–51, 159, 198, 202
  boisterous funerals, 12, 64–7
  compared to Bara, 12, 124, 125
  death songs, 87–9
  migrations, 88–9, 148
  notions of death and afterlife, 87, 89–90

231

Index

Index

Index

and daily actions, 68–70, 72–4
as display, 119, 140, 141–3, 199
function of, 6–7, 47, 93, 141, 143,
    162, 174
indigenous exegesis, 89–90, 94,
    112–3
inversion, 172, 204
nature of, 3, 6, 96, 117, 172, 174,
    179–80, 185–6, 203
and power, 1, 5–7, 39, 162, 166,
    179
and sentiment, 1–5, 43–61, 62,
    201–3
see also civil religion; funerals; kin,
    mourning usages of; regicide; rites
    of passage; sacrifice; secondary
    burial; weddings
Rivers, W. H. R., 6, 75
Rosaldo, Michelle, 5
Rosaldo, Renato, 2, 4–5
rotting. See corpse, decomposition of;
    symbolism, of biological processes

sacrifice, 29, 35, 37, 59, 105, 119,
    126, 184
Saudi Arabia, 134
Saxe, Arthur, 16
Schärer, Hans, 98
secondary burial (secondary treatment,
    secondary disposal, of the dead),
    11–2, 33–5, 191–2
    America, 17
    Asia, 35
    Borneo, 74, 85–99, 150
    Celebes, 99–100
    defined, 97
    Greece, 35
    Indonesia, 35, 97–102
    Jewish, 35
    Madagascar, 47, 108–30
    Melanesia, 14, 35, 192
    Thailand, 136–7
sentiment. See emotions, at funerals
Service, Elman, 15

sexual license, at funerals, 57, 113,
    117, 119, 124–5, 127, 184
shamans, 87, 92, 98, 100
Shilluk, 39, 163–7, 169–70, 172, 174,
    179–80, 186–7
Shyrock, James, 17
Smith, G. Elliot, 192
Smith, W. Robertson, 35, 52
songs, at death rites, 47, 87–9, 94–5,
    122–4, 184
soul
    conception of, 28, 82, 86–7, 90–6,
        105–6
    effect on the living, 34, 81, 93–4,
        96, 97
    fate of, 87, 98, 100
    journey of, 87–9, 106, 124
    spirits of the dead, 70, 86–7, 95, 97,
        100–1, 112
    see also ancestors; death; eschatology;
        land of the dead
"soul loss," 87
Southeast Asia, 11, 68–70, 72–4,
    135–43, 191
spirits. See soul, spirits of the dead
sports. See games, at funerals
Stannard, David, 22, 204
Steiner, Franz, 31
Steward, Julian, 15
Strathern, Andrew, 13
Sudnow, David, 22, 193, 204, 207,
    209
symbolism, 4, 29, 31, 36, 46, 62–75,
    173, 177, 180, 185–8
    of biological processes, 7, 32, 71–4,
        97
    body, 29, 36, 38
    color, 63, 66, 93, 176
    of corpses, 37, 71–2, 84, 90, 100,
        106, 112, 129, 188
    dual, 8–9, 114–5, 128, 155, 179
    of fertility and vitality, 108, 111,
        114–5
    hair, 63–4, 66, 71
    of kingship, 162, 165

235

Index